Maureen O'Hara has starred in sixty films, including such critically acclaimed classics as *The Quiet Man*, *Miracle on 34th Street* and *How Green Was My Valley*. In 2004 she was presented with two Lifetime Achievement Awards: one from the Irish Film Institute, and the other from the Irish Film and Television Network. She has homes in St Croix and Ireland.

John Nicoletti is a Hollywood screenwriter. He lives in Los Angeles.

More praise for *'Tis Herself*

'No Irish actor before or since has ever really rivalled O'Hara's success, either in terms of movie iconography or roles in enduring film classics. With her blazing red hair, piercing green eyes, striking features and independent manner, she was the archetypal screen icon for her era, as strident and confident as the post-war America she played to'

Sunday Times (Ireland)

'She had beauty, a fiery personality, star quality . . . She was fortunate in playing opposite some of the most glamorous leading men in Hollywood, among them John Wayne, Tyrone Power and Errol Flynn. She was a star'

Sunday Independent (Ireland)

'A delightful anecdotal autobiography . . . Hollywood's heyday returns to life in this revealing, insightful memoir. O'Hara treats readers like close friends, and her powerful personality is evident throughout'

Publishers Weekly

'TIS HERSELF

An Autobiography

MAUREEN O'HARA

WITH JOHN NICOLETTI

POCKET
BOOKS

LONDON • SYDNEY • NEW YORK • TORONTO

First published in Great Britain and Ireland by Simon & Schuster/TownHouse, 2004
This edition published by Pocket Books, 2005
An imprint of Simon & Schuster UK Ltd,

Simon & Schuster UK is a Viacom company

Extract on page 367 from *Rubaiyat of Omar Khayyam*, translated by
Edward J. Fitzgerald, 1859

1 3 5 7 9 10 8 6 4 2

Simon & Schuster UK Ltd
Africa House
64–78 Kingsway
London WC2B 6AH

ISBN 0-7434-9535-7
EAN 9780743495356

www.simonsays.co.uk

Simon & Schuster Australia
Sydney

A CIP catalogue record for this book is available from the British Library

Printed and bound in Great Britain by
Cox & Wyman Ltd, Reading, Berks

Acknowledgments

I begin with love to my family, the FitzSimonses and Blairs, for suffering through the hectic chaos that comes with recounting eighty-three years of remembrances. Life will be back to a more comfortable confusion now, I promise.

Valiant Mitchell Waters, God bless you. You slew business dragons and wrestled the devils of detail so this book could live.

Chuck Adams and the gang at Simon & Schuster, you waited for years to do this book with me. Thank you for your faith in this old stuntgirl's story.

I must also send a flurry of thanks to Shirley Stewart and Julia Forster for shining the international spotlight on my life's story. My heartfelt gratitude also goes out to Treasa Coady at Town-House for delivering this memoir with tender care to my beloved homeland, my Ireland, and to all of Ireland's gracious neighbours.

June Parker Beck, for all that you do, I am forever grateful. Danny and you have delivered me with such splendor to the Internet. I don't know a bloody thing about computers and so this was impossible without you.

ACKNOWLEDGEMENTS

My gang: Lucille House, Elaine Parkey, Sally Ryan, Moya Hennessey, Dorothea MacKenzie, and Faye Smyth and Jimmy Barker posthumously, I could thank you a million times and it would never be enough. You have all my love . . .

Marie Mangine for art direction and guidance. Marvin Paige and Laurence Ducceschi, who had photos of me I never knew existed. Sister Margaret Mary and Gina Davis, for your red pens.

My appreciation to the Margaret Herrick Library of the Academy of Motion Pictures Arts and Sciences and the Los Angeles Public Library for keeping sixty years of chronology—records and dates—straight.

Thanks to the staffs of countless restaurants all over Los Angeles—you know who you are—for allowing John and me to work long into the night while sitting at your tables even though you were dying to close and go home.

I also shake a bone of thanks to Maureen FitzSimons Blair herself, for never running out on Maureen O'Hara, no matter how sick of her you got.

And last but not least, thank you, John Nicoletti, for helping me find my voice and make sense of it all. Together we revisited all the hills I once climbed. Most of these paths were easy and pleasant but some were very hard and painful. You were tough and then delicate, but always steadfast in my striving for the honesty and truth that makes for a memorable life's story on paper. Well done, my friend.

For my

daughter and grandson,

Bronwyn and Conor Beau

• • •

And in loving memory of my husband

Charlie Blair

'TIS HERSELF

CHAPTER 1

THE GYPSY AND
THE TWO-HEADED BEAST

*M*y whole life was foretold to me. I peered out the crack of our door and found an old Romany Gypsy standing hunched on our porch in the hot afternoon sun. She smiled down at me and took my five-year-old hands in hers, then turned my palms upward and read my fortune. "You will leave Ireland one day and become a very famous woman known all around the world. You are going to make a fortune and be very, very rich." Then she held my hands in the light and cackled, "But it will all slip through your fingers one day." I pulled my hands away and answered with certainty, "I'll *never* leave Ireland." Then I closed the door.

I thought the old girl was silly. I didn't need a Gypsy to tell me what my place in the world would be. I already knew. I believed from the time I was able to think that I was going to set the world on fire.

You are about to read the tale of the toughest Irish lass who ever took on Hollywood and became a major leading lady of the silver screen. In a career that has lasted for over sixty years, I have acted, punched, swashbuckled, and shot my way through an absurdly masculine profession during the most extraordinary of times. As a woman, I'm proud to say that I stood toe-to-toe with the best of them and made my mark on my own terms. I'm Maureen O'Hara, and this is my life story.

So did the old Gypsy get it right? And who is the real Maureen O'Hara anyway? I bet that's what you really want to know. Before I answer and we begin our journey together, I want to tell you why I've decided to write this book. For one thing, I do feel a sense of responsibility for sharing my thoughts and experiences about the most remarkable era in filmmaking history—Hollywood's golden age. There aren't many of us left who can honestly look back and give you a taste of its delicious insanity and glamour.

More important, though, I'm finally ready to confront my long life with open eyes. I'm ready to revisit those treacherous hills I once climbed, and eager to kill any *fear deargs* (pronounced "far darrigs") that may still be lurking in the shadows. I also want to set the record straight about my life in my own words before some self-serving writer pens a heap of rubbish about me after I'm gone from this earth.

My favorite untrue story ever written about me is that I once lived in a magnificent Arabian palace with tall towers and a long swimming pool filled with waters of sapphire blue. Each night, I descended its marble steps and swam from one end to the other, cooling my naked body, while castrated slaves in white turbans and loincloths pointed flaming torches to light my way.

What fabulous rubbish.

You already know that I am an actress and movie star. Some see me as a former screen siren, while others remember me as the dame who gave as good as she got with Duke. To some I'm the first woman swashbuckler, while others think of me as a pirate queen. I've done as many tearjerkers as I have movies with crazy stunts. I was once called "Frozen Champagne" and "Window Dressing," which still annoys me. I much preferred "Big Red" or "the Queen of Technicolor." Many women have written to me over the years and said that I've been an inspiration to them, a woman who could hold her own against the world. That's lovely. The great director John Ford paid me my favorite compliment by saying I was the best "effin' " actress in Hollywood.

Much of this story, though, is part of a public persona that was carefully sewn together, like a magnificent quilt, by the powerful Hollywood studio system. An entire publicity team had to see to it that at least one item about me was published every day. Many were total lies or studio publicity department inventions. Hollywood gossip queens like Louella Parsons and Hedda Hopper then built on these myths in their daily columns, which were read as Gospel by millions.

Of course, my loved ones know me in a far more intimate way. To them I'm just Mammy, Gran', or Auntie Maureen—a lousy cook but one helluva cleaning lady.

I am and have been all of these things throughout my personal and professional lives, but no one of them defines me. Above all else, deep in my soul, I'm a tough Irishwoman.

Being an Irishwoman means many things to me. An Irishwoman is strong and feisty. She has guts and stands up for what she believes in. She believes she is the best at whatever she does and proceeds through life with that knowledge. She can face any hazard that life throws her way and stay with it until she wins. She is loyal to her kinsmen and accepting of others. She's not above a sock in the jaw if you have it coming. She is only on her knees before God. Yes, I am most definitely an Irishwoman.

My heritage has been my grounding, and it has brought me peace. Being tough and strong have always been my most dominant characteristics, like a fire that burns deep within me. I have always believed that I can do anything I set my mind to, as long as I'm willing to make the necessary sacrifices. I have called upon this fire to achieve my goals and survive whenever I felt my world come crashing down around me. In this way, I am like many of the women I've played on-screen.

And yet you will soon read about two events in my life that caused me to stumble and do exactly the opposite of what you and I would expect Maureen O'Hara to do. They involve my first two marriages and may jolt you. One was a comedy of youth, but the other was a tragedy of inexperience.

Still, if the events of our youth shape us into who we become, then one incident in particular had the greatest impact on me. It happened when I was a young schoolgirl at the Irish Sisters of Charity school in Milltown.

There were two old biddies there who just couldn't stand me. I never knew why they disliked me so, but they jeered at and ridiculed me every day. Miss O'Meara taught English in room 8 and Miss Cook taught maths in room 7. But I never saw them as two old teachers. To me they were one, a large and ugly beast joined at the side like Siamese twins, with two heads that shared one small brain and an even smaller heart. (Allow me just a smidgeon of latitude here. I've waited seventy years for this!)

One day I was sent to school wearing a brand-new sweater. My mother always dressed me and my sisters in matching outfits when we were growing up, but each of us had our own special color and mine was red. I was walking down the hall with my older sister and she looked marvelous in her new blue sweater. At fourteen, Peggy already had a figure, but, at twelve, I was still an awkward girl—big, tall, and freckled.

As Peggy and I made our way to class, we came upon the two old biddies in the hallway. "Peggy," purred Miss O'Meara, "that sweater looks beautiful on you." Miss Cook followed her lead. "Yes it does. Just beautiful." But as I scurried behind Peggy, the two old biddies quickly transformed into the two-headed beast and lashed out at me. "And, Maureen," Miss O'Meara's head went on snidely. "Whatever are you hiding under your sweater? A football?" I tried to ignore her and kept walking with my head down in anger while Miss Cook's head burst into laughter. Their shrill cackles followed me down that hallway.

I was angry, and worst of all, I was hiding. My first class of the day was English, with Miss O'Meara. Should I go or should I run? I wondered. I felt the fire inside me. It told me that I couldn't run. So I turned the doorknob and entered.

Miss O'Meara was standing in front of her desk, before the class, holding the morning edition of the local newspaper, the *Irish Independent*. Over the previous weekend, I had entered a very prominent acting festival and had won the top prize. It was such a big competition that the *Irish Independent* placed the story, with my picture, on the front page of the paper. Miss O'Meara's eyes were fixed on the article, and the corners of her mouth were turned up in a smirk. As the door closed behind me, she turned her attention to me with intensity.

"And here she is at last," Miss O'Meara began, sarcasm dripping from her mouth. "The newest star of Dublin theater, Miss Maureen FitzSimons." I moved quickly across the room to my seat, not saying a word. "Maureen, I was just sharing with the class your triumphant victory at this weekend's festival." Her eyes narrowed on me as she continued. "However did you do it? How could *you* win such an important acting competition?"

The class began to giggle and I felt the heat of the spotlight burning my body. I remained silent, my head down, as Miss

O'Meara continued. "Perhaps you could give the class just a taste of your extraordinary talent. Come up and show us what you did to win the competition." She followed her challenge with laughter and the entire class joined her.

As the sound of it covered me, I felt that fire burning in my belly. It grew in intensity and extended throughout my body. It lifted me, and I knew at that moment that I would never surrender to anyone's jeers. I wouldn't go up there to save my life. I wouldn't give that old biddy the satisfaction. I folded my arms across my chest and locked eyes with her, freezing them. Then I stuck my lower lip out at her defiantly and held it there.

I had never been openly defiant, not ever, and it caught her by surprise. The smile washed from her face. "No? You won't share with the class? I see. Then come with me." She moved toward the door and opened it. We moved down the hall, and Miss O'Meara opened the door that led into room 7, holding it for me to enter.

Miss Cook looked up with surprise as Miss O'Meara and I joined her at the head of the class. They melded together again, transforming into the two-headed beast. O'Meara's head spoke first. "Miss Cook, I thought you would like to share the good news with your class. Our Maureen has made the newspapers for her acting." Cook's head joined in. "Yes, I heard that she had," she said coldly. "How wonderful for you." O'Meara's head continued. "I've been trying to coax Maureen to share what she did to win."

Cook's head picked up fast on where this was going. "Yeeeees. Wouldn't that be fun? Please, Maureen, do perform for the class. We would all love to see what you did to win." I remained silent, unwilling to give an inch. As far as I was concerned, this was a battle between good and evil. "Just give us a little sample," Cook's head went on, "of that enormous talent you must have." O'Meara's head began to laugh and Cook's soon followed. Then the entire class joined in.

I stood there in front of the class with my arms folded, lower lip sticking out, looking at them all with defiant eyes. I was deeply, deeply hurt by their behavior but determined not to show it. Instead, I made a promise to myself. I swore that those two old biddies, that two-headed beast, would never beat me. I would win. I would stand up straight and take it all on the chin. I wouldn't let them or anyone else ever knock me down again.

Just you wait, I promised them in my head. I'm going to become the most famous actress in the world and one day you both are going to boast to everyone you know that I was in your class. Then I'm going to tell the entire world how deeply you hurt me.

That day, I swore I'd keep my promise. If need be, I'd lick the world. And what a big world it proved to be.

CHAPTER 2

BABY ELEPHANT

I was born on August 17, 1920, shortly before midnight. I'm not sure if it was an easy or a difficult birth—I wasn't paying attention—but I entered the world hairless as an egg. Mammy (which we pronounced "Maw-mee") told me she almost sewed fake curls on my bonnet, but my hair started growing just in time to spare me the embarrassment.

I lived without a name during my first three days in this world. Mammy wanted to name me Katherine, but Daddy wanted to call me Kate. Father Joseph Nolan was waiting patiently at the church to christen me and set me properly on the path to becoming a good little Irish Catholic girl; meanwhile the discussion at home was growing very heated. Daddy said, "No. Plain Kate, and that's it." But Mammy held her ground. "No. Katherine, and that's it." My godmother chimed in with, "Well, really she should be named for the godmother—after me—Alice Maude."

With strong, unyielding opinions battling, Mammy and Daddy had little choice but to send for the other priest at our church, Father Keane, to help sort out the whole matter. He took one look at me lying on the bed and said, "Well, she's born on the seventeenth of August, which is close to the Blessed Virgin's Feastday, so she should be called Mary." Mammy, however, wouldn't stand for it: "Absolutely not. No child of mine is going to be called Mary." Father Keane thought another moment. "All right then. How about Mairéad, Gaelic for Maureen?" Mammy shook her head. "I'd never get my tongue around it." Father Keane made one last suggestion: "Well, how 'bout just plain Maureen then?"

No one objected. "All right. Fine. Take her," Mammy said, finally conceding. So I was scooped up and carried out the door to the church where I was christened Maureen FitzSimons. I have no middle name.

I was born into the most remarkable and eccentric family I could possibly have hoped for. I was perfectly suited for them and they for me. My childhood rarely knew pain, sadness, or hardship. In fact, it was joyous—full of love and laughter—and the happiest time of my life.

Mammy was an exceptional woman. Considered one of the most beautiful women in Ireland, even in all of Europe, she once attended the races at the Champs-Elysées in Paris and found her picture in the papers the following day because she was so stunning and well dressed. She had Titian-red hair (I got mine from her!) and the most magnificent black eyes—so black, in fact, you couldn't see the difference between her iris and pupil. She would never go out in public unless she was perfectly made up. Hair, makeup, clothes—everything. She wouldn't even answer the door.

She was the most confident woman I've ever known, and she

was full of pride: proud of herself, proud of her husband, proud of her children. "Always stand up straight. Always be counted," she'd say to me again and again.

Brought into the world as Marguerita Lilburn, Mammy was born and raised in County Dublin, just as her parents were and their parents before them. Very far back in her family tree, someone had come from Scotland. We're not sure who, but we know because there's a town there called Lilburn.

It was Mammy who brought the arts into the house. In fact, she was a fine actress in her own right, performing for years in the theater. She also had the most golden operatic contralto voice you ever wanted to hear, and she often sang with the Dublin Operatic Society at the Gaiety Theatre. As well as she sang, though, her first love was always fashion. I loved going shopping in Dublin with Mammy. She opened my mind to what fashion is all about.

As much as Mammy dazzled me, Daddy comforted me by being the most decent man I have ever known, plus being as honest as the day is long. Charles Stewart Parnell FitzSimons was born on the outskirts of County Meath, to farming folk. It was a country farm and many hands were needed to keep it running smoothly. Daddy, when he was a young lad, was one of thirteen sons who helped his father work the land.

Daddy's real passion, though, was soccer, and indeed, the Irish take their soccer very seriously. He played Gaelic football for the County Meath team until they caught him at a soccer match once and kicked him off the team. There used to be great rivalry between Gaelic football lovers and soccer lovers in Ireland. He later bought into the Shamrock Rovers, one of the most renowned professional soccer teams in Ireland, and swore he would never attend another Gaelic football match again. And he never did.

Of course, County Meath and County Dublin were mortal

Gaelic football enemies, so it was a bit of a miracle that my parents ever married. Mammy was a city girl and Daddy was from the country. She was a Protestant and he was a Catholic. (Mammy eventually converted.) But Daddy was a very handsome man, with piercing blue eyes and thick hair so black it looked as blue as a raven's wing. Curly, curly, curly—he could barely get a brush through it. He was a real charmer and eventually wore her down.

They married after the proper courtship and moved into a lovely six-bedroom house in an area of Dublin known as Ranelagh. This was the house in which all of us were born. They wanted a large family and began having children right away. I am the second oldest of the six FitzSimons children, and we were a close-knit Irish clan. Each of my brothers and sisters was remarkable, and they were my best friends when I was growing up. We gave each other nicknames more meaningful to us than any Christian name our parents could ever finally agree on.

Peggy was the oldest, and we called her "the Dresden China Doll" because she was so beautiful in face and form. A magnificent lyric soprano, she was offered an opportunity to go to Milan, Italy, for training but decided to turn it down. She chose instead to follow her calling by becoming a nun, Sister Margaret Mary, with the Irish Sisters of Charity. Her vocal coach, Mother Clement, was so upset when she heard the news that she cried out, "How dare you take *my* voice to the convent?"

Florrie was "Sneaking Moses." My younger sister was the world's greatest snoop, always lurking in the shadows or hiding behind a corner. She was a wonderful ballet dancer and earned an advanced diploma in teaching classical ballet. She was also a fine actress, performing under her stage name, Clare Hamilton. She acted with James Mason in the 1944 service picture *Hotel Reserve* but gave up her career for love.

Young Charlie was known as "Rusty Gullet," the little boy

who always tried to talk like a grown man. My brother lived an incredibly successful life. He earned a barrister-at-law degree (with the distinction of being the youngest person ever to be called to the bar at that time, an honor previously accorded William Penn). He was also a fine actor and under contract to the famed Abbey Theatre. Charlie was later brought to Hollywood by John Ford and Merian C. Cooper as their protégé and became a successful producer of hit television shows. He finished his career as the founder and executive director of the Producers Guild of America. I was always especially close to Charlie. He had a brilliant mind and I could never manipulate him, which made me love him all the more.

Margot was called "the Banshee" because she cried so much. No one could wail louder than my youngest sister. Margot was also an actress and made two very good films in the mid 1940s, *I Know Where I'm Going!*, with Dame Wendy Hiller, and *The Captive Heart*, with Michael Redgrave. But her real love has always been horses and she became a highly accomplished dressage champion, winning international titles.

Jimmy was the baby of the family and we called him "Pooooor Jimmy" because he was his mother's little darling. Like every good FitzSimons, he was an actor. John Ford suggested the stage name James Lilburn and cast him as Father Paul in *The Quiet Man*. He also worked with me in *Flame of Araby*. He was on his way to becoming a star in his own right until John Ford got mad at him and ended his career, but more on that later. As a young man, Jimmy was a well-known motorcycle racer in Ireland and won the famous Leinster 500.

I had more than a few nicknames. Daddy called me his "Maisín." It was a pet name that is pronounced "maw-sheen." His brother called me "the Glaxo Kid" because of my apparent fondness for a certain breakfast food. My brothers and sisters sometimes called me "Fatzer" but much preferred the name I remember most—"Baby Elephant." A dainty little lass I wasn't. I looked twice my age until I turned ten or eleven, a harsh truth I was forced to accept at my first Holy Communion. I didn't feel any different from the other seven-year-olds as I towered over them in my white dress and veil. But as I made my way down the aisle, toward the altar, I saw an old woman look me up and down and whisper to her friend, "The last time that girl saw seven was on a door knocker!"

My favorite childhood memories are of all of us together. "Here come the beautiful FitzSimons," the neighbors would say as our family strolled across Beechwood Avenue on our way to Mass each Sunday. We walked in rows of two, with heads high, Charles and Rita FitzSimons behind their six children, always in gorgeous clothes that Mammy had designed. Daddy always with his silver-handled walking stick and his spats, Mammy never without a magnificent hat and eye veil, we were an elegant family and we knew it and loved it and were proud of it.

We later moved out of Ranelagh to 13 Churchtown Road where we were raised in a strict house. Daddy and Mammy were very old-fashioned by today's standards. We were shown great affection, but could also be disciplined with a strap when it was deserved. No nonsense was tolerated. Church every Sunday, since God was at the heart of our family life. Impeccable manners and proper etiquette were expected at all times. Rudeness or showing off was never appropriate. We were taught a strong work ethic. When Mammy or Daddy told me to do something, I was told with a smile and I accepted it with a smile. "Give your best day's work for a day's pay," they would say.

We kids always ate in the kitchen, and were allowed to eat in the dining room with Daddy and Mammy only on certain holidays. They ate alone every evening; this was their special time together.

They both had demanding careers. Mammy began as an apprentice to a local high-fashion couturier and eventually went out on her own. She opened a showroom and had four floors of workrooms where tailors, seamstresses, and millinery workers made the one-of-a-kind clothes she designed—nothing off the rack. Daddy was also in the clothing business as the manager of the Irish operations for a large British manufacturer, mostly working in fine hats.

Before dinner was served each night, we all had to line up in front of Daddy and tell him what we had done wrong during the day. We all squirmed in our shoes, trying to find the right words to use so that whatever we had done wouldn't sound so awful. It taught us diplomacy.

But I loved our nights together most of all. Every night, just before we went to bed, the whole family would snuggle in front of the fireplace and listen to Mammy and Daddy sing. Mammy sang classical music, German lieder and opera arias. She sang them in German, Italian, French, and English. My favorite was *"Den Hammer er Schwinget"* ("The Hammer He Swings"), about a blacksmith making shoes for horses. Daddy sang old, old Irish folk songs, like "There Was an Old Man." I loved it so much that I also dreamed of being an opera singer. Each night ended with us all saying our prayers before we drifted off to sleep.

I know this sounds so corny, but we've been this way our whole lives. We were an Irish version of the Von Trapps, right out of *The Sound of Music*. Our lives were centered on each other and how we lived in a world full of music, drama, dance, and fashion. We were introduced to the arts at the earliest age by our parents and encouraged to participate and explore our God-given talents. Each of us did.

I started acting with my own shadow on our back lawn when I was about five. Then the old Gypsy came to our door and everything started to happen. My performances moved from the lawn to a backyard shed that Daddy built as a clubhouse. Inside this magical and secret world, my brothers and sisters and I had our first taste of the theater. We created characters and acted out all kinds of situations and stories. Our imaginations blossomed and went wild there. I started directing my brothers and sisters in every kind of play we could think of. I thought I was the greatest director ever, but they only let me do it because I was the bossy one.

My very first dramatic performance on a stage occurred in 1926 when I was six years old. My school gave a concert for our families and friends and I was chosen to read a religious poem between scenes while the curtain was down and the scenery was being changed. I loved being in front of an audience. It felt comfortable and very natural. I was bitten by the acting bug that night and knew after the performance was over that I wanted to be an actress. Not just any actress, though—I wanted to become the greatest actress of all time! This would be my mission. I would become a grande dame of the theater! I had no thought of movies at that time.

Of course, Mammy had come to see the concert and brought her musical accompanist with her. After my reading, Mrs. Hayden told Mammy, "That girl should be in drama class." So Mammy sent me to the Ena Mary Burke School of Elocution and Drama, the finest drama school in Dublin. I studied and performed plays and recited great poetry there. But the most important thing Mrs. Burke taught me was that my first duty as a performer was to be understood by the audience. I watch and listen to movies today and am shocked by the way actors deliver their lines. I find myself asking, "What did they say? I don't understand one bloody word they're saying!" Everybody mumbles now and I don't quite know why.

I started taking singing and dancing classes. (I was never a good classical ballet dancer. Just imagine Baby Elephant teetering on point!) My early training in drama, music, and dance started at the age of six and continued for eleven years, until I made my first movie. Each class twice a week, a total of six days in all, with only Sundays off. A pretty tough schedule for a young girl. I went to school every day until three o'clock, then walked or rode my bicycle to whichever lessons I had that day. When I turned ten, I joined the Rathmines Theatre Company and worked in amateur theater in the evenings, after my lessons.

After I began my rigorous training as an actress, I didn't have the usual kind of childhood. The commitment I made to my goal didn't leave much time for fun and games. I completed my schoolwork on time and got good grades, but not the best grades in the family. When time allowed, I played sports at school or with the neighborhood kids because I was a tomboy. My size gave me an advantage in *camogie*, an Irish hurling game. I also excelled in fencing, and so was later able to hold my own with Cornel Wilde and Errol Flynn in my swashbuckler pictures. But in great contrast with being a tomboy, I also collected dolls—and still do—beautiful, handmade antique dolls. I love the craftsmanship involved. One time when I was eight, the tomboy came to the rescue of the doll collector when my favorite doll, a perfect replica of a real baby, met with a sinister fate. My brother Charlie and his friend Sam Lombard kidnapped my plastic doll and then burned her at the stake in a game of cowboys and Indians. It felt like my only connection with other little girls had just been severed and now I was different from them in every way. I was so traumatized by it that I swore revenge, that I'd make Sam Lombard pay for what he had done.

Later that summer, our family went on our usual vacation to Bray, and Sam came with us. We were all at the beach and I was making a sand castle. I watched Sam playing in the sand, without a care in the world, and decided that the time finally had come for him to be punished. I sneaked up behind him while his back was turned, locked my arms around him tightly, and then carried him out to the sea. I walked him right into the water and held him down under it, letting him up for air only when I saw the panic in his eyes. "That's for my doll," I said with a smile. Then I casually went back to the shore and continued with my sand castle.

This cemented my reputation as the toughest girl in the neighborhood. When most other girls began blossoming into young women, and boys were becoming young men, the opposite sex didn't seem very interested in me. This was fine because I really wasn't interested in it either. Mammy wouldn't permit her daughters to date until we were at least eighteen. I don't remember having a crush on a boy when I was a girl. I don't even remember my first kiss. Nearly every kiss I experienced before I got married was on camera, with my handsome leading men. I didn't have any experience for those scenes (which makes me pretty damn lucky; a girl could do a lot worse than to have Walter Pidgeon and Tyrone Power to practice on). I might have been called Frozen Champagne for appearing overly ladylike in my earliest love scenes, but what everyone didn't know was that I was scared as hell doing them. I didn't know how at all!

By the time I turned ten, the Gypsy had set my acting career well on its way. Word of my natural talent and determination was making its way through the theatrical gossip grapevine. I was becoming known in theater circles as a bright new prodigy, to be watched and followed. I began entering important and prestigious amateur acting competitions and winning them. I won the Rathmines Feis (the competition that brought the scorn of the two-headed beast down upon me), the Myra Feis, and the Father Matthew Feis. As a result, I was contacted by Radio Éireann (RE) and hired to perform classical plays over the radio. RE was the only radio station in Ireland in those days and so my performances reached nearly every household. I was paid the handsome sum of one pound for each performance. I was so proud that after each show I gave most of what I made to Mammy. Of course, they didn't need it, but she took it with great drama, in a way that made me feel as though I were feeding the whole family.

My radio performances and winning all of the Feis competitions made me a most sought-after young actress by the time I was thirteen. The Gypsy was now turning the wheels of my destiny with dynamic force, and no one, including myself, would be able to stop her.

CHAPTER 3

THE STAR WITH
BLACK-CHERRY EYES

*E*very star has that certain "something" that stands out and compels us to notice them. I loved watching James Cagney because he was so tough and gruff, and I couldn't wait to hear Irene Dunne sing in her movies. As for me, I have always believed my most compelling quality to be my inner strength, something I am easily able to share with an audience. I'm very comfortable in my own skin. I never thought my looks would have anything to do with becoming a star. Yet it seems that in some ways they did.

When I was young, I didn't think I was at all pretty. I was told only that I had a sulky, pouty face. Ironically, after I got to Hollywood, I resented that I didn't get a crack at more dramatic roles because I photographed so beautifully. More than anything, though, it was the way I used my eyes that caused audiences to look deep inside my characters to see what else was there.

When I finally turned fourteen, I had reached the required age to pursue a wild obsession that I'd had from the time I'd begun my acting training. In Ireland, every young actor on her way up wanted to be with the Abbey Theatre – the National Theatre in Dublin. It was one of the most renowned dramatic theaters in all of Europe, and the natural next step if you were serious about a career in the theater. W. B. Yeats and Lady Gregory were two of the greats who helped found it, and many great Irish actors like Sara Allgood and Barry Fitzgerald had honed their craft there.

I wasn't completely surprised when my acceptance letter came. I wasn't an unknown talent to the Abbey. They knew who I was because I had already won every major acting award that could be won in Ireland. I joined the Abbey in 1934, and it was there that I began to learn what acting life in the theater was really all about. I started at the bottom of the ladder, painting scenery, building sets, sweeping floors. I was impatient in the beginning; I wanted to perform.

About this time, I also started working at nonacting summer job assignments that I got from school. My first assignment was at Crumlin Laundry, where I typed tags for the bag wash. My second job was with the Eveready Battery Company. I later worked for the Northern Assurance Company, where I typed letters, took shorthand, and reconciled accountancy records. I enjoyed the work there, but was surprised when I was called to the manager's office one day and asked, "Is it true, Maureen, that you are a Catholic?" "Yes I am," I answered. "But you don't look like one," he replied with surprise. I never did figure out what a Catholic was supposed to look like but was happy to be the first Catholic Northern Assurance had ever hired.

I continued working hard at the Abbey for almost a year before I finally got to carry swords and spears across the stage in classical plays. It took several more months before I moved up to one-line bits. I waited three long years before I was finally given a major role. When I turned seventeen, I was cast as the lead in a new play. I couldn't wait to start rehearsing, but I would never get to play that role.

A few days after I was cast, I went to dinner with my parents at the Gresham Hotel, on O'Connell Street. The hotel manager greeted us in the lobby and then said, "I want to introduce you to Harry Richman. He's performing here in town this week." He looked over his shoulder to the bar and called out, "Harry, come and meet my friends the FitzSimonses."

Harry Richman staggered toward us and slurred, "Very nicc-cce to meet you." He was absolutely crocked. Richman was the first American I had ever met and I was appalled. I thought, Good God, do all Americans drink like this? It was a brief encounter full of the usual "How do you dos?" I didn't think anything of it at the time and had no idea how profound a change that chance encounter was about to make in my life.

Within a week, Mammy received a call from the Abbey saying that Elstree Studios, a motion-picture company in London, had contacted them and wanted to know if I could come to London to make a screen test. Harry Richman was apparently a very popular singer in the United States. He had stopped off in Dublin for the week to perform at the Gaiety Theatre before going to London to make a movie at Elstree.

That was the very first time something happened that would continue to happen over and over throughout my career. Richman, though drunk, had seen something special in my eyes. Whatever it was, it must have made a positive impression on him because he suggested they screen-test me right away. I had never even thought of being in the movies. I seldom went to the movies and never thought they compared in any way to the theater. I came from a theater family, and as a result was the biggest theater snob imaginable. So I turned down the screen-test offer and kept my eye on the brass ring in front of the footlights.

I had some sense knocked into me the very next day, however. Mammy and I went for coffee on Grafton Street with an old friend, May Carey. May was a great Irish theater actress and Mammy and I both respected her. She almost fell off her chair when I told her we had declined the invitation. "You're a damn fool," she said, shaking her head. "You might never be asked to take another screen-test in your whole life, but the Abbey will always be waiting for you." A few days later, Mammy and I were on the mail boat heading to London.

The first thing I did when I arrived in London was to go and see Harry Richman and thank him for recommending the screen-test. He was at Elstree filming a comedy called *Kicking the Moon Around.* Mammy and I stopped by the set and Richman introduced me to the film's director, Walter Forde. Since I was there, Forde asked me if I would deliver a line in the movie. Later, after I became a star, I was surprised when the film was released billing Maureen O'Hara as a star in the movie. It's not true. I was not a cast member and do not consider *Kicking the Moon Around* part of my official filmography. I only agreed to deliver the line as a favor to Harry Richman for his having helped me with my screen test.

I wasn't nervous about my first screen-test. I really didn't care one way or the other about it, which, perhaps, was for the best. They rushed me to wardrobe and makeup as soon as I arrived. What happened next still makes me laugh. They dressed me in a gold lamé gown with accordion pleats that hung from my arms like wings, and transformed me with heavy makeup into a Mata Hari look-alike. The result was that I looked like a ten-dollar hooker. It was ridiculous.

The set was completely empty except for a round table with a telephone on it. I was told to walk across the set, pick up the phone, and say, "Hello." I did it. Next, I was told to walk across the set, answer the phone, listen, slam it down, and storm off the set. I did that too. Then they sat me in a chair in front of the camera and said, "Say something." I told them about my training and about a play by Schiller that I was studying.

I was mad as hell and disappointed by the whole unprofessional event. They had wasted my time and we had made the trip for nothing, or so I thought. I told Mammy, "If that's the movie business, then I want nothing to do with it." I was going back to the theater, where real acting happened. But the Gypsy was working her magic without any regard for what I wanted.

Right after my screen test, but not because of it, I was invited to Connie's Agency, the biggest talent agency in London. Connie Chapman and Vere Barker owned the agency and represented Cary Grant and other top British actors. I needed strong representation, so I signed the standard 10 percent deal with them. The ink was barely dry on my contract when Vere said, "Before you go back to Dublin, there's someone I want you to meet."

I had never heard of Mayflower Pictures before I arrived there; the man I was about to meet, however, was known throughout the world. I was caught completely by surprise when I entered the office. Charles Laughton rose from his chair and fixed his eyes on me. "Mr. Laughton, I'd like you to meet Maureen FitzSimons," Vere announced like a cat with a bird in its mouth.

Charles Laughton was, in my eyes, the greatest working actor alive in those days, and I was a huge fan. I had worshiped him ever since *The Private Life of Henry VIII* and *Mutiny on the Bounty*. Laughton was radiant. He reached out his hand and said in that magnificent voice of his, "Hello, Maureen. Very nice to meet you." I answered with a firm handshake, taught to me by my father, and a "It's very nice to meet you too, Mr. Laughton."

Laughton introduced his partner, Erich Pommer, who rose

from behind his large mahogany desk. Born in Hildesheim, Germany, Pommer was not only Laughton's business partner but also one of the most highly regarded film producers in the world. He had produced most of Emil Jannings's films and the world-renowned classic, *Congress Dances*. He was also the man who'd discovered Marlene Dietrich. The energy in the room was electric. It poured from us as Laughton led the conversation. "Where are you from, Maureen?" I smiled and answered, "I'm from Dublin."

He motioned for us all to sit and continued to question me. "I understand you're from the theater. Do you like the theater?" Laughton studied me as I answered him. "Oh yes," I replied, "I love the theater. I've been in the theater since I was six years old."

He smiled, and his eyes twinkled, and he asked, "Do you like movies?" The truth was, I didn't care that much for movies and had to think quickly of how to reply. "Oh, I don't go to many movies. I only go to Charles Laughton movies and Laurel and Hardy movies," I said, which was the honest truth.

He answered "Clever" with his eyes and then reached for a script that was on the desk. "Maureen, would you mind reading a little for us?" As he handed it to me, I was sure this would be a big mistake. Knowing the story and its characters is very important to giving a strong performance, and the weight of his tone told me that this was a very important moment. I made my decision.

"Mr. Laughton, I don't know anything about your script or what the story is about, so I am afraid that I couldn't read for you now." He raised his brow. "But if you would let me take it home, I'd be very happy to come back tomorrow and read for you."

He shot Pommer a did-I-hear-her-right look. "No, no," he said with a wave of his hand. "That's quite all right." He took the script back from me and said, "It has been very nice meeting you." The meeting was over. I half-expected him to pat me on the head. I don't think anyone had ever refused to do a reading for him, let alone an obnoxious teenager from Dublin.

I stood up with my head high and shoulders squared, then I turned toward the door. As I reached it, Laughton asked politely, "Is there any film on her?" Vere answered quickly, "Yes, at Elstree. I'll arrange for you to see it." Laughton nodded, saying, "That would be fine." I didn't feel guilty about not reading. I would never perform a cold reading at an important moment like that—not even for Charles Laughton.

The next morning, we headed back home to Dublin. While we were on our way home, however, Laughton had driven himself down to Elstree Studios and watched my Mata Hari screen-test. He thought it was horrible and couldn't believe he had wasted his time driving there, but on his way back, it happened again. Laughton apparently couldn't get my eyes out of his mind. He later said they were all he could think about.

When he reached home, he called Pommer and said, "Erich, you better get out there fast and look at this film. We better sign her quickly. Go see it tonight." So Pommer did, and he hated my screen-test too. Pommer was furious that Laughton had made him drive all the way out to Elstree Studios in the late evening to see it. But then it happened again. On his drive back, Pommer had the same reaction to my eyes. He called Laughton as soon as he reached London and said, "You're right. We better sign her fast." By the time Mammy and I reached home that evening, there was a telegram waiting there for me. Laughton and Pommer were offering me a seven-year contract with Mayflower Pictures.

My parents read the telegram over and over that night. I was still a child in their eyes, and this was a very serious offer. Despite their concerns, they decided to accept, because they knew it would further my aspirations of being an actress. They sent their answer to Laughton and Pommer the next morning. A few days later, the formal contract arrived by courier. It needed to be witnessed, so my father sent for our local priest, Father James Doyle, who rode to our house on his bicycle. Then they all signed it together, and suddenly I was, at the age of seventeen, officially under my first movie contract, to Charles Laughton and Erich Pommer.

Being under contract to Laughton and Pommer meant many things. It meant that I would learn how to act in movies under the eye of the biggest movie star in the world. I would be Laughton's only protégée, and he would introduce me to the entire world at a very young age. It meant that I had to leave the theater and the joy of performing before a live audience, including bowing out of my starring role at the Abbey Theatre. It also meant that I had to leave my family and my homeland to live in London. It was just as the old Gypsy had foretold all those years before. Mammy arranged for me to live with her sister in London.

I moved there a few weeks later and immediately went to work, learning the movie business while at the same time continuing to take singing, dancing, and acting lessons. Laughton arranged for me to make my first picture, a low-budget musical called *My Irish Molly*. It's the only picture that I made under my real name, Maureen FitzSimons. I was to play a young woman named Eiléen O'Shea who helps rescue a little orphan girl named Molly. I knew the film was going to be a flop the minute I read the script.

But Laughton wanted me to become more comfortable with both being on a movie set and being in front of the camera. He wanted me to learn how a studio actually makes a motion picture. The most important thing I learned on *My Irish Molly* was that in the theater, I had been acting for the people in the back row; in the movies, I was acting for people in the front row, where the mere flick of an eyelid can say a lot.

The film wrapped without any attention and that was just fine by me. I was so disillusioned by the whole experience that I wasn't sure I even wanted to be in the picture business anymore. I quickly got over those feelings when Laughton called me to his office to discuss another project. He had cast me as his leading lady in his next movie, *Jamaica Inn.* Alfred Hitchcock was set to direct.

It was a big-budget picture. The plot involved a local minister, played by Laughton, who is also the shadow head of a gang of shipwreckers and smugglers. The gang's headquarters is at Jamaica Inn and the innkeeper, played by Leslie Banks, is one of the smugglers. My character was the innkeeper's niece, Mary Yellan, the heroine who is torn between her love of family and her love for a lawman in disguise.

I read the script and loved it, but hated what I then learned often happens in the preproduction phase of filmmaking. The studio selects the scripts they are willing to invest in. Since Paramount Pictures in Hollywood was distributing the film in America, Laughton's villain role was changed from a Protestant minister to a Cornish squire named Sir Humphrey Pengallan. The script had been adapted from the best-selling novel by Daphne du Maurier and the press blamed Laughton for ruining her story. This accusation was wrong and terribly unfair. It was the American Hays Office (then the mavens of taste and always ready to censor anything they didn't like) that insisted the change be made, not Laughton.

Laughton's character wasn't the only big change that happened on the picture. Just before we began shooting, Laughton sent for me. He greeted me in typical Laughton fashion, with a compliment: "Maureen, you're going to be just marvelous in this picture." I thanked him and watched the smile fade from his face as he continued. "But your name is too long for the marquee and we have to change it."

My jaw dropped open and I could barely sputter a response. "But . . . but I don't want to change my name." My protest fell on deaf ears. "Well, I'm sorry, but you have to. You can either be Maureen O'Mara or Maureen O'Hara. Which do you prefer?" I tried to hold my ground. "Neither. I'm Maureen FitzSimons." Laughton dismissed my protest and made the decision for me. "Then you're Maureen O'Hara," and so I was and so I am. With this last hurdle crossed, Laughton felt I was ready to meet the film's director.

I first met Alfred Hitchcock during a preproduction meeting with Laughton and Pommer at Mayflower Pictures. Since it was Laughton who had cast me in the role, I wasn't sure how Hitchcock felt about me. He was already a top director by this time, while I was an unproven film actress.

Hitchcock put any worries I had for myself to rest right away. We liked each other from the start. I never experienced the strange feeling of detachment with Hitchcock that many other actors claimed to have felt while working with him. I know some of his leading ladies have said that he treated them with devotion one minute and then turned cruel the next, but it never happened with me.

The honest truth is that Hitchcock never wanted to make *Jamaica Inn* to begin with. He wanted to go to Hollywood and begin his film career in America. He hated period pieces and thought the costumes actors wore pulled audiences out of the story. He only agreed to direct the picture because he hoped it would assure him of the chance to direct the film adaptation of *Rebecca*, which had also been written by du Maurier. His gamble paid off, of course, and *Rebecca* was later a huge success for him.

That's not to say there weren't things about *Jamaica Inn* that Hitchcock became excited about. He loved the Jekyll-Hyde duality of Laughton's character and he had a lot of fun with the shipwrecking sequences. In fact, he was absolutely giddy about luring unsuspecting ships into the rocks by having the smugglers use fake lights. While shooting those sequences, I could see the devilish boy hiding within his gigantic frame.

His physical appearance was very much a part of his eccentricity. He was always very neat and tidy in his appearance, but he moved very awkwardly because of his weight. He rarely socialized on the set and usually spoke in a low Cockney whisper to keep the set quiet. I thought it was very odd watching him sitting patiently in his director's chair, remaining absolutely silent for hours. No one dared break the mood he had set—no one, that is, except Laughton.

Jamaica Inn was the first artistic collaboration between Laughton and Hitchcock. Both men were powerful forces on the set, with huge egos, and this made for some very exciting and tense moments. Laughton was not only the star of the film, but also its coproducer, which gave him a lot of latitude. They had very different filmmaking styles. Hitchcock wanted a subtle and delicate approach to the story, while Laughton wanted it grandiose and larger than life. Laughton frustrated Hitchcock, and it is very evident when you watch the film that it is far more Laughton's than Hitchcock's.

As interesting as it was working with Hitchcock, I was looking forward most to working with Charles Laughton. I adored Laughton. By this point, I looked up to him like a second father, and he treated me as if I was the daughter he had always wanted. He once asked my parents if he could adopt me. Laughton and his wife, Elsa Lanchester, were never blessed with children. Years after he died, Elsa wrote her autobiography and claimed they never had children because Laughton was homosexual. That's rubbish. Whether or not Laughton was gay would never have stopped him from having children. He wanted them too badly.

Laughton told me the reason they never had children was because Elsa couldn't conceive, the result of a botched abortion she'd had during her earlier days in burlesque. Laughton told me many times that not being a father was his greatest disappointment in life.

No one brought characters to life like Laughton. As an actor, Laughton painted a physical portrait. He was very focused on the physical and oratory aspects of Pengallan. Before each scene, I watched him use a humming ritual to lower the pitch of his voice, beginning with tenor, followed by baritone, and finally bass. He was very concerned about pitch and tone, as compared to dialect, and believed that they revealed certain aspects of the character's back story that were not revealed in the script.

Movement had to be consistent with sound, just as a dancer must be in step with the music. Laughton used his body in his performance much as a dancer would. He dressed in full costume during rehearsals and used music to find a rhythmic motion for his walk and other physical business, all the way down to simple hand gestures. I've never seen any other actor do it. It was beautiful to watch. Of course, he could also make a character completely unforgettable by the mere gleam in his eyes.

This combination gave him a superior screen presence, and the magical thing is that it brought out the best in me. Knowing that Laughton could easily steal my most important scenes brought my creative process to a higher level. It forced me to find hidden qualities of strength within the character of Mary Yellan to project through the camera and keep hold of the audience. It's a technique I've used ever since.

Shooting began on the first day of September 1938, and ended by the middle of October. My day started at four A.M. and didn't end until ten P.M.—six days a week. I was exhausted every day. I'd love to say I made a fortune for working that hard, but no such luck. We didn't get million-dollar paychecks for movies back then, and I never have anyway. I was under contract to Mayflower Pictures for pounds that equaled about eighty dollars a week. That's seventy-five cents an hour for a starring role and I don't even get residuals for the picture!

During the filming, I didn't have time for a social life, but it wouldn't have made any difference if I had. My aunt Florence made it her business to watch every move I made, like some frustrated ex–prison guard. The mere thought of dating exhausted me. I had no interest in it at all.

Interest or not, however, I seemed to be expected to date. There was one date, however, I never should have gone on. It all began when I returned a professional hello to George Brown, a production man on *Jamaica Inn*. I just felt it was appropriate that I be polite whenever he greeted me. I said hello and never thought anything of it. Then one day I was talking to Max Setton on the set and he mentioned George Brown. Max was Laughton and Pommer's lawyer and he and I had become good friends after I signed with Mayflower. Max was also friends with Brown, and he asked me if I would go on a date with Brown as a favor to him. I couldn't say no to Max and so I stupidly agreed. It was one of the biggest mistakes of my life.

Brown called me right away to see if I would go horseback riding with him. I felt strange about it because I knew him only as a production man on the picture. We had never had a single conversation. I barely remembered who he was when Max mentioned him, but I said yes because I thought a date would be harmless. I was wrong. It was a disaster. We could only exchange polite pleasantries and talk about work. There were no sparks whatsoever. Plus, it's hard to talk when you're horseback riding. You have to shout at each other. We trotted around for almost an hour and I was running out of things to shout. Then I got an unlucky

lucky break. My horse stepped into a pothole and lunged forward. I wasn't expecting it and flew over its head and landed hard on the ground.

I quickly sprang to my feet, but was very embarrassed. That didn't last long. I knew this was my chance to get off the hook, and so I asked gingerly, "George, would you mind if we took the horses back now? I have a long day on the set tomorrow and think I should go home and rest." What could he say to that? He sure as hell didn't want to be the reason Hitchcock's to-the-second schedule got held up. "Oh . . . of course. You're all right, aren't you?" I faked my answer as only an actress could with an unsure "I think so."

A few days later, he called and asked me out again, this time for dinner and dancing. I was really feeling uncomfortable about the whole thing by now. I didn't want to go, but I felt obligated because of Max, and I didn't know how to get out of it. So I agreed to have dinner with him, but planned on making it the shortest evening in dating history.

We went to a very nice hotel where they had dinner and dancing and I quickly ordered my meal before the waiter had finished unfolding my napkin. When the food finally came, I ate faster than I ever had before. He remained clueless. He was getting into the swing of the music while the waiter cleared our plates from the table. "Would you like to dance, Maureen?" I forced a smile and answered, "Sure."

He led me to the dance floor, which was packed with dancing couples. We started to dance, but the song ended quickly and my opportunity arrived. I looked up at him and delivered the line I had rehearsed in my head, "George, this has been lovely, but I really have to get home early. I have my last scene with Mr. Laughton tomorrow and need to get ready for it tonight. Would you mind terribly if we made it an early evening?" That was the last time I planned to go out with him. Little did I know that George Brown wasn't through with me yet.

The final week of shooting was grueling and everyone on the set was completely spent at the end. On our last day, I was almost asleep in my chair when Laughton came and sat down next to me. He had his business face on now, and whenever Laughton did that, he always spoke to you very directly. "Maureen, we're going to America to make *The Hunchback of Notre Dame* and you are going to play Esmeralda." That woke me up. "That's wonderful. I can't wait to call home and tell everyone," I shouted with excitement. "When are we going?" Laughton was pleased that I was so eager. "Around June. After the premiere."

The premiere for *Jamaica Inn* was the first I had ever been to. You would think that my family and I would have been excited about going to the premiere of my first starring movie, but in true FitzSimons form, none of us was. We were never impressed by the trappings of stardom and fame. Besides, my family was very prominent throughout Dublin, and we were theater and opera people.

Of course, my career did have its perks, and one of them was the beautiful evening gown I wore that night. It was a magnificent aquamarine dress with a matching pleated chiffon cape that Mammy had designed. My parents went with me and we arrived at the Regal Cinema in a limousine provided by the studio. As we pulled up in front of the theater, we saw that hundreds of excited fans had gathered, eager to catch a glimpse of Laughton and Hitchcock. I'd never seen so many people except at a soccer match. They didn't make any fuss over me. Why should they? I wasn't a star yet. They were kind and politely said hello to me as I walked by, but it was nothing compared to the frenzy that erupted when Laughton arrived.

It was a very big event. The public was there. The press was there. I smiled to this flash and that flash until my eyes began to burn. Then we entered the theater to watch the film.

The magnitude of the moment finally struck me as the lights faded to black and the beautiful curtain slowly opened. I saw my name appear for the very first time on the large silver screen—after Alfred Hitchcock and Charles Laughton—and a feeling of intense pride washed over me.

I became impatient, though, and began fidgeting in my seat as I waited for Mary Yellan to arrive on-screen. She finally came by stagecoach, demurely dressed, and it overwhelmed me. I couldn't believe what I was seeing. The black-and-white celluloid images made me see myself in ways I never had before. That wasn't Baby Elephant up there. It wasn't Fatzer or that awkward tomboy I had been in my early youth. Nature had taken its course without any help or effort from me, and I was the last one to see it. I thought the girl up there was beautiful, and for the very first time in my life, I actually felt pretty. I could finally see what Laughton and Pommer had seen. The black-and-white film somehow made my eyes a rich, deep black. It enhanced significantly the effect I was intending when using my eyes to communicate with the audience.

I watched my performance very closely. I had never seen myself perform before because, of course, it's not possible in the theater. Watching myself confirmed what I had always believed to be true: I was on that screen opposite Charles Laughton and I was holding my own. I peeked around the theater and watched the faces in the audience. I thought of the old Gypsy and knew right then and there, with certainty, that *Jamaica Inn* was going to make me a star.

When the movie ended, the audience showed their approval with thunderous applause. My life would never be the same again and the change was instantaneous. Outside the theater, the crowds greeted me very differently as I made my way toward the car. I heard them shouting my name, but could barely see them through the brilliant flashes from the cameras. They fell upon me and I felt the walls of private life crumble around me as I embraced and became the public person known as Maureen O'Hara. I had arrived at the theater that night a young and aspiring actress, but I left a star.

It's rare when a film receives only positive reviews from critics, and *Jamaica Inn* was no exception. They were mostly positive and very kind to me. My favorite one said, "She creates an impression of reserves of strength that give her a delicate vigor. Here, undoubtedly, is a star of the future." Laughton might have changed my name to Maureen O'Hara, but newspapers throughout England that next morning were talking about "the girl with black-cherry eyes."

CHAPTER 4

THE HUNCHBACK OF NOTRE DAME

*T*he *Queen Mary* was the most civilized and luxurious way one could travel to America in the late 1930s. At the time, she was the largest ocean liner in the world, and had countless successful crossings to her credit. Yet my voyage aboard her was headed for a collision of its own—not with an iceberg, but with Mammy and Charles Laughton. Neither of them knew when we boarded her that I was hiding a terrible secret.

We set sail on Mammy's birthday in June 1939, and expected to be in America for only about three months to make *The Hunchback of Notre Dame* for RKO Pictures. Laughton and I were already scheduled to go straight to Paris after *Hunchback* wrapped to make our next film together, *The Admirable Creighton*.

I was only eighteen years old and so Mammy was required by the immigration laws to go with me. Elsa Lanchester decided not to go with us and would be joining Laughton later in Los Angeles.

The press was already having a field day with Laughton. The day we left, one headline in a large British newspaper read "Beauty and the Beast Leave for Hollywood."

None of this was of any significance to me, however, when I arrived at the *Queen Mary*. I was oblivious to everything, in a total state of shock. I didn't notice the immensity of her thousand-foot frame, though I had never been on a boat that large in my life. I couldn't hear the sound of the three steam whistles blowing or smell the scent of burning coal flowing from her smokestacks. I wasn't on the promenade deck with Mammy and Charles Laughton. I wasn't on that boat at all. I was out in the ocean, completely within myself, drowning from the weight of what I had done just before we set sail.

The anchor that was chained to my feet and dragging me under was George Brown. George had continued pursuing me after *Jamaica Inn* was finished. I had hoped he would've gotten the hint from our two quickly ended dates, but he hadn't. Quite the opposite, in fact. He was calling me more than ever, and the more I tried putting him off, the harder he pursued me. I should have been honest with him and told him straight out that I wasn't interested in seeing him, but I didn't. I was too inexperienced with dating. That was my first mistake, but it was nothing compared to my second.

Earlier that morning, Mammy and I had been frantically packing our bags and readying to join Laughton on the *Queen Mary*. We were running terribly behind schedule and thought we might miss the boat. Brown was relentless, and kept phoning me every five minutes. To make things worse, my apartment building had only one shared telephone, in the hallway on the floor above me. Every time he called, I had to run upstairs to speak with him.

Mammy kept telling me to get off the damn phone. But each time I hung up, he'd call back within minutes. Then he dropped the bombshell. "Maureen, you can't go," he pleaded. "I'm in love with you." I couldn't believe my ears. I had never shown the slightest bit of interest in him. We had never had a kiss. "Well, I'm terribly sorry, George," I answered. "But I'm leaving for America in two hours."

George didn't miss a beat. "Then marry me," he shot back. "Before you go." I almost dropped the phone. "George, I can't marry you. We hardly know each other." He paused. "Then at least see me one more time before you go."

"George, I can't," I replied. "I'm running late as it is. Good-bye." Still, George kept calling and calling, while Mammy kept worrying and worrying about missing the boat. I worked myself into hysterics and couldn't see straight. I didn't know what to do. He kept asking to see me before I went and I suddenly heard myself saying, "Okay, George, okay. Where do I meet you?!" I went back down to my apartment and scribbled down the address. Then I turned to Mammy and said, "Finish packing, Mammy. I'll be right back."

My taxi raced to the address George had given me. I asked the driver to wait for me as we pulled up in front of a small house. George opened the door. He put his arm around me and led me inside.

What was waiting for me was something you'd expect to see in a movie. Standing in the corner of a small room was a very official-looking man. I didn't know why he was there. He seemed surprised by my appearance, and then asked, "Is this the bride?" I was paralyzed with shock when George answered, "Yes. This is Maureen." My heart began to pound. "How old is she?" the man asked. George answered again, "She's over twenty-one." That was a lie, and I knew I should speak up, but my mouth wouldn't work. I was an inexperienced eighteen-year-old on very unfamiliar ground. I just stood there frozen, unable to speak, stunned and scared into absolute silence. I knew I should get out of there right away, that minute, just run for the door—but my feet were frozen to the floor.

The man said, "Then let's get started. I know we're pressed for time." I felt a part of me—the part with an intellect—separate from the rest of me and leave my body. I was having an out-of-body experience, and my brain had just abandoned me when I needed it most. I was numb, beyond feeling, and watched my intellect move to a chair and sit in the corner. It just watched me as I joined George before the man.

It all seemed to happen faster than an eye blink. I saw that the man was speaking, but I didn't hear a word he said. I watched George slide a ring on my finger, but I couldn't really feel it. The only thing I heard was, "Do you take her to be your wife?" George said he did. "And do you take him to be your husband?" My intellect shouted at me from the corner. "Don't do it, Maureen! Don't be a fool!" But I was a girl without any brains in her head. I rationalized the whole thing: "Just get this thing over with and make that boat. Arguing with George will only waste time. Do it, then get as far away from him as you can—all the way to America." I finally spoke, but could hardly believe the words were coming from my own mouth. "I do," I replied. George kissed me; it lasted a nanosecond. I saw my intellect rise from the chair and move toward me. It took my hand and began tugging me toward the door. I looked to George and said, "I've got to go, George. I'll miss the boat."

I climbed back into the taxi and we sped off again. I sat in the seat and hyperventilated. The horror of what I had done was choking me. I was scared to death. I wanted to scream at the top of my lungs, "Maureen FitzSimons, what have you done?!" But my intellect spared me the effort by reminding me, "You stupid ass. You just married George Brown!"

I ripped the wedding ring off my finger and threw it into my purse. I said nothing to Mammy when I got back to the apartment. Two hours later, we were aboard the *Queen Mary* and sailing for America.

Of course I was scared. I might have found a degree of celebrity but I was still just a teenage girl. I didn't know how to tell Mammy that I had married George Brown. I spent the first day on the *Queen Mary* hiding at the pool, scared half out of my wits. I was very quiet the whole day, and Mammy knew me well enough to know that something was wrong. When I returned to the cabin, all hell broke loose. While I was at the pool, Mammy had found the wedding ring at the bottom of my purse. She held it out in front of me and asked, "What is this, Maureen?"

I broke down and confessed, very much like a criminal. Mammy was shocked and furious, but she didn't scream or yell at me. She just kept asking the big question: "Why?" All I could say was, "I don't know." I didn't know how to tell her how scared I had been in that house. Then she turned to the details. When did you get the marriage license? I didn't know. I never got a license. Who were the witnesses? There were no witnesses. Nobody else was there. Did a priest marry you? I didn't know who that man was, I had never seen him before. I just wished I had a magic wand to make it all go away.

It was Mammy who broke the news to Laughton, and he took it worse than I'd expected. He was shocked and very angry. What I didn't know was that this couldn't have happened at a worse time. Mayflower Pictures was in serious financial trouble, and *Jamaica Inn* was not going to save it. Since my star was now on the rise, my contract with Mayflower was a valuable asset of the company's. Laughton and Pommer wouldn't want any bad press about me. Damage control would be required, and I was instructed not to speak of the marriage to anyone.

• • •

We arrived in New York on June 23, 1939, to a tremendously warm and exciting welcome. The press greeted us at the dock, and countless photographs of Laughton and me were taken. Laughton was hamming it up for the camera and obliged a photographer's request by wrapping his arms around me. Snap and flash. Of course, that picture appeared in a British newspaper, causing rumors to fly in England.

It was all so ludicrous. But when word of it reached Elsa in London, she was livid. A reporter from the *Evening Standard* asked her, "What about your husband traveling abroad with that young girl?" Elsa resented the insinuation and seemed to blame me for it. She said, "Well, I don't know what Miss O'Hara or any others have been saying, but she's an actress who is going to appear with Charles in his next picture. He found her, discovered her, and so on—and there's just nothing to it."

It was perfectly natural that the press would greet us at the dock when we arrived. *Jamaica Inn* had just been released in the United States by Paramount that week, and all the newspapers were writing their reviews of it. Despite what some papers were saying back in London, the American press was wonderful to me. The kindest welcome came from Bosley Crowther, the powerful film critic for the *New York Times*. He wrote, "She is the emerald shower which succeeds the initial explosion of a skyrocket." I didn't see any skyrockets as I peered out the window of our car and took in New York City for the very first time. My first impressions of America were of bald heads and billboards. I had never seen so many of both.

After two days in New York, I was put on a train that took Mammy and me to Los Angeles—and Hollywood. Laughton stayed in New York for a few extra days to complete some important business with RKO and to wait for Elsa to join him. The studio had made all the living arrangements for us and had rented an apartment in the Pasadena area. It was quite a sight to see: all pale pink—very anemic, very swank, very cold. When Laughton finally reached Hollywood, he took one look at the place and said, "Good God. You're moving out of this," and transferred us to the Garden of Allah Hotel on Sunset Boulevard where he and Elsa were staying.

I was happy to move to more comfortable living quarters, but a bit apprehensive about living so close to Elsa. She was tough, and had a special talent for being really mean when she wanted to be. I never felt she really liked me. I think she was jealous of my friendship with Laughton, but I'm not sure. Perhaps she was jealous of my career. She always seemed to enjoy a good laugh at my expense and delighted in my problem with George Brown. "All this time we thought our little Maureen was so fresh and innocent," she later said. "Who would have thought she'd already been wedded and bedded?" Wedded yes, bedded no—and she damn well knew it.

We just didn't click personally. I never understood the changing of her last name from Sullivan to Lanchester because it sounded more elegant. Nor did I understand her hatred of religion of any kind. She was a very fine character actress, though, and she was good to Charles. She was witty, and down deep, she was decent, but she always seemed to want something outside her reach, and I never knew what it was.

I spent my first week in Hollywood at Paramount Pictures working on publicity for *Jamaica Inn*, mostly interviews and photo sessions. It was the first time I had ever been on a Hollywood studio lot and, not surprisingly, I found it quite different from the small, intimate surroundings of Mayflower Pictures and Elstree Studios. Everything was so large and grand in scale. One minute you're walking down Chicago's streets, then you turn right and you're on a set lost in the trees of a forest. Craftsmen from every discipline of the medium were scurrying about, hundreds of them. I had never seen a more concentrated population of artists in a single place. I knew instantly that a Hollywood studio was a filmmaking machine of precision unlike anything I had experienced before.

After I finished the publicity campaign for Paramount, I went right to work on making *The Hunchback of Notre Dame.* RKO wanted to remake the 1923 silent film that had starred Lon Chaney and there was great anticipation about Laughton's portrayal of Quasimodo. The plot of the film is well known, of course. Set in fifteenth-century Paris, the deformed bell ringer of Notre-Dame cathedral, Quasimodo (played by Laughton), falls in love with a Gypsy girl, Esmeralda (played by me), and tries to save her from the gallows when she is falsely accused of murder.

The script was excellently written by Sonya Levien, based on Bruno Frank's adaptation of Victor Hugo's classic novel, *Notre-Dame de Paris.* A first-rate supporting cast included Sir Cedric Hardwicke as Frollo, the king's high justice; Harry Davenport as King Louis XI; Thomas Mitchell as Clopin, king of beggars; and, making his screen debut, Edmond O'Brien as Gringoire the poet.

In the first week of August, I was summoned to RKO to meet my new director. RKO sent a car, as they always did in those days, and I was instructed to ask for Mr. Dieterle when we reached the gate, where I was to show them my pass allowing me on the studio lot. Of course, nothing went as it was supposed to. The driver arrived without a pass and I forgot Dieterle's name. There I was at the gate pleading with the guard to let me in, but he wasn't budging. He thought I was a fan trying to crash the studio. Luckily, Pandro Berman spotted me in the car and recognized the girl he had just cast as Esmeralda and took me inside to meet Dieterle. It was not the best first impression to make on the boss.

My first impression of William Dieterle was that he would be a tough, no-nonsense director. Of German origin, Dieterle was very tall, six-five or so, and had a commanding presence. That first encounter was mostly a get-acquainted talk, so meaningless I don't remember what we actually said. I do recall, though, that he hated my curly hair and told me to have it straightened before filming began. He had a very thick accent and his English was quite flawed. Typically German, he was autocratic and businesslike. Dieterle was best known for the historical epics he directed at Warner Bros. and for his ability to film masses of people in large, glorious scenes. He had begun as an actor, and later worked under the great German director Max Reinhardt. He was a devout Christian Scientist and always wore white gloves on the set because he was deathly afraid of germs. I always suspected he also wore them so we actors could see his directions during the crowd sequences no matter how far away we were.

After our meeting, I was sent to wardrobe to be measured and fitted for my costumes. Later, on location, I was impressed with the efficiency with which big studios handled wardrobe. There were hundreds and hundreds of extras on the picture, and there was an enormous wardrobe tent where they went each morning to pick up their costumes and to be fitted. It was an assembly line of mass production. I was amazed that they could process so many people through each morning in time to meet the shooting schedule.

But I was the one who ended up having a problem with the shooting schedule, and it led to one of the biggest disappointments of my career. A few weeks before we were scheduled to finish filming, Alfred Hitchcock called and offered me the leading role in *Rebecca*. It was going to be his first picture in Hollywood, and I guess he had felt comfortable working with me on *Jamaica Inn*. I wanted the part very badly, but Dieterle had to agree to accelerate the shooting of my last few scenes in *Hunchback* if I was going to make

Hitchcock's shooting schedule for *Rebecca*. Dieterle refused, and so Hitchcock cast Joan Fontaine in the role. I was crushed, and Joan received an Oscar nomination for her performance.

We began filming *The Hunchback of Notre Dame* during the second week of August out in the San Fernando Valley at the sprawling RKO ranch. When I first arrived on the set, the sight of it awed me. The outdoor sets were astounding. A fifteen-acre re-creation of fifteenth-century Paris had been designed from a four-hundred-year-old wood carving of the city, then had been built in intense summer heat on a $250,000 budget. That was big bucks back then. Every scene in the film was shot on a set. We didn't go on location to Paris, but anyone who watches the film would believe that we had.

Unfortunately, Los Angeles was having the hottest summer in its history, and I knew from day one that it was going to be a physically demanding shoot, with the temperature averaging 100 degrees. Though it was tough on all of us, it was especially taxing on Laughton because of the heavy makeup and costume requirements for Quasimodo. When I saw Laughton for the first time made up as Quasimodo, I almost fell over. I took one look at him and gasped, "Good God, Charles. Is that really you?" He answered me with a wink and then limped off. The transformation was unbelievable, and was accomplished without any of the advanced technology used today. Of course, to get Quasimodo just right, RKO spared no expense. Perc Westmore, at the time the number one makeup man in the picture business, was brought in at Laughton's insistence to create the disguise, at a cost of $10,000. That was a fortune in those days.

Quasimodo's appearance was the result of a collaboration between Laughton and Westmore; they had started working together on it weeks before we began filming. Westmore made numerous versions, but Laughton rejected each of them until he finally got what he wanted. Laughton wanted the hunchback's face to look lopsided, and so the mask had to pull the right side of his face up and the left side down. A false eye was placed on the left cheek and Laughton wore a colored contact lens in his right eye to give it a cloudy look. The hump itself weighed four pounds and consisted of an aluminum scaffold filled with foam rubber and then covered with a thin layer of elastic. Laughton wanted it to be heavy so he could feel the physical pain of walking with it. He also had an inch added to the sole of his left shoe so that one leg would be shorter than the other, creating a natural limp.

I was well prepared for my role as Esmeralda. I knew my character, my lines, and how I would deliver them. I spent time with dance directors Ernst and Ginny Matray mastering the tambourine dance sequence. And since I had already worked with Laughton, I was familiar and comfortable with his style of acting. I was meeting Dieterle's expectations and he seemed happy with me. I never found him to be the tyrant other people say he was on the set. My only complaint after the first month of shooting was that I had painful bruises on the soles of my feet from running around the cobblestone streets all day.

There had been only a few surprises, funny ones. One morning I arrived on the set and was shocked to find the town square full of live chimpanzees, baboons, and gorillas. They made a mess all over the place and it smelled like a zoo. The day before, Dieterle had said, "I vont two hundred monkey on ze set tomorrow morning." His poor English had failed him. I found him running around the cathedral steps with his white gloves flailing, screaming, "*Mein Gott!* Vat iz diss?"

His assistant, Peter Berneis, answered, "The monkeys you ordered, Mr. Dieterle."

"No, you idyet! I vonted two hundred priests. I vonted monks, not monkeys!"

Everything was going smoothly with the picture and I was enjoying my time in America very much. That all changed on the first day of September when Hitler and his Third Reich rolled over Poland. The whole world had known Europe was a ticking time bomb, but we all seemed to believe that everything would somehow work itself out. We arrived on the set that day and the usual calm was noticeably absent, replaced with fear about an uncertain future. The whole cast and crew gathered in the town square trying to reassure and comfort each other. All but Laughton, who sat in his chair, still and silent. Finally he rose and moved to the pillars of Notre-Dame cathedral. Then he did something absolutely extraordinary. He leaned against the pillars and began to speak: " 'Four score and seven years ago our fathers brought forth on this continent, a new nation, conceived in Liberty and dedicated to the proposition that all men are created equal . . .' "

The entire cast and crew—every one of us—stood mesmerized as Laughton continued reciting the Gettysburg Address, completely from memory, all the while dressed as Quasimodo. "'. . . we can not dedicate—we can not consecrate—we can not hallow this ground . . .' " Time stood still as the words rolled off his tongue and danced in the air, building to astounding, powerful crescendos of eloquence. " '. . . that this nation, under God, shall have a new birth of freedom—and that government of the people, by the people, for the people shall not perish from this earth.' "

It was a prayer, a battle cry, and the single greatest piece of acting I have ever seen. All of us, hundreds of us, just stood there, moved to stunned silence when the speech ended and Mr. Laughton quietly returned to his chair.

Two days later, England and France declared war on Germany. Laughton's homeland was now at war, and he was in agony over it. We were scheduled to shoot one of the most important scenes in the film that day, when Quasimodo rings the bells in the bell tower for Esmeralda. It was supposed to be an expression of the hunchback's love for her. But Laughton was so overcome with pain that the emotion of the scene swept him away. He began ringing the bells and then it grew into something that transcended the film. He rang them with a ferocity that I had never seen in him before. The intensity of it grew and grew, until I was shaking from the power of it. The sound was almost deafening. Everybody, including Dieterle, was so overcome we all forgot we were shooting a scene. Dieterle forgot to call "Cut" when the scene ended, and Laughton kept ringing the bells until he collapsed from exhaustion.

Afterward, I went to see him in his tent. "Charles, are you all right?" I asked. "It just took me over, Maureen," he replied. "I couldn't even think of Esmeralda up there at all. I could only think of the poor people out there going to fight that bloody, bloody war. To arouse the world, to stop that terrible butchery! Awake! Awake! That's all I could feel."

In many ways, the war helped Laughton's performance. It became his nexus. It was the voice through which he could express the world's pain and suffering.

After weeks of shooting, I was finally sent to work with two of the greatest Hollywood stuntmen, Sailor Vincent and Dick Crockett, in preparation for the stunts I had to perform in the film. These were the very first dangerous stunts—but certainly not the last— that I was asked to perform. I had no prior stunt training, and we prepared for many days before shooting them. At eighteen, I was fearless and willing to do anything required for the role. Looking back with wiser eyes, I realize that I was crazy and what I did scares the hell out of me today. My first stunt was the least difficult. As Esmeralda waits on the platform for the hangman to put the noose around her neck, Quasimodo swings down from the cathedral scaffold on a rope, scoops her up in his arms, and then carries her back up to safety, a triumphant rescue. Sailor Vincent performed this stunt for Laughton, and he instructed me to hold on tightly to the rope with both hands while he held me with one arm around my sternum. This was real life. There were no harnesses or safety nets used. If we had missed our mark, we would have crashed into the wooden scaffold and fallen forty feet, to the stone floor below. Fortunately, we got it in one take.

The second stunt was the more dangerous of the two; in fact, it was truly life threatening. We filmed that one the following day. It was Dick Crockett, standing in for Laughton, who raised me up over his head on the cathedral balcony and showed Esmeralda to the cheering crowd below after she had been saved. The stunt had three parts: raising me over his head, holding me there for a period of time, and then getting me safely back down. Again, no safety devices of any kind were used, not even a railing or a board to break my fall should Crockett slip. Had Dick's elbow bent or my weight shifted, I would have fallen hundreds of feet down to the stone steps and been killed instantly. I had a lot of nervous energy before he lifted me up, but I forced myself to smother it. Once he got me up over his head, I kept my body rigid, in a lifeless position, and purged all thoughts of fear from my mind. Fear and panic are killers.

I felt a tremendous adrenaline rush when it was over, which was followed by a great sense of gratitude to Dick Crockett. This began my love affair with stunts and stuntmen. The bond of trust that forms between you is very special, and that's why most performers prefer to use the same stuntmen in picture after picture.

I also met another young man while making this movie, and he would later take me on the longest ride of my life. I don't remember exactly when I first met Will Price, but it had to be on the only dark day amid a remarkably beautiful summer. Price was the dialogue director on *Hunchback*, responsible for making sure all the actors knew their lines. You make a movie, talk to people all day, every day, and along the road somewhere someone suggests that you all grab a bite to eat together at the commissary. I'm pretty sure it was Edmond O'Brien who invited Price the first time, because they were friendly and I was friendly with Eddie. I didn't think much of Will Price one way or the other until then, but he seemed to be a decent enough fellow, full of Southern charm.

Then, while we were sitting down to lunch, Price mentioned that a friend of his would be joining us. A few minutes later, Olivia de Havilland walked through the doors and sat at our table. She and Price had become friends on the set of *Gone With the Wind*, where he had also been the dialogue director and had coached her on her Southern accent. I found Livie de Havilland to be one of the most gracious, kind, and charming people I had met in America—not to mention one great actress—and I liked her instantly. (My opinion of her has never changed. She's a wonderful lady.) I liked her so much that it made me look more favorably on Will Price. I thought that anyone who had a friend like Livie just had to be a great person too. We all enjoyed each other so much that Livie invited us to her home for dinner, and so toward the end of the picture, I began seeing Will Price socially, joining him and Livie for dinners. We went as friends though, not as each other's date. Besides, I was still legally married.

We finished filming *Hunchback* in the first week of October and it premiered on New Year's Eve at New York's Radio City Music Hall to enthusiastic reviews by critics. *Variety* predicted a "rosy" future for me, and Laughton's portrayal was hailed as "masterful." The picture was a huge box-office hit for RKO and earned over $3 million on its initial release, recouping the $1.8 million spent making it. There were high hopes for multiple

Academy Award nominations, but the film earned only two technical nominations, for score and sound. Unfortunately, timing is everything and 1939 was a hallmark year for the movie industry. *The Hunchback of Notre Dame* had to compete with *Gone With the Wind* and *The Wizard of Oz*, both from MGM; *Wuthering Heights*, from United Artists; Warner Bros.'s *Dark Victory*, with Bette Davis; and Columbia's *Mr. Smith Goes to Washington*, starring Jimmy Stewart.

Lost in a crowd of greats.

Not a single Oscar.

That's showbiz.

CHAPTER 5

BOUGHT AND SOLD

*N*othing was as it had been. The world and everything in it had been turned upside down by the end of 1939. And I wasn't immune to it. Shortly after *Hunchback* premiered, I was called to RKO Pictures for a meeting with Laughton and Pommer. I knew right away that it was going to be bad news.

"Maureen," Pommer began, "we won't be going home. We won't be going to France either to make *The Admirable Creighton*. It's too dangerous with the war, and all travel to Europe has been suspended." I wasn't surprised. Mammy and I had been following the news daily and were well aware that travel to Europe wasn't being permitted. "How long do we have to stay?" I asked. "We just don't know," he said. "If the Americans enter the war, and I think they will, it could be quite a long time. Maybe until the war ends." His response took me by surprise. It was naive of me, but deep down I had been secretly hoping that Laughton could some-how use his influence to get us all back home. "Oh God," I said in a low voice. "But that could be years." They nodded in unison. "There's something else, Maureen," Pommer continued. "We don't want you to be upset, but we've decided to sell your contract to RKO Pictures."

Those words hit me like an ax. There had been no warning signs. Still, despite my young age, I knew this was very bad news. I knew being sold to RKO Pictures would trap me in Hollywood forever, and I desperately wanted to go back home to Europe as soon as I was able to leave. I didn't want to leave Mayflower, and more important, I didn't want to stop making pictures with Laughton. "But I don't want to be sold," I protested. "Are you upset with me? Have I done something wrong?"

Laughton finally spoke: "Of course not, dear. We're doing this for you. It's a good thing. It's going to be very good for your ca-reer." I didn't believe him and I began to cry. "I don't care. I don't want to go to RKO. Please don't sell me, Charles," I pleaded. "I don't want to stay in Hollywood. I want to go home." Laughton hugged me and said softly, "I'm sorry, but it's too late. We've already sold you."

Being sold to RKO broke my heart. I felt completely aban-doned in a strange and faraway place. I didn't believe at all that it had been done for the good of my career. In retrospect, of course, I realize that it was. The old Gypsy was still working her magic. Years later I learned that Laughton and Pommer had actually sold me while Laughton was still in New York and I was on that train headed for Los Angeles. Mayflower was going bankrupt and RKO agreed to bail the company out by paying off its debts in exchange for a five-picture deal with Laughton and the rights to my contract. Laughton and Pommer saved themselves from financial ruin and guaranteed me a movie contract. If they hadn't sold me, my movie contract with Mayflower would have been worthless because there wouldn't be a Mayflower Pictures anymore.

Whether I liked it or not, I was now a property of the powerful Hollywood studio system. My life and career would never be the same again. The types of roles I would be cast in were now to be decided by studio bosses. I have always believed that had I returned to Europe, I would have played far more serious, character-driven roles throughout my career. But the studios had different plans for me. Hollywood would never allow my talent to triumph over my face.

Shortly after I was sold to RKO, I received more bad news. Connie's Agency in London sent word to me that MCA (Music Corporation of America), the largest talent agency in Hollywood, had just bought Cary Grant and me, and that they were my new agents. All of my professional ties to Europe had now been officially severed. I was about to be handled by a whole team of agents, led by a young hotshot with black-rimmed glasses, Lew Wasserman. Lew would later become a big cheese in the picture business as head of MCA and Universal, but for now he was representing me and he quickly moved to renegotiate my contract with RKO. He got me a raise from $80 a week to $700 a week, which was more than a small consolation.

But the bad news kept coming. The United States government then announced that it would not extend visa rights to work. I was being thrown out of the country and the government didn't care where I went as long as I left the United States. I didn't know where to go. I couldn't return to Europe because of the travel ban, and that left me with only a few options. I could either go north to Canada or south to Mexico. That's when I learned firsthand just how powerful a Hollywood studio was. RKO stepped in quickly to handle the matter. The studio arranged for Mammy and me to go to Canada, where studio lawyers and Erich Pommer had cleared the way for us to reenter the United States on a quota number and remain as permanent residents.

RKO completed the whole matter swiftly and I was shocked that the studio was able to pull it off at all. The U.S. government was adamant about all foreign aliens leaving the country immediately. But I later came to believe that Hollywood was part of a larger strategy as the nation readied itself for war. Hollywood would be an important instrument in gaining widespread public support for the war effort. Newsreels would later play in movie theaters, showing the heroism of American generals like George S. Patton and Douglas MacArthur, and the villainy of Axis commanders like Field Marshal Rommel. I was later required to promote war bonds to the public to show my support for the war effort, which I did, not only because the studio required it, but because I wanted to and believed in it. Despite these efforts, I was still required to carry the necessary documents on my person at all times, documents that proved I was allowed to remain in the country. It was both sobering and frightening to be singled out and marked by the government because I was not an American.

With the issue of the visa resolved, I was cleared and able to go right to work at RKO. I settled in pretty quickly and became one of the studio's marquee stars, joining Rosalind Russell, Joan Fontaine, Loretta Young, and even RKO royalty, Fred Astaire and Ginger Rogers. I was assigned the same dressing room I'd had while filming *Hunchback*. It was standard issue and perfectly adequate, spacious and nicely decorated, with a sitting room, bathroom, hair and makeup room, and a desk to work from. It was good enough for me at the time, since I hadn't yet learned how to be a demanding Hollywood movie star.

While RKO was deciding which picture I would make next, Mammy and I rented a small house on Horn Avenue, off Sunset Boulevard. I spent the next few weeks digging out of boxes and getting the house in order, but mostly I was fretting about my next picture. I had trusted the choices Laughton and Pommer made for me, but they were no longer in charge; I was now at the mercy of anonymous RKO executives.

Will Price continued to call me; I saw him occasionally at Livie's and sometimes he'd stop by the house. I still had George Brown hanging over my head, but decided to leave that problem on the back burner. A war was on and no one gave a damn about personal problems. I was European and my family lived in an area that could become involved with the war at any minute. Mammy and I were very frightened for their safety should bombs start falling on Dublin. We kept our noses buried in newspapers most of the time. There were no telephone calls allowed to Ireland, so we hadn't spoken with anyone there for over a month. We sent short letters and food packages as often as possible. The mail was slow, but at least it was getting through, and we felt great relief every time we got word that they were all safe.

In the first week of December, I finally received word from RKO that my next picture would be a remake of the 1932 film *A Bill of Divorcement*. I was cast as Sydney Fairfield, the daughter, a role played by Katharine Hepburn in the earlier George Cukor version. Based on a play by Clemence Dane, the film's plot involved a family that is torn apart when the father returns home after spending twenty years in an insane asylum, and complicates his ex-wife's plans to marry another man. Adolphe Menjou was cast as the lunatic father and Fay Bainter would play my mother. Australian-born John Farrow was set to direct.

I was worried about the project from the outset. The screenplay was mediocre at best, and Farrow was nowhere near the caliber director Cukor was. My concerns about Farrow were only heightened after I met him for the first time. His behavior was extremely inappropriate, and he didn't attempt to disguise his obvious designs on me. Farrow was already married to another Irish actress, Maureen O'Sullivan (most famously Jane in all the Johnny Weismuller *Tarzan* movies), and they had already started a family. (The actress Mia Farrow is their daughter.) His demeanor and inappropriate comparisons of "his Maureen" and me put me off. I decided to keep my head down and get through the picture as quickly as possible.

I spent the first few weeks dodging Farrow while we made the usual wardrobe and makeup checks. The costume sketches were made and shown to him and the producers for corrections. Then the costumes were made and I modeled them for a photographer for the final check and approval.

Obviously, I couldn't avoid Farrow anymore once shooting started, in the middle of January. He started right in on me. At night, after filming, Farrow would show up at our home with gourmet dinners from the Brown Derby. He even brought the waiters with him. Mammy would be there alone when he arrived. The director and crew always leave the set before the actors do, as we have our makeup removed and hair set for the next day, so he always beat me home. When I saw that he was at my house, I refused to go in, and instead had to drive around the neighborhood for hours, waiting for him to leave. I'd call Mammy and ask, "Still there?" She'd answer, "Yep," and I'd keep driving. I never ate a single meal with him.

After several nights of my driving around until all hours, Farrow caught on. Then he got very angry, and started bad-mouthing me on the set, saying to crew members, "Well, she must be a lesbian." I was mad as hell when I got wind of that, but really blew my top when I learned he had hung a full-length photo of me on his office door and was throwing darts at it. I decided to teach him a lesson the first chance I got, which finally came during a scene with Menjou. Adolphe was a sweet old man—patron of the elegant Menjou mustache—and known as the best dresser in Hollywood. The scene required me to hit him hard in the face, and I really hated to have to do it. But every time I swung, Menjou ducked and I missed. "No! No!" Farrow yelled as he jumped from his chair and stormed over to me. "Hit him. Hit him hard!" His moment of truth had arrived. "Oh," I replied. "You mean like this?" I hauled off and socked Farrow so hard it nearly knocked him on his ass. It felt wonderful. You should have seen the twinkle in Menjou's eye. The whole cast and crew knew what Farrow had been doing to me, and they knew that he had it coming. Farrow was like a church mouse on the set for the rest of the shoot. I barely heard him squeak. The crew, on the other hand, treated me like a princess. I had won them over with my right hook.

I was so happy when filming for *A Bill of Divorcement* was finally over, and I was also not the least bit surprised that it didn't do well at the box office, not a total stinker, but close. Still, I wasn't overly concerned about it hurting my career. I had given a strong performance and got as good reviews as Hepburn had for the role in 1932. I couldn't complain about that! The studio seemed pleased with me overall, and wasted little time casting me next in a comedy titled *Dance, Girl, Dance.* The plot focused on the relationship between two professional women who battle each other over fame and a man. I was cast as Judy O'Brien, an aspiring ballerina who joins a dance troupe. Lucille Ball was cast as her rival, Bubbles, the brash, man-eating "Queen of Burlesque."

I was looking forward to making this picture. My old boss, Erich Pommer, was producing, and I was happy to be working with Lucille. Before filming started, the entire cast went right into dance classes. Pommer hired Ernst and Ginny Matray again, and they really had their work cut out for them this time. My ballet sequences were far more difficult than the dancing with a tambourine I had done in *Hunchback*, and I struggled to get it right.

Lucille had a much easier time of it because she was a former Ziegfeld and Goldwyn Girl, and a much better dancer than I. We enjoyed a competitive rivalry on petty and harmless things, like fighting over which one of us would get the dance stocking without the ladders or runs.

By the time dance classes were finished, Lucille and I were inseparable chums. We were a lot alike, two tough dames. She wasn't hysterically funny off camera, more of a wisecracker with a quick wit and a short fuse. Lucille wasn't a star yet, but she made no bones about the fact that she planned to be one. She was very ambitious and calculating where her career was concerned.

We started shooting *Dance, Girl, Dance* at the end of April, but the film got off to a rocky start. Roy Del Ruth, our first director, struggled to find a vision for the picture. He had made terrific urban and crime dramas for Warner Bros., but didn't know what to do with a comedy about two women. He and Pommer were clashing creatively from the beginning, and he was dropped from the film within weeks. Dorothy Arzner was quickly brought in to replace him; she demanded that we reshoot every sequence Del Ruth had filmed. Arzner was a filmmaking phenomenon in those days. She was the *only* serious female director of her time and the first woman member of the Directors Guild of America. She fascinated both Lucille and me. She had been an ambulance driver before coming to Hollywood and quickly brought a distinctive point of view to the film. She moved it away from Del Ruth's love-triangle focus and approached the story as a deep exploration of strong-willed, independent women. Everything fell into place after that, and shooting went like clockwork.

Still, everyone in the cast and crew was anxiously waiting for the big confrontation scene between Lucille and me. It was not choreographed and blocked, so it was catch-as-catch-can. Frankly, I was disappointed. Remember, I had worked with great stuntmen on

Hunchback and knew the exciting action you can get when a sequence is properly planned. When we arrived on the set, Lucille and I smiled warmly at each other and made idle chitchat while waiting for our cue. "Everyone safe and sound back home, honey?" she asked.

"Oh yes, thanks. Just got a letter from Daddy yesterday. Everyone is fine," I replied.

The director called, "Action."

I lunged wildly at Lucille, pulling hard on her hair and making her scream. She clawed back at me, digging her fingernails deep into my arms, then ripped a handful of hair from my head. I groaned. She threw a right while I countered with a left. Arms were swinging and flailing. We bounced each other off this wall and that before getting tangled up in the curtain backdrop. We crashed down hard to the floor—screaming out together—then rolled around, savagely swinging at each other in a wild and frenzied catfight.

"Cut and print." Arzner got what she wanted, but for me, it wasn't good enough. It was a missed opportunity for a great action sequence. Those on the set seemed to enjoy it though, and broke into applause and laughter when it was over. I rolled off Lucille and fell onto my back, panting for air. Lucille caught her breath first and casually asked, "Hey, you hungry, kid?"

"I'm starving," I replied. We looked like hell, walking arm in arm across that RKO lot to the commissary—clothes torn, hair like wild birds' nests. While we were in line getting lunch, Lucille started complaining about her next movie, a musical called *Too Many Girls*. She was worried about it because her new leading man was a younger actor who had never been in front of a movie camera. She called him "that Cuban—Desi Arnaz." Lucille hadn't met or even seen Desi yet, but I had had the pleasure of catching his act and meeting him several months earlier in New York. Just as I was telling her how talented and gorgeous he was, Desi walked into the commissary with his agent, Doc Bender. I whispered to Lucille, "But don't take my word for it. See for yourself." Lucille followed my eyes and I could almost hear the bells ringing in her head. The first words Lucille uttered when seeing Desi for the first time were, "Oh my God." It was love at first sight for her.

"I hear he's a real lady-killer," I continued. But Lucille didn't flinch, and responded, "And here's his next victim. Well, don't just stand there, kid," she said with an elbow. "Get ready to introduce me."

I was trying to think of a clever introduction while Lucille straightened her dress. Oops—"Lucille, your socks! They're showing," I said under my breath. She looked down at her feet, but those weren't the ones I was talking about. I was referring to the ones that were hanging out of her bra. She ducked behind me to fix them as Doc dragged Desi in our direction. But Desi was resisting him. "Don't introduce me," he snapped. "Lucille Ball is queen of B movies," he went on in broken English. "I don't do picture with her. Will kill my career."

It was a total snub and I was embarrassed for her. We just stood there watching Desi and Bender slip quickly out the side door. I didn't know what to say. "He didn't mean it," I began, but she wasn't buying it. Instead, her eyes grew determined. "Oh God," I continued. "What are you going to do?" She smiled slyly. "What else? Make him change his tune!" From that moment on, Lucille was on a mission to win Desi's heart. She stopped seeing the finance executive she had been dating and pursued Desi all over the RKO lot. She kept calling him Dizzy, to shake his confidence, and it didn't take long for her to win him over. They started dating, and soon he was all she could talk about. I liked Desi—it was impossible not to like him. He was very charming and very charismatic. But Lucille's Desi this, Desi that, Desi is absolutely wonderful was sure wearing thin. She was driving everyone crazy with it. Even Mammy couldn't take it anymore and finally snapped, "Good God, Lucille! If you're so in love, go run off and marry the man!" They married a few days later.

When the filming ended in late July, Lucille and I were sent on the road to do publicity. We flew all over the country together and I got terribly sick on the planes. I can still hear Lucille wise-cracking while I was getting sick in a bag. *Dance, Girl, Dance* opened with weak box-office receipts and I had a second miss on my hands. The critics were again kind to me, but most felt Lucille had stolen the picture.

To my surprise, despite the film's poor showing, feminists responded to my character in the movie and used her in support of their campaign for women's rights. It rolled like prairie fire all across the country. During the now famous burlesque-house scene in the movie, my character rose above the jeers and sneers of the male audience and castigated them in words that women all over the world had always wanted to say to male chauvinists. I was astounded and flattered by the undeserved credit and attention that was showered on me.

Lucille and I remained close for many years after the picture was over. We'd see each other socially from time to time, but most often spoke on the phone. Frequently, she called in tears, because she couldn't get pregnant and desperately wanted to have children with Desi. I was so happy for her when I called one evening and heard her say, "Maureen, I can't talk now. We're on our way to the hospital." Little Lucie was born later that night. Despite the fact that she now had a family, Lucille still wasn't satisfied with her career. What she really wanted more than anything else was to be a movie star, and it took Desi a long time to convince her to do the *I Love Lucy* show for television.

The big decision came over dinner at the home of our mutual friend Paul Coates. Paul was a renowned newspaper reporter and his wife was a famous ballroom dancer. All night long, Desi kept bugging Lucille about doing the show. He nagged her and nagged her. He wouldn't stop talking about it. But Lucille didn't want to do it. She kept saying, "No, no, no," followed by, "I won't, I won't, I won't." She wanted movie stardom, and that was it. But Desi kept at her until she finally said, in exhaustion, "Oh dammit, all right! I'll do the thing."

She and Desi went on to make television history, and I stayed in films. We lost touch over time. We'd see each other at industry functions and get caught up as much as we could, but then we'd go our separate ways, always meaning to get together but never doing it. It was sad when Lucy and Desi finally divorced. Desi Jr. and little Lucie used to put on *The Parent Trap* and make their parents watch it, hoping they'd get back together. Though they never did, I'm not the least bit surprised that as a couple they are so beloved all over the world.

The end of *Dance, Girl, Dance* also marked the end of my first full year away from home. I was very homesick by this point and missed the rest of my family more than I could bear. There was little hope of going home any time soon, however. Germany had invaded France and the Axis powers were growing in strength and number. With nothing to do but wait for my next picture, I decided the time had come to resolve that which I had left behind in London—my marriage to George Brown. The first thing I did was ask Charles Laughton and Erich Pommer for their help. They advised me to seek an annulment, and so I left it in their hands. At the end of October 1940, they contacted my old agents at Connie's Agency in London and asked them to contact George Brown. With a war going on, finding him proved to be far more difficult than anyone expected.

There was little for me to do but wait and hope. Wait and hope to hear that my family was still safe. Wait and hope that my next picture would be a good one. Wait and hope that I would soon be free of that stupid mistake from my past. I felt helpless, and I was waiting and hoping at a time when hope seemed to be waning all over the world.

CHAPTER 6

HOW GREEN WAS MY VALLEY

I had to make the rounds and be seen at all the right places if I was ever going to be a star of any significance in Hollywood. That's what I was told by the new publicity man at RKO, Perry Lieber, after work on *Dance, Girl, Dance* was over. In those days, only a few establishments were considered the right places to go, and everybody who was anybody went there. Romanoff's was the glitziest of them, with its brilliant orange, yellow, and green wallpaper. It was owned by Prince Michael Romanoff, who claimed to be the cousin of Czar Nicholas. Of course, that was all rubbish. He was really Harry Gerguson, the orphaned son of a Cincinnati tailor. Still, he was a dashing little fellow who sported a carefully waxed mustache and a monocle, and who always wore a pin-striped suit and spats. Romanoff's was where all the boys who made gangster movies hung out, and if you wanted to see Cagney or Bogie or even a real-life gangster, then that's where you went.

Another popular place was Ciro's, a nightclub where Hollywood's elite went wild during the 1940s. Frank Sinatra, Nat King Cole, Marlene Dietrich, Billie Holiday, and Mae West all performed there. There was something about the place that just brought out the worst in people. Fights broke out so often they considered, as a publicity stunt, replacing the dance floor with a boxing ring. A plaque on the wall read "Three-Brawl-per-Customer Limit." When you were feeling naughty and up for some trouble, you went to Ciro's.

Usually, though, everyone went to either Chasen's or the Brown Derby, two excellent restaurants. Most actors preferred Chasen's because it was off-limits to the press, and asking for autographs there was strictly taboo. Stars and studio bosses could go there and let their hair down. One day, Perry suggested I call Lew Wasserman and ask him to join us there. We chose a good night for it. Clark Gable and Carole Lombard were there and so were Lana Turner and William Powell, and even MGM boss Louis B. Mayer was there with his wife. From my red-leather booth, Chasen's was quite a sight, musical tables and musical chairs. That night I met then-child star Jane Withers and we ended up at the same table. Somewhere in the conversation, someone brought up the subject of badminton—I think it was Jane—and how much fun it would be to start a badminton club. Perry and Lew thought it was a great idea that I get involved. I'd never thought much about badminton until then because it is far more an American sport than a European one, but I sure was sick as hell of sitting around the house all day reading newspapers.

A few days later, Jane held a meeting at her home to form the Beverly Hills Badminton Club. Many young stars and starlets soon joined. I was shocked when Lana Turner was refused membership for being over the age limit. She was so gorgeous and youthful that I almost fell over when I learned she was older than I by more than just a few years. I don't know how Lana managed to pull it off, but I was even more shocked many years later when Lana died and I read in the papers at the time of her death that she was now officially younger than I was.

We took our badminton very seriously and even had a professional instructor as our coach. In a typical two-game singles match, you cover nearly every inch of the court and run more than a mile. We started playing every weekend and rotated the matches at each other's homes. I often brought Will Price along to play mixed doubles and to be my escort if matches turned into social events later in the evening.

In November 1940, I was cast in the musical comedy *They Met in Argentina*, RKO's response to the Betty Grable hit *Down Argentine Way*. I knew it was going to be a stinker; terrible script, bad director, preposterous plot, forgettable music. Twenty pages into reading the script, I called Lew Wasserman and begged him to get me out of the picture, but he persuaded me to stick it out. Truthfully, I didn't have much choice. In those days, the studios owned their stars and you had to do what they said. He said, "Maureen, I know it's bad, but you've gotta make this picture or you'll be suspended. You'll be put off salary and won't be allowed to work anywhere else until they finish it. You won't see a cent for months." My back was against the wall, and so I had no choice but to make the movie. It was the typical ten-plus-two-weeks shooting schedule, which went by very slowly; we finished in January 1941.

As I expected, the film was a total flop, and I was furious about it. I had made three consecutive duds with RKO, and knew I desperately needed better vehicles. Despite my anger, I never lost hope that they would come. I had a strong faith in God and believed in my soul that he wouldn't let me down. A week later, my prayers were answered, as the Gypsy kept the wheels turning and I met a man who would help set me on a path to climb to some of the highest peaks of my career.

I didn't know much about John Ford the night I first met him. I had only heard that he was an important director and an Irishman. When I got the call from the studio informing me that I was to attend a party at his home, to me it was just another routine business party. I had no idea that Ford had sent word to RKO asking that I be there, and that he had a reason for wanting me to come. I had evidently caught his eye with *Jamaica Inn* and *Hunchback*, and he wanted to look me over for his next picture. When I arrived at his home the following evening, accompanied by Perry Lieber, it was a different crowd of people from those I usually saw at these events. Mostly they were actors and executives from Fox, where Ford had his offices. Mary Ford, his wife, was greeting guests as they arrived at the door, and Ford was in the middle of a crowd of people. After a few moments of meandering about, Perry dragged me over to meet him. Ford spotted us standing nearby and wrapped up his conversation. Then he turned to Perry, who, after introducing himself, asked, "Have you met Maureen O'Hara?" Ford turned to me without expression and answered, "No, I haven't."

I extended a hand, and gave him a firm handshake, saying, "It's very nice to meet you, Mr. Ford."

He accepted it with a firm handshake of his own and a simple "Hello," and then continued, "So you're from Dublin, are you?"

"Born and raised," I answered proudly.

"I'm Irish too, you know," Ford said, pressing on. "Did you know that?"

I nodded and answered, "Yes, I know."

Then he blurted out, "I'm an Irish rebel, a freedom fighter. Bet you didn't know that."

That was a strange declaration. I knew no one who would ever announce such a thing at a party, for everyone to hear, and I assumed he was testing my reaction. "No, I didn't," I answered with a matter-of-fact manner before changing the subject. "What part of Ireland are you from?"

"Before they came to America, my parents were from a town called Spiddal, in the west of Ireland." I knew the area well and assured him, "It's a beautiful part of Ireland."

Ford was done with me just like that. "Have you met all the big shots here yet?" The only person I had really met was his wife, Mary, at the door. "No. You're the only one so far." He turned to Perry. "Well, make sure she does."

Perry took Ford's suggestion like an order from the president and spent the rest of the party making sure I met everyone there. In the car on our way home, though, he gave me the real scoop on Ford by telling me that he was the most brilliant and controversial director in Hollywood. I would soon learn that firsthand.

A few days after the party, I got a call from Lew Wasserman telling me that Ford wanted to meet with me at Fox the following day. He had apparently liked what he had seen and heard during our brief conversation and wanted me in his next picture, *How Green Was My Valley*. Lew was so excited I could almost hear, over the phone, him jumping out of his seat.

"This is big, Maureen, huge. It's Fox's biggest film of the year. What happened at that party?"

"Nothing at all," I answered. "We only spoke for a minute or two. He must have liked me."

Lew and I arrived at Fox the next day, right on time at two P.M. We were led to Ford's office, where he was already waiting with several Fox executives, including Lew Schreiber, head of casting and Darryl F. Zanuck's right-hand man. I felt very confident going into the meeting, naturally assuming that I had already won Ford over. I was expecting a warm and friendly discussion about the picture. Instead, Ford introduced me with a horrible accusation and lie.

"Gentlemen, this is Maureen O'Hara, the young lady who insulted me. Called all my relatives a bunch of shawlees."

Where had that come from? I wondered. I didn't have a clue as to what he was talking about. What he was accusing me of was terrible. In Ireland, a "shawlee" is a poor country peasant who wears a shawl because she can't afford a coat. It's an unforgivable insult.

"I did not," I protested. "I never said any such thing!" But Ford kept pressing it. "Yes you did. You insulted all of my aunts, nieces, cousins . . . all of them."

"But, Mr. Ford, why would I say that about your family?" I asked, still trying to defend myself. "I don't know your family. I've never met them."

"I don't know, but you did." Now he was playing to the room.

I wasn't about to concede the point. "No, I didn't," I declared. Ford ended the argument with a firm and decisive "You did. Now sit down and let's talk about *How Green Was My Valley.*"

Lew shot me a "sit down and shut up" look and so I settled into my seat and listened to Ford describe the film he wanted to make. *How Green Was My Valley* was going to be a big-budget adaptation of Richard Llewellyn's classic novel. The story revolves around the heartbreaking struggles of a poor coal-mining family who live in a Welsh mining village at the end of the nineteenth century. I was being considered for the role of Angharad Morgan, the eldest daughter, who forsakes her family and true love by marrying into the wealthy family who own the coal mine. I was riveted by Ford's description of the story and by the passion and humanity with which he spoke. I quickly forgot the tiff we'd had at the beginning of the meeting, and by the end of it, I had never wanted to be in a movie so badly.

I wasn't offered the role at the meeting, however. Before it began, I thought my chances were pretty damn good, but by the time I reached home, the shawlee business with Ford was weighing on me again and I was worried that I wouldn't get the part. The following morning, Lew Wasserman called with the good news—the role was mine.

So with a bizarre confrontation and my subsequent casting in *How Green Was My Valley*, an artistic collaboration began that would span twenty years and five feature films. My personal friendship with Ford would last much longer, until the day he died. I was about to work with the most complex man I would ever know, and he would become one of the most important people to ever touch my life.

After I was cast, great things suddenly started happening. Mammy was lonesome for her husband and five other children and decided to get back to Ireland, come hell or high water. She purchased a ticket on a ship that would take her to Lisbon, since Portugal was a neutral country during the war. Once she arrived in Lisbon, she met an English air force officer who offered to get her on a military plane and take her to London. Six weeks later, she was safely back home in Dublin, and the family, excluding me, were all tearfully reunited.

Shortly after Mammy set sail, Perry Lieber from RKO called with exciting news of his own. I had been invited by the White House to attend President Roosevelt's annual birthday celebration in Washington. I would be one of many stars representing Hollywood at the event. As a new Irish immigrant, I was very proud to have been asked and excited about meeting the president.

Honey O'Neill, my new assistant and secretary, whom Mammy had hired before she left, and I boarded a plane on January 29, 1941, and made our way to Washington. The events began the following day with a luncheon at the White House being held for the president by Mrs. Roosevelt. When we arrived at the White House, I was handed an envelope containing my invitation and a seating card. I never expected what was inside. When I looked at my seating card, I saw that I had been seated at the table of honor and in the seat of honor, at the right-hand side of President Roosevelt himself. I was thrilled.

I then found myself surrounded by security men and a sea of unblinking, watchful eyes as I was escorted into the dining room and over to the president's table. My escort announced me, "Mr. President, Miss Maureen O'Hara." The president looked up and greeted me somewhat formally, saying, "How do you do?" I answered with a big smile and "I'm very pleased to meet you, and happy birthday, Mr. President." I took my seat beside the president and began listening to the story he was already sharing with the other guests at the table.

Over the course of lunch, the president went on telling stories about the White House and previous presidents and other residents. He had just finished one about Lincoln's ghost when he turned to me abruptly and started talking about Communism. He shocked me by saying, "Don't you know Ireland is a Communist country?" He wasn't asking a question at all, but stating a fact. I was astounded and insulted. I suddenly found myself defending my own country to the president of the United States. I told him in no uncertain terms, "I've never heard such rubbish in my life." His eyes widened and I felt the weight of stares on me, but I continued anyway. "I don't know where you got your information, Mr. President, but you are absolutely wrong. Ireland is not a Communist country nor will she ever be."

President Roosevelt already had his mind made up and assured me that Ireland would one day be part of the Communist bloc. I said nothing more about it and finished my lunch very quietly. It was terribly disappointing, and on my way back to the hotel, I wondered how the president of the United States of America could have such terrible misinformation. Still, I refused to let it ruin my trip, and went to all six of the balls anyway wearing a gorgeous apricot lace gown loaned to me by RKO Pictures.

When I arrived back in Hollywood, I got word from Connie's that they had finally found George Brown, and that he also wanted "a clean and definite break" so that he could marry again. But George was now on active duty in the war, and it was going to be difficult for him to work through the process in England. It was decided that I should get an annulment in the United States instead. The easiest place to get one in those days was the divorce capital, Reno, Nevada.

Shortly after getting the ball rolling in Reno, sometime in February, I think, I was surprised by a call from John Ford's assistant, Meta Sterne, inviting me to dinner at Ford's home. I assumed he wanted to get to know me better before we went to work on the picture, and I was genuinely interested in knowing him, so I eagerly accepted. I never expected that John Ford and I would become friends before we ever shot a single frame of *How Green Was My Valley*, but we did. It sprouted from our mutual love of all in the world that was Irish. Before I knew it, I was having dinner with his family at their home in the Hollywood Hills at least once a week during preproduction. In his home, away from the studio and away from the business of making movies, John Ford was very different from the man I had previously met. He was kind, charming, and absolutely wonderful to me. It was there, but never on the set, that with great affection I started calling him by his favorite nickname: Pappy.

What I loved most about our evenings together was that they were a celebration of being Irish, which suited me just fine but drove poor Mary crazy. She used to say, "Oh God, Maureen is coming over. It's going to be Irish this and Irish that all night long." But John Ford loved his Irishness. Pappy was born a good Irish lad named John Martin Feeney, but followed his older brother Francis in changing his last name to Ford to further his career in the picture business. (Francis was a star in silent movies.) Pappy also loved calling himself by the Gaelic version of his birth name, Séan Aloysius Kilmartin O'Feeney. The routine was the same every night I visited his home. It always began with Pappy telling many, many glorious stories about Ireland. Him in Ireland. His family in Ireland. The cottage they lived in. How they lost the land they had once owned. Irish history intertwined with Feeney family history. I believed everything he told me, not yet knowing that John Ford was a congenital fibber. I just sat there with Mary, his son, Pat, and daughter, Barbara, and soaked up every word of it.

When we finally sat down to dinner, it was my turn to entertain Pappy. He always made me sing for my supper. Before dinner was served, I would stand at my place at the table and sing some of his favorite Irish songs. "Sing 'Danny Boy,' " he'd insist. "Now sing 'I'll Take You Home Again, Kathleen,' " which he loved most.

Sometimes these evenings included Pappy's extended family. These were a handful of special friends he had made over his years spent in the picture business. Then, on a crisp evening in May 1941, at one of Pappy Ford's dinners, I met John Wayne for the very first time. Duke had cut his teeth on the set of many John Ford films for years before he was given the leading role in *Stagecoach*. So Duke would come to dinner with his wife, Josie, and a casual friendship between us began while sharing food, wine, and song over Pappy Ford's dinner table.

These were wonderful nights and wonderful times. The only glimpse I had at this point of the darker side of John Ford were mean things he occasionally said to Mary. At times they were so downright mean and nasty that I thought, I'm going to get up and leave, but I never did. I just ignored it and chalked it up to a somewhat strange relationship between husband and wife. As we readied to make *How Green Was My Valley,* I became part of John Ford's family and inner circle. I knew the man, or so I thought, and I adored him. Now I was about to know the director.

How Green Was My Valley was Darryl Zanuck's baby from the time he'd finished reading the novel, in 1939. He hoped it would be the next *Gone With the Wind* and wanted a four-hour epic that would be shot in Technicolor on location in Wales. The first director Zanuck hired for the picture was William Wyler. Wyler spent three months on the project, working out early drafts of the script, but he was having problems satisfying Zanuck and the studio. The top brass in New York felt Wyler and screenwriter Philip Dunne had crafted a story about labor problems instead of a great human drama about real living people. Fox executives were already worried about possible cost overruns and so they put the picture on hold.

That *How Green Was My Valley* was ever made speaks volumes about the kind of studio boss Darryl Zanuck was. He was not solely driven by bottomline profits, even though his favorite saying was "Time is money." Zanuck loved the art and process of great filmmaking. He was very concerned with story. In fact, it was Zanuck who insisted that *How Green Was My Valley* be told through the eyes of the young Huw, the character played by Roddy McDowall, rather than by an older Huw, who was originally supposed to be played by Tyrone Power. Zanuck made that change, and so Ty Power was dropped from the picture. When the studio put it on hold, it was rumored that Zanuck fought so hard for the movie that he actually threatened to send it to another studio. By the time he was finally given the green light, Wyler had already moved on to direct *The Little Foxes*, so John Ford was called in to replace him.

Zanuck's choice of Mr. Ford was calculated and brilliant. I think he knew Mr. Ford would bring out the humanity of the story despite the script, just as they had done when they collaborated on *The Grapes of Wrath* (for which John Ford won his second Academy Award as best director). Mr. Ford earned my respect and admiration while making *How Green Was My Valley*. I saw the genius in him and quickly knew his talent dwarfed that of any director I had previously worked with in the theater and movies, even Hitchcock. That opinion has never changed over the years. My opinion of him as a person, though, did change over time, but I'll get to that later. The filmmaking achievement of *How Green Was My Valley* is remarkable and, in my opinion, much of the credit belongs to Zanuck and Ford. Would a film about sociological problems like coal miners forming a union be so captivating today? I doubt it. It is the story of this poor Welsh family and a town in decline that continues to endure and rivet us because it shows the right and wrong doings of simple people who are trying to correct themselves by learning from the mistakes they've made.

One of the first things Mr. Ford did was to recast the picture. Mr. Ford was far too proud to ever let another director cast his movie, and only one of the originally cast actors appeared in the film. He chose Donald Crisp and Sara Allgood as the father and mother of the Morgan clan. He wanted Walter Pidgeon to play the village preacher, Mr. Gruffydd, to give the film its needed star power. Anna Lee was chosen to play the role of Bronwyn, and as he had done in the past, Mr. Ford turned to Barry Fitzgerald for comic relief by casting him as Cyfartha. The only actor originally cast by Wyler that Mr. Ford kept was young Roddy McDowall as the boy Huw.

After Mr. Ford offered me the role of Angharad, Lew Schreiber refused to cast me unless 20th Century-Fox owned part of my contract. He said it was too big and too important a movie for the studio not to own at least part of all the leading characters. Here's where an agent comes into the process and helps the studio finalize casting for a film. Before I was officially announced for the role, Fox worked with Lew Wasserman and purchased the right to make one picture a year with me. I don't know how much RKO got in exchange, but it was another important turning point in my career because it led to my being cast later in *Miracle on 34th Street.*

We began filming *How Green Was My Valley* in June 1941, on an eighty-acre set built at Brent's Crags, in the hills near Malibu, some thirty miles outside Hollywood. Because of the war, not a single scene was shot in Wales as Zanuck had originally hoped. Also, the film's budget was scaled down to about $1,250,000. Still, Zanuck had his publicity team hold to the story that *How Green Was My Valley* was the biggest-budgeted picture in the studio's history, but plans to shoot the picture in Technicolor were lost in the cost cutting.

When I arrived on the set, I was again overcome by the magnificence of it, but for different reasons than I had been on the set of *Hunchback.* Our Welsh village was so perfectly constructed that when the Welsh Singers finally arrived on the set, the whole choir fell to their knees and wept.

At a cost of $110,000, our Welsh village was modeled and built after the Cerrig Ceinnen and Clyddach-cum Tawe in Wales. Since the coal mine was such an important part of the story, Mr. Ford had blocks of coal weighing over one ton each brought in to build the mine tunnels. The tunnels had to be made of real coal so

Mr. Ford could film the workers actually mining from the walls. He also wanted real coal slag to cover the surrounding hillside, but he was unable to move that amount of coal across the country because of the war. He was forced instead to paint the eight-acre hillside black, and it took twenty thousand gallons of paint to cover it.

If the sight of this gorgeous set took my breath away, then I can only say that the first time I saw Mr. Ford on a movie set I was left speechless. There he was, slouched in his director's chair, like a king on his throne, while feverishly chewing and pulling away on a super-size white handkerchief. Though he was only forty-seven, Mr. Ford looked like an old man to me, never vital or athletic despite his ropy six-foot frame. Thick eyeglasses protruded from under the rim of a weather-beaten hat, and his rumpled clothes looked as though they never made it to the cleaners. He appeared the kind of untidy rumpled man you would expect to find on a farm rather than a movie set. But Mr. Ford's presence on the set was unlike anything I had ever experienced. Commanding and demanding, his dictatorial manner was matched only by the ease of his competence. I had never seen a more tyrannical personality with a more steady hand on the rudder. It was exhilarating because I felt both safe about the future of this picture while close to personal danger at every turn.

John Ford had been making movies for nearly a quarter of a century by the time I started working with him. The dos and don'ts on a John Ford picture were already well etched in stone by this point, and so members of the John Ford stock company, cast and crew who followed him from picture to picture, helped me out by explaining for the first few days the way everything worked. Men like Jack Pennick, Eddie O'Fearna (Mr. Ford's brother), or Wingate Smith (Mr. Ford's brother-in-law) advised me on how to stay out of trouble and out of the barrel. You never ever wanted to find yourself in Mr. Ford's barrel, which meant you were on John Ford's list to be tortured, made fun of, and tormented.

Over the course of the eight-week shoot, I watched John Ford with great interest. There was much about his style that to me seemed different and unique. He was far more visual than my previous directors. I quickly surmised that Mr. Ford was a painter of celluloid who masterfully composed every frame of his scene, down to the smallest detail. I watched him paint these scenes with lights. There were many times I saw him instruct Arthur Miller on how to light a specific scene, and Miller was one of the most famous and highly regarded cinematographers in the picture business. Mr. Ford took my breath away in one of my early scenes with Walter Pidgeon, which involved a chair in the kitchen. He looked through the lens and said, "No, no, no. I want the shadow of the back of the chair to be huge on the wall, to be bigger than they are." I looked at its enormity, its imposing presence, and thought, My God, look what he's doing. It's magnificent.

My favorite shot in the film takes place outside the church after Angharad is married. As I make my way down the steps to the carriage waiting below, the wind catches my veil and fans it out in a perfect circle all the way around my face. Then it floats straight up above my head and points to the heavens. It's breathtaking. I later read a book about the picture in which the author praised the scene and said it was "typical John Ford luck" that the wind gave him such a beautiful image. Rubbish. The book made me so damn mad. Mr. Ford had wind machines blowing until he got that shot exactly the way he wanted it.

He was the most efficient director I had seen. He usually got what he wanted in a single take, never shot more than three, and I can't recall a single retake being shot on the picture. *How Green Was My Valley* was camera cut, and nearly every inch of film that Mr. Ford shot ended up in the picture. He left hardly anything on the cutting-room floor. There were two reasons for this. First, Mr. Ford the painter constructed exactly the image he wanted before the camera rolled. Second, he didn't want any extra footage. He made certain that no other versions of the picture could be made by anyone else. There was only enough film shot to make John Ford's version of the movie.

But the most wonderful thing in watching Mr. Ford work was the freedom he gave his actors. He was treating everyone with artistic respect and trusted us all to give every scene exactly what it needed. He never gave specific directions and I learned over time that this was the best compliment Mr. Ford could give. If John Ford gave an actor detailed directions, then you knew he thought that actor wasn't very good.

On *How Green Was My Valley*, Mr. Ford was the most pleasant and relaxed I can ever remember him being on a set. In fact, far more than usual, there was a special camaraderie that developed among the cast and crew because of the times in which the picture was being made. We were a group of Celts making this wonderful movie together. Nearly everyone on the picture was Irish, Welsh, or Scottish. For many of us, being in this make-believe Welsh village was the closest we had been to home and our families for nearly two years. I truly believe this magic touched the picture in special ways.

Mr. Ford was cordial to me on the set but offered no special consideration because of our personal friendship. The only time Mr. Ford treated an actor poorly on the set of *How Green Was My Valley* was with me. I found myself in the barrel one day when I broke a sacred commandment and called a potential mistake to his attention in front of the entire cast and crew.

We were setting up the scene in which the men return home from the coal mines after being paid, and they place their wages in baskets being held by the women of their families. I recognized that the basket Sara Allgood and I were about to use would be inappropriate for the time period in which the story was set. I opened my big mouth and said, "Oh, Mr. Ford, we can't use this basket. This is a modern Kraft cheese basket," thinking I was being helpful. But Mr. Ford answered, "Well, it doesn't concern you anyway because you're not in this scene." Of course I was in the scene, at least until that moment. The set went silent as he continued, "You can go up there on the hill now and wait until I need you."

I had never in my life been instructed to leave a set. I stormed up the hill and tried to hide my anger, but John Ford could read me like a book and knew I was mad as hell. I sat under a tree wondering why he had done it. I knew he was wrong. It was obvious that the basket was a modern Kraft basket, an anachronism that an audience would surely recognize. Apparently, John Ford didn't eat Kraft cheese. I waited up there for nearly an hour, stewing the whole time. Then a struggle of nature, very much like the struggle I was going through with the director, caught my attention.

Up in this beautiful tree outside the church, I spotted a bird making an awful fuss. A snake was making its way down a long branch, toward the bird's nest. She was fluttering about in the air and then diving, taking the snake up into the air and then slamming it down hard on the branch again. I was fascinated by it and watched intently, as if I were watching my battle with Mr. Ford unfold. It went on and on and yet the snake made no progress. It was just being attacked by the bird and I thought, Good for you, bird. That snake is going to eat your eggs. Then the snake finally had enough and conceded. The bird had been consistent in its approach and won, while the snake had been aggressive in its approach and gave up. I thought, Well, I'll just do the same thing with Mr. Ford. Just then, Ford's assistant reached the top of the hill and said, "Mr. Ford wants you down at the camera." When I got there, Mr. Ford handed me a new basket and instructed me to stand next to Sara Allgood and for the camera to roll. I was back in the scene. He never mentioned the incident again and I kept my mouth shut.

For the remainder of the shoot, which wrapped on August 12, 1941, Mr. Ford and I got along wonderfully. He was nice to me, smiled at me often, spoke of working together again, and even tried to get me to date his son. I took all of this to mean that he was pleased with my performance. I was pleased with it as well. I felt that I captured the sincerity of Angharad's tragedy when she has to turn her back on love to climb out of poverty. I was also grateful that I had the opportunity to work with so many fine actors.

I thought Walter Pidgeon, who played Mr. Gruffydd, the village preacher, was very easy to work with and a real gentleman. I was stunned when I heard that the schoolteacher hired by the studio had accused him of making sexual advances to her and tearing her blouse. I found it very hard to believe. The whole mess was handled very quickly and quietly because I never heard about it again, and Walter continued with the project.

Young Roddy McDowall was only thirteen when he gave that remarkable performance as young Huw Morgan. It is arguably the finest performance by a child in movie history, though Roddy, ever modest, always believed that distinction belonged to Jackie Coogan in *The Kid*. He used to call me "Sister Maureen" on the set, but always had his real sister, Virginia, by his side. Years later, I would take them both for long drives along the California coastline, and eventually got my only speeding ticket thanks to those kids. Roddy remained one of my closest friends for over fifty years, until the day he died.

Anna Lee was one of the gentlest and most charming people I had met working in the picture business, a lady in every sense of the word. What made her performance as Bronwyn Morgan so powerful was that it was so very delicate. I was so proud to have Anna as my friend that I later named my own daughter Bronwyn, after her character in the movie.

More than anyone, though, the strongest relationship that grew from my making *How Green Was My Valley* was the one I developed with John Ford himself. By the time the picture finally wrapped, I thought John Ford was a walking god. I liked him personally and admired him professionally. I knew the picture was going to be a hit, but contrary to popular belief, Darryl Zanuck did not. After seeing the daily rushes, Zanuck ordered his name, as producer, removed from the film. He thought he had a huge flop on his hands. It wasn't until the final cut had been finished that he reversed himself and ordered his name back on the movie.

How Green Was My Valley opened on October 28 and its success was meteoric. Theaters were packed—huge box-office receipts—and there was overwhelming critical acclaim. After three misses in a row, I finally had more than a hit—I had a bull's-eye. My reviews were wonderful, but my favorite came from the Welsh Singers, who had been in the movie. The day the picture opened in Europe, the whole choir sailed across the sea from Wales to Dublin and made their way to our family home, where they serenaded my family. I'd have given anything to have been there.

How Green Was My Valley earned ten Oscar nominations and won five Academy Awards, giving John Ford his second Oscar in a row for best director. In addition to Donald Crisp winning as best supporting actor, the film also won for best cinematography and best art direction, and beat Orson Welles's *Citizen Kane* and John Huston's *The Maltese Falcon* as best picture of the year, proving once and for all that making movies is just like betting on horses at the racetrack.

CHAPTER 7

OVERPRICED

*I*t was like one of those recurring nightmares that jolt you from a deep sleep and you wake up to find yourself lying in your own sweat. My brain must have abandoned me, seeping out through my pores, because I had gone and done it again. I wasn't free of George Brown for more than seventy-five days before I married another man I wasn't in love with. Like a half-witted idiot, I jumped from the frying pan into the fire and became Mrs. William Houston Price.

I've never done well with men who nag and berate me for my affections. I know many women who are wonderfully savvy at turning away men they aren't interested in, but I've never been one of them. While others brushed off, I married. *Crikey!*

Will and I had been spending time together on and off since we'd first met. I never thought of it as a serious relationship, though. We were just company for each other. Dinners, badminton, occasional parties—that kind of thing. Will, on the other hand, couldn't get us to the altar fast enough. "Maureen, I think we should get married," he'd say over and over, to which I would give my stock answer, "Will, I can't. I'm still legally bound up in that mess with George Brown." It was an easy and safe response.

But as soon as we wrapped *How Green Was My Valley*, Will was pressuring the hell out of me to resolve the whole Brown problem. He saw my inaction as an indictment of him. "Am I wasting my time here, Maureen?" he asked. "I can't and won't put up with this. You have to straighten out your life and pick a date." Then he turned it on me: "Or maybe you're just not very serious about us. If you were, you'd be out of it by now."

He didn't know how right he was. I thought he was fun and very charming, but I didn't dream of spending the rest of my life with him. As his nagging persisted, I should have said, "Will, I have a lot of fun with you and enjoy your company, but I don't want to marry you." But something completely different came out of my mouth. "Will, I know it's been frustrating for you and I'm sorry. I can get an annulment in Nevada in just a few weeks."

During this early period in my life, when it comes to my relationships with men, I still don't fully understand the decisions I made. How could I have made the same mistake again? I was a strong-willed, bright young woman who I thought had her head on straight. I didn't let anyone push me into things I didn't want to do where my career was concerned. So why did I crumble when it came to men?

The best rationale I've come up with is that I was too naive and inexperienced. I had always been a tomboy—I still am, at heart—and had never had a real boyfriend. At the age of twenty, I still didn't know how to properly read the interest, intentions, and desires of men. I enjoyed their company, but I didn't know how to keep one step ahead in that game called "dating." And I sure as

hell didn't know how to reject a man. I was also from a very conservative country, which, compared to Hollywood, was a
completely different world. I was not the typical American movie
star; I was very different in this way from the other stars and starlets. Where men were concerned, I was ill prepared to navigate
confidently through Hollywood's sometimes murky waters.

So in the first week of September, Honey and I drove to Lake
Tahoe, where the petition had been filed to have the marriage to
George Brown annulled. About two weeks later, I started having
terrible pains in my midsection and became quite ill. Honey
drove me to Reno Hospital, where I was admitted and then taken
straight to surgery for the removal of two ovarian cysts and my ap-
pendix. My attorney took my deposition from my hospital bed and
then went before the judge on my behalf, and on September 15,
1941, the marriage to George Brown was legally annulled.

Any hope of a peaceful recovery went right out the window
when I got a disturbing call from Lew Schreiber at 20th Century-
Fox. News of my surgery had apparently hit the papers and
Zanuck was reportedly furious. A few weeks earlier, Zanuck had
been so pleased with my performance in *How Green Was My Valley* that he had purchased my contract from RKO and reversed
positions with them. Fox now owned all of me except for one picture a year with RKO. Zanuck wanted to cast me opposite his
biggest male star, Tyrone Power, in an adventure-drama called
Son of Fury. Though I was lying flat on my back in a hospital bed,
Lew made no attempt to sugarcoat his message. "This whole hospital thing is very serious, Maureen," he began. "Mr. Zanuck is
very annoyed. If you've checked yourself into that hospital to get
out of making this movie, you've made a very big mistake." I was
livid. The nerve of studio bosses was something you just had to
learn to accept and deal with when you were in the picture business. But to accuse me of masterminding an elaborate scheme

that included undergoing risky surgery just so I could avoid making a picture was not only ludicrous, it was insane.

My first reaction was to blow my lid, but I didn't. I didn't want to alienate Zanuck, or even Lew, for that matter, since *How Green Was My Valley* had been such a success. I kept my cool and answered calmly, veins bulging from my neck, "Lew, I'm not faking this, if that's what you think. You've got to convince Mr. Zanuck that it doesn't do either of us any good if I'm forced to return and then drop dead on the set." They still weren't convinced. A day later, Zanuck flew in 20th Century-Fox's top doctor to verify my condition. All he did was review my charts and talk with my doctor, but he never bothered with something as trivial as examining me. Instead he simply told me, "Oh, it's probably just a fragment left over from an abortion." I was outraged. If I had been able to get out of that bed, I would have socked him in the jaw for his crude insult. I was genuinely unable to make the picture and Zanuck was forced to cast Gene Tierney in the role.

When I was finally released from the hospital in the middle of October, I went right into costuming for the next film that Zanuck had cast me in. *To the Shores of Tripoli* was the first film I made with John Payne and also the first film I made in Technicolor. Based on a story by Steve Fisher, Lamar Trotti crafted a patriotic script. It had unfurling flags, marching men, and martial music. Bruce Humberstone, or "Lucky Stumblebum" to those who couldn't understand why the quality of his pictures never seemed to match their impressive box-office receipts, directed this film about a spoiled recruit named Chris Winters (played by John Payne) who joins the United States Marine Corps after being kicked out of the military academy. Randolph Scott was cast to play Dixie Smith, the iron-jawed drill sergeant who finally makes a man and a soldier out of him. I was cast as Second Lieutenant Mary Carter, the rank-pulling navy nurse being pursued by John Payne's character.

Lucky Stumblebum got another break. The film's timing was right on the nose. Halfway into the shoot, which began in early November, Japan bombed Pearl Harbor and forced the United States into the war. Never one to miss an opportunity, Zanuck quickly had the ending changed from a happily-ever-after love story to one with us all sailing off to combat. He also had a second camera unit sent to the Pacific to film the Pacific fleet.

Audiences ate it up. *To the Shores of Tripoli* was a smash hit, and was credited with more new enlistments in the United States Marine Corps than any other promotional campaign that year. The picture became the model for other "service pictures" that were widely produced once the war became real.

But neither the attack on Pearl Harbor nor my busy shooting schedule were enough to slow Will down. With the annulment done, he wanted to get married right away and I didn't have an excuse anymore. Telling the truth was the simple and right thing to do, but I couldn't do it. I began to rationalize marrying him. "He comes from a good family. A girl could do worse." (As it turned out, I couldn't, but I didn't know that yet.) "I want children one day, and who knows when or if I'll ever get back to Ireland? Anything can happen with the whole world at war." And most important of all, "I'm all alone here."

All of these reasons were true enough, but at the heart of it was an honest attraction to him. In the beginning, before he changed and things became ugly, I liked Will. I was attracted to his personality and his infectious Southern charm. More than anything, though, Will had the ability to make me feel special when he wanted me to shine. This time, I married knowingly, with open eyes.

Will Price was born and raised in McComb, Mississippi, and was a "son of the South" in every way, full of Southern charm. In his mind, Yankees were bums, while Southerners were more than gentlemen. He thought they were brave, elegant, and the rightful leaders of the country. He wasn't a particularly handsome twenty-eight-year-old—rather ordinary, if the truth be told, with dark brown hair and eyes. Not tall, a bit shorter than I, but stocky, although not fat. But as I've said, Will's finest quality was his Southern charm. He had that special ability to make the people he was interested in knowing like him. After graduating from Duke University, he moved to New Orleans for a short while, where he met George Cukor and they became friends.

It was Cukor who later brought Will to Hollywood to work as the dialogue coach on *Gone With the Wind*, helping the cast speak with a proper Southern accent. That credit got him the job on *Hunchback* and thus our meeting. After *Hunchback*, Will never had another job while we were dating (which only further supports how stupid I was). He spoke of his family's estate, and I just assumed he was living off family money until he landed another Hollywood job.

On my way to the airport, I had second thoughts about marrying Will and almost didn't board the plane. My publicist, Jean Pettibone, was driving me to the airport and on the way there, I told her, "I'm making a big mistake. I shouldn't marry him." Instead of listening to my own warning, though, I ignored my feelings and went through with it. Will and I were married on December 29 in a simple ceremony at the St. Mary of the Pines Convent in Will's hometown of McComb, Mississippi. I wore a powder blue dress with a small collar edged in brown lace, and a matching hat. My bouquet was made of white camellias from his family's estate.

None of my family or friends were present, just members of his immediate family. Will's father, K.G., was a lawyer and the son of a Supreme Court justice from the state of Mississippi. Although he was confined to a wheelchair with Lou Gehrig's disease, my first impression was that he was a braggart. Will's mother, Margaret, was a sweet Southern belle who stood quietly at her husband's side. I liked her. Will's younger brother, Kenneth, was a decent young man who made a very good impression on me when I first met him. That changed later. He was intelligent—a lawyer like his father—and a teetotaler. Sadly, Will's only sister was severely handicapped and later hidden away in an institution. They never spoke of her after that.

My family didn't know about the marriage until minutes before we took our vows. Will's grandfather was able to use his connections and arrange for me to call home and deliver the news. I was allowed to say just one sentence into the mouthpiece. "Will and I are getting married." Absolute silence until Mammy just said, "Oh." Her disappointment shattered me, but, always an actress, I put on a good show for everyone that day. I smiled and laughed and leaned my head against Will's shoulder whenever he hugged me. I glowed and sparkled for all to see, while on the inside, I was sad and full of fear.

After the ceremony, Will and I drove to New Orleans, where we spent our wedding night. I did wait until I got married, just in case you're wondering. I know the experience wasn't special for me because I don't remember it. All I can remember thinking is, What the hell have I done now? We caught a plane back to Hollywood the following morning. Zanuck had given me only a few days off, because *To the Shores of Tripoli* had a few more weeks of shooting. The truth is, I couldn't wait to get back to the safety and security of a movie set. I have always found the set to be a great escape from my problems and worries.

The ink was barely dry on our marriage license when the real Will Price revealed himself. I don't mean the way most newly married couples begin discovering each other's quirks as they settle in and start living together. That's just a period of getting comfortable with each other. No, I was about to meet a completely different Will Price—one I had never seen before. As soon as we got back to Hollywood, Will and I found a small two-story apartment that was down the street from Schwab's Drug Store, just off Sunset Strip. It was temporary until we found a house we liked, and it was not anything fancy: one bedroom, living room, dining room, kitchen, and bath. That's when it happened for the very first time. Just a few days after we moved in, I came home from the studio after a long day's work and found my new husband passed out on the floor, drunk out of his mind.

I had seen Will drink more than he should before I married him, but I had hoped it wasn't a serious problem. I should have known better, but because there were no heavy drinkers in my family, I didn't recognize the symptoms when I saw them. I had never been around an alcoholic before, yet there would soon be no denying that I had married one. Every few nights after that, I would come home and find Will reeking of liquor, and in one of three conditions: drunk, skunk drunk, or passed out cold. I'd find him on the kitchen floor, on the stairs, or lying in the hallway.

I knew then and there that I should get out of the marriage fast, but I just couldn't bring myself to do it. The worry of again hurting my parents stopped me. I couldn't put my mother and father through the shame of a public divorce. I knew that news of it would surely make its way overseas and hit the papers. My pride wouldn't let me do it. I couldn't walk out of this marriage just days after the ceremony, only weeks after my annulment—it was just too embarrassing.

I was scared and overwhelmed, but I kept silent. I tricked myself into believing that if I ignored Will's drinking problem, it would somehow magically fix itself. When I came home and found him passed out on the floor, I just stepped right over him and went about my business.

It didn't get better, of course. It went from bad to worse. Once his drinking was out in the open, Will made it clear that he wanted to upgrade our standard of living. "I'm from the South," he began, "and everyone in the South has help around the house." He had a talent for leaving me speechless. I finally managed, "But, Will, we live in a small apartment. It's just the two of us." Will wasn't very interested in what I had to say. Before I knew it, he had hired a full-time maid, a lady from the Caribbean, to work seven days a week at our little apartment, and he soon had her waiting on him hand and foot.

Meanwhile, I was breaking my back every day at the studio. I had finished *To the Shores of Tripoli* around the middle of January 1942, and gone right to work making *Ten Gentlemen from West Point*. It was a forgettable film mostly because John Payne dropped out of the picture during our first week of filming. John was a real talent, a triple threat; he could sing, dance, and act. Fox usually starred him in musicals that paired him with Alice Faye or Betty Grable. (He was also the first person in Hollywood to option the movie rights to the James Bond character, but unfortunately he never made the film.)

A few days after we started the picture, poor John had come home from the set and found that his wife, Anne Shirley, had walked out on him. I liked John very much and we had become good friends on our last picture, even though he used to tease me because he thought I didn't smile enough. The day after Anne left him, John came to my dressing room and sobbed and sobbed. He never saw it coming, and just kept asking me, "Why didn't she tell me? Why didn't she tell me she was so unhappy?" I gave him a tight hug and wondered how I would feel if I came home and found Will gone. Would I be sad at all?

I got my answer. In early February, Will came home and announced, "I've joined the marine corps." I went into shock again, which at this point was becoming my regular state of mind. I don't know whether he had been so drunk that he'd enlisted or whether he truly did it out of patriotism. I wasn't sad or relieved by Will's news. Instead, I was upset. It made me worry, Oh God, now what's he doing? Going off to war is something a husband and wife discuss together. But it bothered me that he joined so soon after we were married, and without the courtesy of first talking it over with me.

Finally, a ray of sunshine broke through the dark clouds. After weeks of searching, I found a little house in Bel Air to buy. It wasn't a movie-star mansion by any means—I couldn't afford one—but it was lovely and reasonably priced at $19,500 (which I borrowed from a bank). Situated at 1435 Stone Canyon Road, it was a cozy two-bedroom house with a beautiful garden and a badminton court. Will loved it too, and in purchasing it, I finally seemed to have done something that pleased him. Will wanted the house to be perfect, and to him that meant elegant. Now that we had a house, we naturally would need a staff. He insisted on hiring live-in servants right away. His parents already knew and recommended a husband-and-wife team, Wilmon and Dan (Dan was the wife), from Mississippi, who would come to live at the house, Dan as maid and cook, Wilmon as butler and chauffeur.

I knew we couldn't afford servants. In fact, we could barely afford the mortgage on that house. Will didn't have a job and wasn't even looking for one. My weekly paycheck from the studio was the only money coming in. But I agreed to hire the couple because getting our home in order had brought some signs of positive life back into Will. I didn't want to break the momentum or do anything that might send him back on a drinking binge. Besides, he would soon be leaving for basic training down in San Diego, and from there he'd be shipped overseas. I didn't want to be left in the house all alone, so I agreed to hire the couple.

Things appeared to be looking up as we settled into our new house. But just as the knot in my stomach started to loosen, another new side of Will emerged more prominently: Will the lavish spender, Will the Hollywood husband, Will the man of means. It was all an illusion, of course, because he didn't have two nickels to rattle on a tombstone. On my way home from work one night, I turned my 1939 Packard coupe onto Stone Canyon Road and stopped dead in my tracks in front of our house. I couldn't pull into the driveway because parked there was a brand-new 1942 Cadillac. That feeling of stunned panic had returned as I asked myself, Did Will buy a new car? I calmed down by reminding myself that Will Price couldn't have bought that new car. Will Price couldn't buy an ice-cream cone because he didn't have a job. What he was able to do, however, was go to the dealership that day and commit Maureen O'Hara to buying that car. While I was putting in sixteen hours a day at work, my twenty-eight-year-old, unemployed husband was spending his last few weeks as a civilian being driven by a chauffeur all over Beverly Hills in a flashy new car.

The car provided mobility, and this gave Will the freedom to be out on the town again. It didn't take more than a few days before he was back on the booze. Now he was out until all hours, going wherever it was he went to drink, until he finally staggered into the house in time to pass out. Sometimes I went to social events with Will, but they typically turned out to be bad experiences.

In the middle of February, I went with Will to a small party at the home of Don "Red" Barry and his wife, Peggy Stewart. Red had received a modest amount of attention for starring in the adventure series *Red Ryder*, from Republic, but had been relegated to supporting parts in B westerns by the time he'd become friends with Will. At the party, I was glad to see my old friend Mickey Rooney with his new wife, Ava Gardner, but I didn't know any of the other people there. Will was in his element with a bunch of men all getting very drunk. I couldn't stand it. I went downstairs and into the kitchen, found a comfortable chair, turned out the light, and closed the door. I just sat there in the dark, relieved that I didn't have to watch Will and the rest of them boozing it up. I had been there for a while when I heard a couple, both of whom were well-known reporters, come downstairs with Ava and sit in the little dining area right outside the kitchen door. I could hear their entire conversation.

Ava started ranting about Mickey: "I can't do this anymore. I hate him. I hate him so much!" I was surprised. Mickey and Ava seemed so happy, unlike Will and me. "I want out," she went on. "I want a divorce. I want out of this marriage right now!"

Their response was even more shocking. "Don't be a damned fool, Ava," the husband said. "You've only been married a few months. You won't get anything." Then his wife interjected, "Stick it out a little longer. Then you can skin him and take him for everything."

Ava listened as the couple continued to coach her on what to do. She took their advice, of course, and left Mickey just over a year later. I should have told Mickey that he was about to be taken, but I didn't, and I have always regretted it. I was so young then and didn't want to get involved in someone else's marriage problems. I had my own to worry about.

Shortly after that party, there was one night when Will didn't come home at all. His absence stretched into days. I was frantic, thinking that he might have been in an accident while driving drunk. He wasn't at any of the hospitals. There were no police reports. Then, late one night, I got a telephone call. A woman on the other end of the phone asked, "Is this Maureen O'Hara?" I was half asleep. "It's very late. Do you know what time it is?" I asked cautiously. She didn't answer but gave me instructions instead: "Write this address down," she said, which I did. "I've got your husband here. Come and pick the son of a bitch up and get him the hell out of here!" Then she slammed the phone down.

I went downstairs and asked Wilmon to go get Will. He found him in a drunken stupor right where the lady had said he would be, at a whorehouse in a seedy part of the city. He'd apparently been there for days, bragging and shooting his mouth off. We had been married less than sixty days.

Any hope that I had of finding true happiness with Will died that night. I was certain that it was going to be a very difficult marriage and that life with him would be a constant trial. I'd be lying if I said that what he did that night hurt me deeply. The sad truth is, it didn't hurt, and if I'd really cared about him, then it should have hurt me very much.

A few days later, Will was on his way to boot camp in San Diego, California, at the same marine base where I'd made *To the Shores of Tripoli*. It had come around full circle and I was relieved that he was gone and that some normalcy would be back in my life.

I was still working on *Ten Gentlemen from West Point,* and filming was nearing completion. Zanuck had recast the John Payne role with George Montgomery, a former heavyweight prizefighter who in college had studied interior decorating. I found him positively loathsome. During a love scene we had together, Montgomery got out of line by giving me an open-mouth kiss and damn near choking me to death. I was livid. You just didn't do something like that in those days. I know today they practically lick each other's faces clean, but back then it just wasn't done. I broke loose, restrained myself from belting him, and—for the only time in my career—walked off the set.

I stormed out the stage door, up the lot, and into Lew Schreiber's office. I told him what had happened, and demanded in no uncertain terms, "This had better be taken care of." He knew I was fuming and so he just calmly nodded his head as I went on, "I want it made clear that this sort of thing is never to happen again. Tell Mr. Zanuck that I don't mean to be difficult, but I'm very serious about this." I half-expected Schreiber to tell me I was overreacting, but he was wonderfully supportive. He said, "Difficult? Maureen, when you walk out of the room, who do you think he hopes his daughters will turn out to be like? We'll handle it." He lived up to his word and Montgomery behaved like an angel for the rest of the picture.

I had some time off while I waited for my next film to start production. Lew promised that it was going to be a big one. With Will gone, I was invited to John and Mary Ford's house for dinner a number of times. Mary wanted someone to commiserate with and help her at the Hollywood Canteen, a free club for the servicemen who frequented Hollywood. After *How Green Was My Valley* was finished, Pappy had gone into the navy as a lieutenant commander in charge of a film unit. Sometimes I'd see Duke and Josie Wayne there, and we were becoming closer friends. Then I got the strangest invitation from the most unexpected fellow.

CHAPTER 8

DINNER WITH HOWARD
HUGHES, THEN TEA
WITH ERROL FLYNN

ohn Farrow's jaw must have felt much better, for he asked me to join him and Maureen O'Sullivan for dinner at their home. I don't hold grudges, so I accepted. The evening felt bizarre from the moment I arrived. Farrow was in the living room, speaking softly into the ear of a very strange-looking man. I was surprised when he said, "Maureen, I'd like you to meet Howard Hughes." I needed the introduction because I wouldn't have known him otherwise. I had never seen Hughes before. Stories and rumors about him were widespread at every major studio—picture people love to gossip—but all I really knew about him was that he was in the motion-picture business, he was a pilot who had been in a lot of crashes, and his body was held together with wire and string.

At thirty-six, to me Howard Hughes looked like an old man, nothing like the dashing womanizer you read about today. I got a strange vibe from him as soon as I shook his hand, and it wasn't a good one. I tried to be polite and make small talk with him, but I found that having any sort of conversation with Hughes was nearly impossible. Whenever I asked him a question, he wouldn't answer, and I thought, Oh, he can't hear. He has a hearing problem. But then when I asked Farrow or Maureen O'Sullivan a question, Hughes heard it fine and answered the question for them. He did it so much that, to me, Farrow started to resemble a Charlie McCarthy doll.

When we finally sat down to dinner, everyone else was so exhausted by the rigors of that kind of conversation that they stopped talking. The only thing breaking the silence was the sound of silverware on plates. Finally, I couldn't stand it anymore and decided to ask him the one question that had fascinated me: "Mr. Hughes, I hear you've been in a lot of plane crashes. Is it true you're held together with wire and string?" I was shocked at myself for asking it, and I could tell by Farrow's and O'Sullivan's open mouths that they were too. Hughes never flinched or even appeared to have heard the question. I was never again invited back to the Farrows' home for dinner.

In the middle of March, Will called to say he had finished his basic training in San Diego and was being sent to Marine Corps Base, Quantico, in West Virginia, for officers' training. From there, he would be sent somewhere in the Pacific. Will asked me to come to Quantico for a few weeks before my next picture began.

The next week, I took a train from Los Angeles to Quantico. I'd stupidly left my money on the dresser at home, and I boarded the train with just enough in my wallet to tip the purser. I had no money for food and, in no time, I was starving. I was doubled over from hunger pains. I started eating the vitamins I had in my purse, but the bottle ran out quickly. I had to get out of my elegant travel car and walk up and down the aisle to work out the cramps. I was so dizzy and light-headed I could barely stand. I was in serious trouble. And then I got a lucky break that I have never forgotten.

A woman suddenly rounded the corner, and she, thankfully, turned out to be a big fan. As soon as she spotted me, she rushed over and said, "Oh my goodness! It's Maureen O'Hara. I'm your biggest fan." The questions came rushing at me, but I was so delirious from hunger that I was struggling to answer. "Where are you going? Are you off to make another movie? Who's the leading man?" My head was spinning and I could barely hear her. Then she finally asked the magic question: "Would you do me the honor of letting me take you to lunch?"

"I'd love to join you for lunch," I answered. "The pleasure would be all mine!" I was so hungry that I beat that dear woman to the lunch car. I'm sure she was expecting quite the elegant and proper little luncheon, but I could focus only on the lamb chops, potatoes, and mint jelly that I had ordered. She was wonderful and dear and kept trying to engage me in conversation, but all I could do was stuff food in my mouth. Her eyes widened when I started licking my fingers, and then her mouth fell open when I made sure to hit the thumb area twice. I've never eaten so fast or enjoyed a meal more. The food helped, and my wits finally returned to me. I knew I had to stock up on rations for the rest of my journey; a chance like this might not come again. I reached for the bread basket and started stuffing rolls in my purse. That's when she gasped.

I can't tell you how many times over the years I've thought about that dear lady. I wonder what she told her friends about her lunch with that awful Maureen O'Hara.

I had made arrangements to stay in Quantico with my old stand-in Sue Daly, who had quarters on the base in the noncommissioned officers' building. Her husband, Jimmy, a cameraman at RKO, was now a marine stationed there. I was hopeful Will would be as changed as he sounded on the phone. My visit was an important test of him; unfortunately, he failed it miserably the first weekend.

I caught the first train out as soon as Lew Schreiber called with the news that Zanuck had made good on his promise and had cast me opposite Tyrone Power in *The Black Swan*. It had everything you could want in a lavish pirate picture: a magnificent ship with thundering cannons; a dashing hero battling menacing villains (Ty Power, Laird Cregar, *and* Tony Quinn!); sword fights; fabulous costumes; and a damsel in distress draped in oodles of jewelry. We filmed much of the picture on Tyrone Power Lake, a large body of water behind the Fox studio named after its biggest swashbuckling star. *The Black Swan* proved to be a super-smashing box-office success and, even today, is renowned for its superb Technicolor photography.

Working with Ty Power was exciting. In those days, he was the biggest romantic swashbuckler in the world. Murderously handsome, Ty was the fourth in a long line of actors named Tyrone Power. His father was a famous Irish Shakespearean actor who had died tragically in his son's arms when Ty was just seventeen. The experience affected Ty deeply, and he often spoke to me about his own children—sons and daughters he didn't yet have, but wanted in the future.

But what I loved most about working with Ty Power was his wicked sense of humor. He was an absolute devil and quickly figured out that I was a naive young Irish lass. I was the perfect stooge.

"Gee, Mr. King looks awfully low today," he'd begin, referring to our director, Henry King. "Did you notice that, Maureen?" I would shake my head no. "Why don't you go tell him a little joke to cheer him up?"

I'd fall right into it. "But, Ty, I don't know any jokes to tell." Not to worry, Ty had just the joke for me. "Oh, Mr. King, I have a story I'd like to tell you."

I'd watch the warm smile fade from Henry King's face to the sound of Ty Power choking with laughter somewhere out of sight. Ty would tell me off-color stories with hidden double meanings, knowing damn well I wouldn't understand a word he was saying. Then he would make me repeat them to Henry King, a distinguished man who was an industry pioneer and cofounder of the Academy of Motion Picture Arts and Sciences. King began in silent films, directing actors like Richard Barthelmess and the Gish sisters. He was one of the most important directors of his time and I really wanted to make an impression on him. Thanks to Ty Power, I sure did.

In those days, I was very strict about what I would and wouldn't do in the picture business. It was always important to me to remain true to myself and to the teachings of my family. When I first came to America, studio executives wanted to bob my nose. They said it was too big, which it is, but I like it anyway. I told them, "I'm very sorry, but if you don't like me the way I am, then I'll get back on a ship and go home. We'll forget the whole thing." I kept my nose. I refused to pose suggestively for magazines or perform scenes in which I would be drinking liquor or smoking cigarettes (I softened on these points later, as I got older).

These restrictions sometimes put me at odds with the studio because of the way the system worked. While I was under contract to a studio, that studio considered me their property. In some ways, they were right. They paid me a weekly salary whether I was making a picture or not. If they wanted me at a charity event or at a premiere for one of their movies, I went because they were paying for my time. This was how the studio used you between pictures.

I liked doing events that supported the war effort. Everyone in Hollywood was doing his or her part. Jimmy Stewart had gone to war. So had Clark Gable and Ronnie Reagan. Ty Power went in late 1942, and Hank Fonda followed him, right after we finished filming *The Immortal Sergeant* together. I can still see Hank with his nose buried in books between takes, studying for his service entrance exams. The studio publicized our love scene as Hank's last screen kiss before going to war. These were serious times, and they were serious men who loved their country. Even Pappy was wounded at the Battle of Midway, and was later awarded the Navy Cross and the Purple Heart.

One of the small ways in which I was able to contribute to the war effort was by promoting war bonds. Sometime between making *This Land Is Mine,* my last film with Charles Laughton, and *The Fallen Sparrow* with John Garfield (my shortest leading man, an outspoken Communist and a real sweetheart), Fox sent me to an evening dinner engagement in Texas to sell war bonds. Studio functions were always well planned, down to the tiniest detail. I never went to them alone. I was part of a team that included my publicist, Jean Pettibone, and my hair and makeup team, Faye Smyth and Jimmy Barker. It was Jean's job to get me to these events prepared, and Faye and Jimmy's to make sure I looked like a star when I walked into a room. I was on the dais with all the other speakers for the evening. Below were dozens of tables jammed with guests who were usually selected for their ability to write big donation checks.

Suddenly, there was a commotion at the door, including camera flashes, hushed chatter, and a rush of energy. Then Errol Flynn strolled into the room as if he owned it. Errol was scheduled to speak that night, and he was seated on the dais next to me. He was very poised. We made the pleasant chitchat you always do at these events, as we dined and listened to the first few speakers. I looked around the dining room for a moment, but noticed out of the corner of my eye that Errol was hiding something under the table. I glanced down and saw that he was holding a whiskey bottle between his knees. He saw me looking, but it didn't seem to bother him in the least.

One after the other, speakers went to the podium and pressed the message: "Buy war bonds." With each new speaker, Errol secretly unscrewed the cap of his whiskey bottle and filled his teacup under the table. I'm sure that countless women in the audience that night were gazing up at him on the dais and thinking, What a dashing and proper gentleman he is, sitting up there so handsomely sipping his tea.

But then came my vintage Errol Flynn moment. Errol leaned toward me—feeling no pain and now more than a bit frisky—and began whispering lewd propositions out of the corner of his mouth, the likes of which, if repeated, would turn this book into a cheap X-rated exposé. Suffice it to say, it was crude and ugly stuff and not the slightest bit erotic, which I would have expected from this legendary Casanova. Clearly he had to be drunk if he really thought I'd ever be part of a seedy Errol Flynn sex orgy. I tried to ignore him and not let his behavior make me mad. I still had to get up there and speak, and so did he!

I moved my chair away from him slightly, but he pressed on anyway, one dirty and lascivious suggestion on top of another. They mounted in their vulgarity, yet Flynn never lost his elegant poise. He just sat there with that Errol Flynn arrogant smirk on his face. I was fuming. He didn't give a damn about what he was saying. He was treating me like a Hollywood whore, like a little sex doll from the back streets. I would have loved to have knocked him on his ass, but knew I couldn't make that kind of scene. I finally whispered, under the guise of a smile, "Listen here, Errol, knock it off right now. You better get the hell out of here or I'm going up to that microphone and tell everybody what you've got in that teacup of yours, plus I'll repeat everything you've been saying to me—word for word."

Errol knew he had gone too far and was about to be exposed. I watched him slowly slide off his chair, down to the ground, where he began to crawl on all fours under the table, trying to make his escape. He was like a mouse trapped in a maze. Right turn, then left turn—and he was still under the table. People down the length of the table were jumping slightly as he startled them from beneath. When he finally reached the end of the long table, he stood up and looked back at me—arrogant smirk intact—and waved good-bye playfully. I saluted with my closed fist and returned his smile. He never spoke at the dinner that night.

Will returned from battle in August 1943. He was now stationed down in San Diego at the marine base, but would come home to Los Angeles on weekend leave from time to time. Unfortunately, war had only made him worse. He had turned angry and mean. This new dark side came out whenever he drank. In the morning, however, he wouldn't remember any of it.

One evening in early October, he staggered into the house with another marine who claimed to be a minister. I didn't even know Will was off the base. They were both falling-down drunk, and Will started in on me about something nonsensical. Eventually, Will passed out in the hallway, and the minister thought he'd try to have some fun with me.

I was shocked, and I shouted, "What kind of man are you? You're a minister, and here you are trying to have sex with your friend's wife! You're a disgrace!"

He looked down his nose at me and snickered, "You stupid bitch. You don't even know where we were last night or what he was doing." Clearly, he was about to tell me: "Your husband was with another woman last night. Her name was Jane. He begged me to marry them. He doesn't give a damn about you, so why don't we have some fun?"

"I don't give a damn where he was last night," I shouted. "I want you out of my house!"

"I'm too drunk to drive," he persisted. "I'll have an accident."

I didn't want that. I didn't want anyone hurt, so I gave a little. "Fine. I know you're drunk, and it's late. If you're too drunk to drive, then you can stay here until the sun comes up. That's it. Then you get the hell out of my house!"

I moved to the bedroom and made one more thing clear: "If you so much as come one step toward my door, I'll report you to the police and to your base immediately. Then I'll kill you."

The next morning they were both gone. I never saw that minister again. I looked at the mess they had left and felt sick to my stomach. I knew Will was in serious trouble. I knew then that for him, any recovery was going to take a tremendous effort on my part. Despite all that I already knew about him, however, I felt without any reservation that I had to do my utmost to save him. I had no choice. The day before, I had learned I was pregnant.

CHAPTER 9

MAMMY'S THE QUEEN
OF TECHNICOLOR

*A*s the end of 1943 neared, I was busy wrapping up my first western. In *Buffalo Bill*, Joel Mc-Crea played legendary showman William F. Cody, and I was cast as his wife. I thought the picture would be forgettable, but it turned out to be one of the biggest moneymakers 20th Century-Fox had that year. I didn't feel McCrea was tough enough to play the lead in a western. He was a very nice man, a good actor, but not rugged like Duke or Brian Keith. Critics mostly panned the film, except for the positive way in which Native American Indians were portrayed.

I think the picture did so well with audiences because of its masterful use of Technicolor. *Buffalo Bill* was an outdoor panoramic feast for the eyes. Director William Wellman and cinematographer Leon Shamroy used these special cameras to capture the majestic coloring of the canyons, mountains, and plateaus of Arizona and Utah. The film's climax was a spectacular battle at War Bonnet Gorge between the U.S. Cavalry and a Cheyenne tribe. It was gorgeous to watch on-screen.

Though *Buffalo Bill* was my third picture in Technicolor, it's the one that best shows how using color could sometimes save a picture at the box office. Moviegoers then watched color films with the same wonderment that audiences do dazzling special effects today—forgiving almost every flaw in story, performance, and direction. No one ever sets out to make a bad motion picture, but despite all the best intentions, it happens from time to time. The use of Technicolor was more costly, but a good hedge of one's bet if you were a studio boss like Darryl Zanuck and determined to make the most out of every project.

I didn't know a thing about the technology and made my first picture in Technicolor (*To the Shores of Tripoli*) because Darryl Zanuck told me to. Apparently my features—red hair, hazel-green eyes, and a fair complexion—had photographed so well in Technicolor that when other actresses saw what I looked like on film, it calmed their fears. Studio requests for Technicolor went right through the roof. Almost overnight, everyone wanted to be shot in Technicolor. Dr. Herbert Kalmus, who had invented the Technicolor process, was so pleased that he started saying, "Maureen O'Hara is *my* 'Queen of Technicolor,' " and since he owned the technology, I became known as *the* Queen of Technicolor.

In the beginning, the honest truth is that I hated working in Technicolor. On *To the Shores of Tripoli,* the special cameras required so much light to capture images that it burned my eyes horribly and I got klieg eye. I reached the point where I could barely open them to face the cameras. I was in so much agony that I told Zanuck, "I don't want to make another Technicolor picture. I can't stand the pain."

When I was later cast in *The Black Swan* and heard it was

going to be shot in Technicolor, I wanted out of the picture. But Leon Shamroy was a magnificent cinematographer and he promised that he could film me without the lighting problems. I reluctantly agreed to a test so he could prove it. When I arrived on the set, I asked him, "When are you going to turn on the lights?" He just grinned at me and said, "They're already on." I didn't believe him. "Come on, Leon. We're in the dark here." He assured me that this was how he was going to light the movie and so I threw caution to the winds and made the picture. Shamroy was a master, and we worked together again several times in Technicolor. To this day, *The Black Swan* remains one of the greatest examples of Technicolor photography and is used in schools to train cinematographers.

The year 1944 came with the excitement of my first trimester ending without any problems. In February, I began working for Paramount on *Till We Meet Again,* with Ray Milland and director Frank Borzage. On my way home from the set one evening, I started feeling extremely hot. I felt as if I was dripping with sweat all over. I checked myself and pulled up a hand covered in blood. There was quite a bit of it and I started to panic. My first thought was, Oh my God, I'm losing the baby. I rushed home and then to the hospital emergency room. The doctor gave me a choice: "Do the movie or keep the baby." There was no decision to make, so I dropped out of the picture. I had to stay in bed until the bleeding stopped and was told to rest and avoid stress for the remainder of my pregnancy.

Shortly after I was back on my feet, Wilmon and Dan went on vacation to visit their family in Mississippi. I didn't want to be alone in the house in case I had more problems, so I hired a temporary housekeeper I found through an agency. Elena was a hard worker who claimed she had been a German countess before the war broke out. She told me the awful story of how, to survive, she went from living in palaces to cleaning other people's homes. I didn't know if her story was true, but I thought she was a good person and she certainly was doing a fine job. Having her in the house set my mind at ease and I could relax. I slept and napped to my heart's content. Peaceful bliss.

CRASH! SMASH! The sudden sound was followed by another and another. I heard screaming. I leaped out of bed and rushed to the dining room where I found Elena in a state of hysterics. On the table in front of her was my magnificent yellow Dresden china set that I had fallen in love with and bought at an estate auction some months before. Her eyes were on fire as she reached for a teacup.

"What in God's name are you doing?" I demanded. She turned to me, enraged, and shook the teacup at me. "How . . . dare . . . you? How dare you have this in this house? How dare you have this china in this country!" She shattered the cup against the wall and then grabbed a dinner plate.

"Don't!" I pleaded. Too late. The plate was in flight. *CRASH!*

"It's German! It's German, and I'm going to break it all. Every last piece of it!"

She was like a maniac and kept grabbing pieces and breaking them against the wall. "Stop that this instant!" I demanded. I rushed over to her and had to wrestle her out of the house. I needed peace and quiet, not rage and aggravation. Thankfully, Wilmon and Dan were back a few weeks later, and things were back to normal in no time.

Unfortunately, so was Will. He showed up on leave, skunk drunk. He was in a particularly nasty mood when he arrived and started right in on me. "I'll need some money." Ice cubes clinked into his glass. "I'm going out to meet some friends."

I asked him a question without offering him any cash. "How

can you need money, Will? You get a paycheck, and everything is provided for you at the base."

"It's barely anything," he snapped. I decided to retreat to the bedroom to escape his belligerence, but he followed me. He fixed on my gorgeous antique doll collection. "You and those god-damned dolls. They're everywhere." I loved my dolls even then. I used to sit them up on my bay window every day. I had them beautifully displayed, and they always brought a smile to my face when I saw them. "You know how much I love them. I've had them ever since I came to America."

"Well, I hate them," he snarled. "Get them out of here." I wasn't about to get rid of them, no way. "Well, I'm sorry, Will, but they're staying," I said forcefully. "They're mine and I want them here. They make me feel good."

"I don't care. Get rid of them or I will." I didn't like his tone, so I changed the subject. "There's money in my purse. Take what you need." That did the trick, and Will was on his way to the kitchen to freshen his drink and find my purse. The more I thought about his threat, the more it worried me. He was more ag-itated than usual and I didn't want to chance his doing anything crazy. I boxed up the dolls and asked Wilmon to take them down to the basement where they would be safe. Will didn't stay home long and I barely saw him again while he was in Los Angeles. I asked Dan if she had seen him, and she told me he had gone back to the base. I was relieved. I asked Wilmon to go down to the base-ment and bring up my dolls. He came back with an ashen face in-stead. "Where are my dolls, Wilmon?" He looked at Dan with sad eyes. I raced down to the basement and was sickened by the sight of it. Will had gone down to the basement before he left and had pulled all my dolls out of the boxes. Some he had burned and others he had doused with water. The rest of them had been smashed to bits. He had destroyed them all.

I never confronted Will about the dolls. It bothered me that I hadn't because that's not like me. I never really confronted him about anything because it would just end up in a fight. The more I thought about it, the more I realized that I had become afraid of Will. I was afraid of the dark side I had seen and of his growing instability. I didn't have a clue as to what he was capable of or what he might do.

As my due date neared, Will's mother, Margaret, called and asked if she could be there when the baby was born. She arrived in Los Angeles the first week of June and was very kind to me. The more I got to know her, the more I liked her. I felt that my child would be fortunate to have her as a grandmother. I also thought very seriously about whether or not I should tell her about the problems I was having with her son. Will answered the question for me when he arrived the second week in June. I was due any day, at this point, and the marines had given him leave until the baby was born. He made no attempt whatsoever to hide his drinking from his mother. I knew instantly that she was aware of how severe his problem was. I could see the pain in her eyes.

I don't know whether my hormones were all mixed up, but I was very emotional the last few weeks of my pregnancy. Will got drunk and wanted to go out on the town by himself the very first night he was home, but I pleaded with him not to. "Please stay home tonight, Will. The baby could come anytime and I need you here." He wouldn't listen. He didn't give a damn about what I needed. "Don't tell me what to do," he snapped as he made his way to the door. I grabbed his arm and tried to pull him away from the door. "Will, I mean it, please." He pulled his arm free and I never saw it coming. Will swung around and buried his fist in my stomach. I cried out in pain and doubled over. Will's face didn't seem to register what he had just done. He was just blank—a shell. I rose and clung to the wall to get my balance and then made my way slowly across it, away from him.

Will's mother had been standing behind me in the hallway the entire time. She saw everything. When I reached her, I saw the horror in her eyes. Will stormed out and left us there. "Are you all right, Maureen?" she asked in a shaky voice. "Is the baby . . . ?" My breath was back and the pain was gone. I was more scared than anything else. "I think I'm fine." That was a lie. Everything was far from fine. The baby might still be safe and unharmed in my womb, but we were in danger. Will's mother took me by the arm and faced me with the most strength I had ever seen her show. "Maureen, if my son ever hits you again, I want you to call the police. Do you understand me? Call the police!" I suspected then that she had probably suffered the same kind of treatment from Will's father. I felt sad, and strangely close to her. We sat together in silence for the rest of the night.

One week later, I went into labor and was taken to Hollywood Presbyterian Hospital. I don't know where tough and gruff Maureen O'Hara was, but she sure as hell wasn't in that delivery room with Maureen FitzSimons. Visualize the most ridiculous birthing scene in any movie you can think of—one in which the mother is behaving histrionically—and you have a glimpse of how I was in labor. I was in agony. All I remember is Dr. Krahulik telling me to push. He *had* to be kidding. I said, "Oh no. No way. I'm not pushing." He gently reminded me, "You know you have to push for the baby to come out." To which I responded, "Why?" He started pleading with me, "Oh please. Just one little push. That's all I'm asking. One little push." I gave in—pushed just a little—but then I couldn't stop. The pain intensified and I spewed venom. "You son of a bitch! You knew if I pushed, I wouldn't be able to stop!" He laughed at me as nature took its course. On June 30, 1944, my beautiful baby girl was born. She was a healthy eight pounds, ten ounces. As I've already said, I named her Bronwyn after the character my dear friend Anna Lee played in *How Green Was My Valley*.

Bronwyn entered my life like a glorious sunrise brightening the sky. There was warmth in the house now, the kind that comes only with the innocence of a newborn baby. I was starting the most important role I would ever play—one far more meaningful and enriching than any Hollywood could ever offer.

Will was barely able to utter anything about becoming a father. "Her tiny hands are so beautiful," was all he was able to muster, followed by an occasional "Coochee coo, coochee coo." I could barely stand to see him touch her, and was eager to have him get back to the base. His mother stayed for a few more weeks and helped me hire a nanny before she left. I knew it wouldn't be long before the studio would be expecting me back at work.

A few weeks after Bronwyn was born, I got the call from Joe Nolan asking if I would be ready to come back in early August. Joe was the number two man at RKO Pictures and I still had a one-picture-per-year commitment with them. The studio had lined up an action picture for me called *The Spanish Main* and was hoping to piggyback off Fox's huge success with *The Black Swan*. I said I was able to work, but sensed that Joe was holding something back. I asked him if everything was okay. He said, "I don't know how to tell you this, but I have a big concern." He was dancing around something. "What's wrong, Joe?" I pushed. "It can't be that bad, whatever it is." He paused for a moment, then said, "Well, a young actress was just in here to see me and said that I should cast her in the picture instead of you. She said you were as big as a horse, as big as a house, and will never be able to make another picture again. Is that true?"

I knew what was going on. "Joe, for God's sake, don't get caught up in petty studio jealousies. Of course it's not. I've had a baby. Women do it every day and still manage to go on with their lives." He was still quiet. "Listen, I'm still recuperating, so I'm not going to get in a car and drive down to the studio. But if you send a car and a driver to me, I will get in, provided I can stay in my robe, and come in and let you see that I am not as big as a house." That offer eased his concern. "That's not necessary. I'll see you in August."

You learn very fast in the acting profession that there isn't anything an aspiring actress won't do to steal your part. If you're thinking of becoming an actress, here's another tip: Never take your eyes off the rearview mirror. There's always an Eve Harrington out there somewhere, creeping up, who'll try to run you off the road.

The truth is, I had gained the usual pounds during my pregnancy, so I put myself on a diet to drop the extra weight. I ate the same dinner every night: lamb chops with stewed tomatoes and fresh fruit. After dinner, I took a long walk down to Sunset Boulevard and back with our dog, Tripoli. On one of those walks, a young actress named Kathryn approached me and asked, "Miss O'Hara, can I walk with you?" I said, "Sure. That's okay. I don't mind," thinking nothing of it. The next thing I knew, she spread an absurd rumor that I'd made a sexual advance toward her in an elevator at MGM. It was an outrageous charge, of course, and it rolled right off my back. Fledgling actresses will say or do *any-thing* in the hope of jump-starting a career. The big laugh was that at that time I had never even been to MGM. Her story gave her five minutes of notoriety around the studio, at my expense, but in the long run, her modest talent revealed itself and her career never amounted to anything.

In October, I was back in front of the cameras shooting *The Spanish Main*. It was good swashbuckler fare, pairing me with Paul Henreid, the Austrian actor best known for his role as Victor

Laszlo in *Casablanca*. Some in Hollywood called him "Cracker-butt Hemorrhoid" because he had no behind at all. Truthfully, he was too charming and not tough enough for the role in our film. Frank Borzage directed the picture and it was shot in Technicolor by cinematographer George Barnes. With a camera, George could make you look like milk and honey, sugar and cream. We had a good supporting cast that included Walter Slezak, Binnie Barnes, and Nancy Gates. Nancy and I later became good friends when we made *This Land Is Mine* together, and she stayed with me for a short time while she was looking for a place of her own in Hollywood. Shooting was going on normally until the day John Ford made an unexpected visit to the studio.

He was back from the war, and early one day, he drove himself to the RKO studio to see me. But when Mr. Ford arrived, the young guard at the gate refused to let him on the studio lot. John Ford had shown up unannounced, as he always did, dressed in an old jacket, an old pair of pants, and an old hat. The young man thought, No way. This isn't anyone important. He's trying to crash the studio, so Ford was turned away.

Ford went back home and was furious, absolutely livid. He called Joe Nolan and really let him have it. Nolan rushed down to the set in a panic and said, "Maureen, my God, there's been a terrible mistake. The guard at the gate wouldn't let John Ford on the lot. He sent him away, and Ford is outraged. He was coming here to see you about something." I wanted to laugh, but I didn't. I could only imagine the hell Ford had put poor Joe Nolan through. Nolan was very upset and continued, "I don't know what to do. To insult John Ford like that!" I wanted to help him out of his pickle. I offered, "Well, maybe he'll come back tomorrow and we can straighten it out." Nolan and his team put their heads together and came up with the perfect olive branch. My job was to extend it.

I called Ford later that day and said, "Mr. Ford, the studio is so upset by what happened today. They're just sick about it. They sincerely regret it." He remained silent. "If you will please come back tomorrow," I went on, "the studio will roll out a red carpet for you, from the gate all the way out to the set, and I will be waiting for you." This must have tickled John Ford's fancy. He came back the following day and RKO did roll out a red carpet, just as they had promised—from the gate all the way through the studio, right to my set. John Ford drove through the gates of RKO that day and, like a king, rolled across the studio lot on that red carpet.

I didn't know why John Ford was coming to see me that day. When he arrived on the set, I greeted him as I always did: "Hello, Mr. Ford, it's so good to see you." We shook hands, and he then got right to the point. He called out to Borzage, "Frank, can you come here for a moment? I'd like you to witness this conversation." Borzage obliged the request as Mr. Ford continued: "Maureen, I am going to make a movie in Ireland called *The Quiet Man* and I would like you to play the female lead." I knew Ford wanted to make a picture with me in Ireland because he had dropped hints about it at his home over dinners ever since *How Green Was My Valley*. He had given no specifics, only the intention. It was on the set of *The Spanish Main* that I finally knew his intention of making a picture in Ireland was both serious and real. It was the very first time I knew specifically what picture we would make there. I answered with a firm handshake and, "Mr. Ford, I accept your offer and will be thrilled to play the female lead in *The Quiet Man*."

Borzage chimed in, "Mr. Ford and Miss O'Hara, I am delighted to have witnessed your agreement that Miss O'Hara will play the female lead in *The Quiet Man*." From that day forward, John Ford and I had a binding legal agreement that I would play the role of Mary Kate Danaher. Of course, we didn't know it would take another seven years before the cameras would finally roll in the village of Cong.

No matter, because my work on *The Quiet Man* began as soon as I finished filming *The Spanish Main.* I received an invitation to spend the weekend with Pappy and Mary on their boat, the *Araner.* One never declined an invitation to join Pappy on his beloved yacht. I had never been on the *Araner* before and she was a splendid sight—a glorious double-mast sailing vessel that ran 110 feet in length. Her superstructure and decks were done in a rich, varnished teak, and her hull was as white as virgin snow. Plush red carpets gave her the feel of luxury, as did her fireplaces, four-poster beds, and dressing quarters. Several crew members scurried about, jumping to every one of Captain Ford's commands.

It was on the *Araner* that I began working closely with Pappy as he started crafting his very first ideas for the manuscript of *The Quiet Man.* While Mary, her grandchildren, and Bronwyn enjoyed the beaches of Catalina Island, Pappy began this artistic process by having me share with him everything about my life growing up in Ireland. I watched as Pappy immersed himself completely in all that was Ireland, and more important, in life experiences and customs that he had never lived himself. In the very beginning, the first role I played in *The Quiet Man* was not Mary Kate Danaher, but that of John Ford's muse.

From this moment on, Pappy and I continued working on *The Quiet Man* aboard the *Araner* every weekend unless one of us was working on a picture. The process didn't end until we left for Ireland to make the film.

CHAPTER 10

PINUP GIRL

*S*pending so much time together brought Bronwyn
and me even closer to Pappy, Mary, and their kids.
I'd have them to my home for dinner or they'd have me there. It
was wonderful, all good, until the night I attended one of their
parties in early December 1944. The usual gang was there, and
after mingling with the guests downstairs for a bit, I went upstairs
and found Pappy on a chaise longue in the middle of telling a
story to some friends. Frank Borzage was one of them. Frank was
not only a friend of John Ford's but was also the brother of Danny
Borzage, who was the most unusual member of the Ford stock
company. If you were ever allowed to visit a John Ford set (and
very few people ever were), you could count on seeing Danny
Borzage there, playing an accordion all day long. Danny
wouldn't be a cast member in the pictures; Mr. Ford had him
there to create atmosphere.

At the party that night, I waited at the door for a moment, listening to Pappy, and then I took a seat next to him as he continued with one of his favorite fibs: how he had once ridden with Pancho Villa. When Pappy finished the story, Frank Borzage asked me a simple question. I don't remember what it was or how I answered him. Whatever I said, though, infuriated Ford. Without any warning at all, he turned on me and socked me square in the jaw. I felt my head snap back and heard the gasps of everyone there as each of them stared at me in disbelief and shock. I didn't know why he hit me, and, to this day, I still don't have a clue. Was it a test of my loyalty and respect? Was he waiting to see if I would challenge him? No one said a word. Not one of them was about to challenge the old man by rising to my defense, and I wasn't about to fail the test either. I stood up without a word and walked downstairs and straight out the front door. I never mentioned the incident again.

In the middle of April 1945, a few days after FDR died and Harry Truman became president, I went to work shooting the musical *Do You Love Me?* It was one of the worst pictures I ever made. Neither Dick Haymes nor Harry James could save it. It was rocky from the start, and a bad omen for worse to come. A couple of weeks into shooting, the film's producer, former vaudevillian George Jessel, came to see me in my dressing room. He said we needed to talk about the shooting schedule. Jessel was well known as having a lecherous eye for young girls. A few years earlier, he had raised more than a few eyebrows when he'd married a sixteen-year-old girl only months after his scandalous divorce from silent-screen star Norma Talmadge. I was at my makeup table when he came in, and within minutes he was standing behind me, massaging my arms and shoulders.

Then he started pawing me and I went into orbit. I stood up and chewed out "America's Favorite Toastmaster," yelling so loudly you could hear my voice echoing outside my trailer. As now, there was great market value for good Hollywood gossip back then. Someone on the set heard my explosion and sold the story to the trades. The incident was all over the papers the very next day and Jessel kept his distance after that.

Later that morning, I was summoned to Zanuck's office. Going to see Zanuck was always an experience. His office was an oddly shaped room, oblong, so that you had to walk quite a distance from the door to reach him. As I entered, I could see him, at the other end of the room, seated rigidly behind his expansive desk, positioned squarely on a raised platform. He rose and greeted me when I had passed the halfway point. "Maureen, come and sit. I'm about to make you very happy." That was a relief. I was sure he wanted to discuss the Jessel matter.

I felt awkward sitting in a chair that was so much lower than his, which, of course, was his very intention. It forced me to look up at him and take notice that he was also looking down at me. Studio bosses had good sport playing head games and engaging in power struggles with their stars, and Zanuck was an Olympian at it. He might have had an oversize cigar in his hand, but Zanuck needed that platform to compensate for being so short. This Hollywood kingpin with a legendary libido was at least a few inches shorter than I was.

Zanuck continued, "I like your chemistry with Ty Power. I like what you did with *The Black Swan*. I'm casting you in *The Razor's Edge* with him." I was thrilled and could hardly contain myself. I knew Ty and I had a strong chemistry on-screen, and I was eager to sink my teeth into a great dramatic role. After I thanked him repeatedly, Zanuck cautioned me. "Listen to me. I'm planning a big publicity campaign for this picture. You are not to discuss this with anyone until the formal announcement is made. Is that clear?"

I stood and extended my hand *up* to him. "Oh yes, Mr.

Zanuck. Perfectly clear." I promised, "I won't say a word. Not a single word." I had every intention of obeying his order, but I was bursting with excitement when I got back to the set. It kept building and building as the day went on, and I had to tell someone or I was going to burst. So I stupidly met Linda Darnell at the Fox commissary for a bite of lunch and told her everything. Linda was a close friend and I figured that she would keep her mouth shut after I told her how important the secrecy was. It was a monstrous mistake.

By the time I got back to the set, there was a phone call already waiting for me. It was Mr. Zanuck. He said, "Maureen, I told you not to discuss our conversation with anyone, and you did. You're out of the picture." He slammed the phone down. I was so disappointed that I ran to my dressing room crying. I was absolutely devastated and couldn't return to the set. Director Gregory Ratoff finally came to me and asked what had happened. After I told him, he started to chuckle and said, "Oh you silly, stupid girl. Don't you know what you did? You told Zanuck's mistress."

But there were many reasons to be happy. I was set to star in *The Quiet Man* with John Wayne. I had also found the script for *Sentimental Journey* floating around the Fox lot and had persuaded Lew Schreiber to make it, even though he wasn't sure it would be a success. Far more important, though, not just for me but for the whole world, was that the end of the war was at last at hand. Hitler killed himself, Berlin fell, and Germany surrendered to the Allies on May 7.

After wrapping *Do You Love Me?*, all I wanted to know was how soon I could go home to Ireland. It would take another full year for the Marshall Plan to be put in place and for the world to start rebuilding Europe. In the meantime, life went on as it had for me. I had to wait. But as sure as I was that I would be going home soon, I was also certain that Will would be coming home too.

I went right into making *Sentimental Journey* and it was every bit the smash hit that I thought it would be. It was a rip-your-heart-out tearjerker that reduced my agents and the toughest brass at Fox to mush when they saw it. Lew Wasserman sobbed so loudly that he embarrassed himself. Audiences ate it up, Fox made a fortune, and I was hoping that critics might actually mention my performance for a change instead of focusing on my looks.

I hadn't received a positive review on my acting abilities since *How Green Was My Valley*. I was growing damned tired of the suggestion that suddenly all I knew how to do was "sit tight and look pretty." Picture after picture, the reviews were always the same: "Maureen O'Hara is luscious in Technicolor" or "She looks lovely and pouts beautifully." Dorothy Manners of the *Los Angeles Examiner* went so far as to write, "If they gave an Academy Award for gorgeous, Maureen O'Hara would win hands down."

Such comments were awful unless you were a beauty-pageant contestant. I was an actress. Being "the Queen of Technicolor" hurt my career rather than helped it. Many of the great, great roles that came along were given to less attractive stars because studio bosses assumed they had to be better actresses. I was passed over because executives reasoned, "Oh, she's so gorgeous we don't have to worry about anything else. All we have to do is put her in beautiful costumes and photograph her." They were using me to push their lousy scripts while the other girls were getting all the good parts. I would have loved the chance to play one of those really nasty bitches that Bette Davis always got to do.

I decided to take my complaint to the source and granted a very candid interview to Edwin Schallert, drama editor for the *Los Angeles Times*. The interview ran the following day under the headline:

MAUREEN O'HARA IRKED BY HER OWN BEAUTY
IRISH STAR REBELS AT DECORATIVE ROLES
DEMANDS OPPORTUNITY TO ACT

(Here's just some of what Schallert printed.)

I am living in the hope that somebody will chance to remark that I have given a good performance as an actress, and not simply say something about how good I looked in the production . . .

When I was with the Abbey Players in Dublin I had acquired a reputation for ability and I was proud of that. Ever since I've been in pictures, with a single exception or two, any capacity I might have for interpreting a character seems to have been ignored completely . . .

I'm not blaming this on the critics of my work. I seem to have fallen heir to a lot of decorative roles, which don't register, except pictorially. I want a part to play now in which I can win approval for accomplishment. I have grown to detest praise for any beauty I may have . . .

No more duchesses, countesses, or great ladies with hoopskirts, bonnet, bangs, and parasol! If I don't get the parts that I want, I shall just "sit tight and look pretty" until I do.

My plea for better roles fell on deaf ears. RKO quickly announced that I had been cast in the first of their planned action-adventure tales, *Sinbad the Sailor.* I would be playing Shireen, the glamorous adventuress who helps Sinbad (played by Douglas Fairbanks Jr.) find the hidden treasure of Alexander the Great. Ridiculous. I made the picture because I couldn't afford a suspension—not with a daughter, a husband, and a household to support. I was also happy to be working with Doug Fairbanks, but my image of him went right out the window when I heard he wore a padded jockstrap to bolster the bulge in his tights. The picture made a pot of money for RKO—action-adventures almost always did—and the *Hollywood Reporter* concluded that "Maureen O'Hara is one of Hollywood's best arguments in favor of tinted photography."

But it wasn't an awful movie review that ran in the newspapers on January 26, 1946, and put me in the middle of an international controversy. The day before, on January 25, I completed a process I had begun in late 1941: I officially became a dual national, a citizen of both the United States of America and of Ireland. If you recall, I had come to the United States in 1939 on a work permit to make *The Hunchback of Notre Dame.* RKO and Erich Pommer later arranged for me to obtain a quota number so that I could stay and live in the United States permanently. I did not have to become a citizen of the United States, because I already had the right to live here. I came to love her as I do my beloved Ireland, and so I wanted to be counted as an American, just as I am counted an Irishwoman.

In those days, the process of becoming an American citizen was a lengthy one. You applied for your first papers, then second papers, and, finally, your third papers. Then you took and passed the exam and were granted citizenship. I had applied for my first papers through the law offices of Wright, Wright & Milliken, but after months of waiting, hadn't heard a thing. I called and asked them to check on the status of my application and we found out that the U.S. government had lost my application. I had to apply again, only by then the law had changed.

This time I didn't have to apply for first and second and third papers. I just had to apply and then they would schedule me for an initial interview and to fill out the required paperwork and take the exam. There must have been a thousand questions on their standard questionnaire. After I completed it, I went in and took the exam. I must have passed because I was then sent before a woman, an officer of the court, who instructed me to raise my right hand and forswear my allegiance to Great Britain. FULL STOP!

Forswear my allegiance to Britain? I didn't know what she was talking about. I told her, "Miss, I'm very sorry, but I cannot forswear an allegiance that I do not have. I am Irish and my allegiance is to Ireland." She looked at me with consternation for a moment and then said, "Well, then you better read these papers." She handed me back the stack of papers I had filled out before my exam. I perused them and was stunned to see that on every page where I had written "Irish" as my former nationality, they had crossed it out with a pen and written "English."

I told the woman, "I'm terribly sorry, but I can't accept this. It's impossible for me to do. I am Irish. I was born in Ireland and will only do this if I am referred to as an Irish citizen." She seemed perturbed that I would break the routine of the allegiance ceremony, and said, "I can't do that. You'll have to go to court to obtain the order for me to do it."

"Fine," I said. "When shall I come back to go to court?" I didn't have to come back. I did it right then and was taken straight to the courtroom. No attorneys were allowed in the courtroom with me, only my two witnesses. I stood in front of the judge, whose name I can't remember, and listened as the clerk explained why I was there before the court. Then I told the judge, "I am Irish. I will not forswear allegiance to Great Britain because I owe no allegiance to Great Britain. I was born in Dublin, Ireland."

The judge and I then went into a very long discussion of all of Irish history. He challenged my assertions. We kept going over it and over it, back and forth, but I wouldn't give an inch. I couldn't. Finally he said, "We're going to have to find out what Washington thinks." He instructed the clerk, "Check Washington and see what they consider a person like Miss O'Hara." The clerk left the courtroom and returned shortly after that. He told the judge,

"Washington says she is a British subject." I was furious and told the judge, "I am not responsible for your antiquated records in Washington, D.C." He promptly ruled against me.

I had no choice but to thank him and tell the court, "Under those circumstances, I cannot accept nor do I want to become an American citizen." I turned to walk out of that courtroom, but having the kind of personality that I do, thought I couldn't give up without taking one last crack at him. I was halfway out of the courtroom when I turned back to him and said, "Your Honor, have you thought for one moment about what you are trying to force upon and take away from my child and my unborn children and my unborn grandchildren?" He sat back and listened intently as I went on, "You are trying to take away from them their right to boast and brag about their wonderful and famous Irish mother and grandmother. I just can't accept that."

He'd had enough. The judge threw his hands up and exclaimed, "Get this woman out of here! Give her anything on her papers that she wants, but get her out of here!" The clerk moved in my direction and I simply said, "Thank you, Your Honor."

I didn't know at that time that my certificate of naturalization had already been created, and that they had listed my former nationality as English. Sometime between that date and the date when I was called to be sworn in as an American citizen, they changed my certificate in accordance with the order of the court. Where my former nationality was printed, they had erased "English" and typed over it "Irish." On the back of this document it states that "the erasure made on this certificate as to Former Nationality 'Irish' was made before issuance, to conform to petition. Name changed by order of the court." It is signed by the clerk of the U.S. District Court.

This was the first time in the history of the United States of America that the American government recognized an Irish person as being Irish. It was one hell of a victory for me because otherwise I would have had to turn down my American citizenship. I could not have accepted it with my former nationality being anything other than Irish, because no other nationality in the world was my own.

The controversy arose when a story hit the papers claiming that I had challenged the court at the ceremony in which the oath of allegiance was taken. Federal judge J. F. T. O'Connor presided at that ceremony and was outraged that the incident had reportedly occurred in his courtroom. Judge O'Connor sent letters to every major Irish organization in the country saying that I was a liar and that the incident had never happened. He claimed that the entire story was phony and had only been made up as part of a Hollywood publicity stunt. He was correct that the event did not happen in his courtroom, but very wrong that it didn't happen at all. I still have the certificate with the changes and signatures that prove it did. He was also wrong about my motives. In fact, I had never discussed what happened with anyone until now. I never defended myself against O'Connor's charges because I knew what the truth was. I did it for myself, not to get my name in the papers.

The story and the controversy grew so big that it made its way to Ireland in a matter of days. Apparently, the Irish government was unaware that its citizens were being classified as subjects of Great Britain. On January 29, Taoiseach (head of government) Éamon De Valera issued the following statement:

We are today an independent republic. We acknowledge no sovereignty except that of our own people. A fact that our attitude during the recent war should have amply demonstrated. Miss O'Hara was right when she asserted she owed no allegiance to Britain and therefore had none which she could renounce.

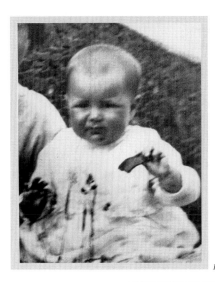

The Baby Elephant

1

At my first holy
communion, I
towered over all the
other seven-year-
old girls.

2

3

Charles Stewart Parnell
FitzSimons (Daddy)

A portrait of
Marguerita Lilburn FitzSimons
(Mammy)

4

The beautiful FitzSimons children:
Left to right: Peggy, me, Florrie, Charlie Fitz, Margot, and Jimmy

Going over lines on the set of *Jamaica Inn*. I was minutes away from filming my very first scene with Charles Laughton.

Charles Laughton signed me to my first movie contract at seventeen. He later asked my parents if he could adopt me.

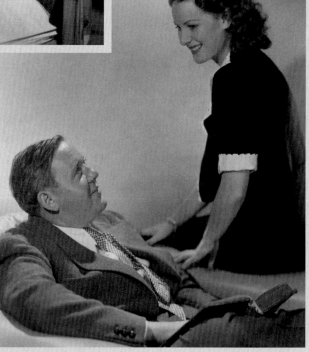

The Hunchback of Notre Dame, 1939. Quasimodo (Laughton) confronts Esmeralda (me).

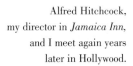

Arriving in America with Mammy at eighteen to make *The Hunchback of Notre Dame.* Audiences in London called me "the girl with black cherry eyes."

Alfred Hitchcock, my director in *Jamaica Inn*, and I meet again years later in Hollywood.

Lucille Ball and I pose during a
publicity tour for *Dance Girl, Dance.*
Days later she left the tour
and eloped with Desi Arnaz.

Ginny Matray (left)
coaches me in ballet for
Dance Girl, Dance
in 1940.

My makeup test for *How Green Was My Valley*, 1941. After a strange confrontation with John Ford at the studio, I wasn't sure he'd cast me as Angharad.

With Roddy McDowall and Anna Lee in a scene from *How Green Was My Valley*.
We have remained dear friends for over fifty years.

Séan Aloysius Kilmartin O'Feeney,
alias John Ford

Part of the eighty-acre set
built for *How Green Was My Valley*.
Its beauty made the Welsh Singers
fall to their knees and weep.

With William Houston Price

Bronwyn was born on June 30, 1944.
I named her after Anna Lee, but loved
the name of her character in *How
Green Was My Valley*.

In 1946, I fought to be recognized as Irish when I became a dual national, a citizen of both Ireland and the United States. It was the first time in history that the United States government recognized an Irish citizen as Irish.

A prominent federal judge later claimed that my fight to be recognized as Irish never occurred and was a cheap studio publicity stunt. This signed amendment on the back of my Certificate of Naturalization proves just how wrong he was.

I hereby certify that the erasure made on this certificate as to Former Nationality "Irish" was made before issuance, to conform to petition.

Name changed by Order of Court from:

MAUREEN PRICE - - January 25, 1946.

Edmund L. Smith, Clerk U. S. District Court,
Southern District of California

By _____ Deputy

Ireland's prime minister, Eamon De Valera, sent envoys to Washington to change the process for all the Irish immigrants who followed me. Irish papers ran this cartoon calling me his "Pin-Up Girl."

Tyrone Power and I steam it
up in the lavish 1942 swashbuckler, *The Black Swan.*
After its release, I was called
"The Queen of Technicolor."

As the Countess Francesca
in RKO's 1945 adventure *The
Spanish Main.* Audiences
loved the film but I consider
the countess one of my more
decorative roles.

24

Arriving at a garden party in
London. I was there filming
Britannia Mews.

Clowning around before my
flight. It's hard to believe
she later became the first
woman president of a
scheduled airline in U.S.
history.

25

John Payne, Natalie Wood, Edmund Gwenn and me in *Miracle on 34th Street*

Making a movie is hard work, even if you're Kris Kringle. Left to right: Edmund Gwenn,
director George Seaton, producer William Perlberg, me, John Payne, and
assistant director Artie Jacobson. Natalie Wood is already in bed.

With Duke in our most famous moment together—*The Quiet Man*, 1951

Pappy, Meta Sterne and I sit on the side of a road. We were thrilled to finally be filming in our beloved Eire.

I was caught napping during a break on *The Quiet Man.* John Ford later spun the yarn that we shot in horribly wet weather, but it was sunny and gorgeous almost every day.

Many fans thought Duke swept me off my feet in real life, but this is just a publicity shot from *The Quiet Man.*

The taoiseach then dispatched his envoys to Washington, D.C., where the Republic of Ireland formally requested that this policy be changed. The policy was changed, and my stand had paved the way for every Irish immigrant to the United States, including my own brothers and sisters, to be legally recognized as Irish from that day forward. Days later, Irish newspapers weighed in on how Ireland felt about what I had done. They ran a cartoon of Taoiseach De Valera working hard at his desk. On his lonely wall was tacked a single picture of me. The caption read simply, "Pinup Girl."

When I later went to England to make *Britannia Mews*, I was a little worried that the English might have been offended by what I had done. But at the very first interview I gave, the British reporter walked into the room, stuck her hand out, and said, "Congratulations! I would have done exactly the same thing if anybody asked me to say I was anything other than English."

On October 25, 1946, I boarded an American Overseas Airlines plane with my daughter and her nanny and began my journey back to my native land of Ireland. After seven long years, I was finally going home. As I sat in my seat and readied for takeoff, I looked at my young daughter in the seat beside me and was reminded that I had been a young girl when I'd boarded the *Queen Mary* and sailed away. Now I was a young woman and a mother. I was a wife and my husband was an abusive alcoholic. I was a Hollywood movie star. I was a dual national, both an Irish and an American citizen. My life had changed in so many ways, and yet I had not changed at all. I was still Maureen FitzSimons and I was finally going home.

I was still terrified of flying, especially after my rough trip with Lucille Ball, and was comforted when I saw the pilot making his way down the aisle toward me. As they always did back then, he was introducing himself and welcoming all of the passengers.

When he reached me, he said, "Hello, Miss O'Hara. Welcome aboard. I'm Captain Charlie Blair." I returned the greeting and he moved on to the seat behind me. I would never have guessed that he would later become one of the most important people ever to touch my life.

The flight to Ireland from the United States was long, and the anticipation that was building made it seem even longer. Words can't adequately describe the thrill I felt as our wheels touched down on Irish soil. Daddy and Mammy and their driver, Kevin Lawlor, were waiting for us at the gate, and it was a long and loving embrace that greeted me. But the attention quickly shifted from me to the granddaughter neither of them had seen before.

It was wonderful to be back home again and I wanted to go and see all the places I had missed for so long. I visited old school friends and went into town with Mammy, showing Bronwyn off to those who had known me most of my life. I went to the Abbey Theatre, St. Michan's Church, St. Stephen's Green, Grafton Street, O'Connell Bridge, and to the Dropping Well, the place where I had bought ice cream and candy as a little girl.

The evenings were quiet, and I enjoyed the comfort of resting in my old room at 13 Churchtown Road. Then, late one night, shortly before eleven o'clock, a large black limousine pulled up to the house. We watched from the window as several men and a woman, all strangers to us, got out of the car. We had no need for a car and wondered aloud, "What is a limousine doing here?" Mammy opened the door and asked, "Can I help you?"

The woman answered, "We've been sent by Radio Éireann to take Miss O'Hara to tonight's midnight broadcast. Is she ready?" I had no plans to attend the function and Mammy knew it. She said, "Miss O'Hara has other means of transportation. You're not needed, thank you." But the woman persisted. It was all so very strange. It took Mammy several tries before they eventually went on their way. Naturally, we called the radio station to check it out. They said it was good that I hadn't gotten into the limousine because they had not sent it. The following day, the story hit the papers all the way back to America: "Irish Report Plot to Kidnap Miss O'Hara."

I don't know what would have happened if I had stepped into that car. It's all guesswork, really. Maybe I would have been held for ransom, or worse, and maybe I would have been treated to a wonderful dinner by some overzealous fans. This too was the price of fame.

A few days later—though it felt like only five minutes from the time I'd arrived in Ireland—I received a call from 20th Century-Fox ordering me to report back to work in the United States immediately. After waiting seven years, my reunion had been cut short by the studio. I was heartbroken, furious and reduced to tears. I almost refused to go back, but knew I had no choice. I was madder than a wet hen the whole flight back. "How dare they," I fumed. "How dare they force me back just to make a silly little movie about Santa Claus!"

CHAPTER 11

MIRACLE ON 34TH STREET

hen I arrived in New York City, I wasn't very full of Christmas cheer. The first thing I did was read the script that I was so urgently brought back to make. *The Big Heart* was the story of a department store Santa named Kris Kringle who claimed to be the one and only Santa Claus. The film's director, George Seaton, also wrote the screenplay, based on an original story by Valentine Davies. Over the course of shooting the film, its title was changed twice, first to *It's Only Human*, and then to *Miracle on 34th Street*. My mood changed as soon as I finished reading the script. I knew the movie was going to be a hit, but I was not clairvoyant enough to foresee it becoming a classic. It was warm, charming, and sentimental, but more than anything, it captured the spirit of Christmas.

I was playing Doris Walker, a single working mother who doesn't believe children should be taught the nonsense of fantasies like a belief in Santa Claus. A remarkably endearing eight-year-old Natalie Wood was cast to play my daughter, Susan, the little girl who is befriended by Kris Kringle. John Payne was cast in our third picture together as Fred Gailey, the young attorney who must prove that Kris Kringle truly is Santa Claus. And, of course, Edmund Gwenn played Kris Kringle; by the time we were halfway through the shoot, we all believed Edmund really *was* Santa Claus. I've never seen an actor more naturally suited for a role.

I spent the first week in costuming, and by Thanksgiving was in front of the cameras filming. It went unusually fast. I later learned that the reason I was so urgently brought back to New York was so we could film the Macy's Thanksgiving Day parade sequences live while the parade was actually happening. They weren't going to run the parade more than once on our account. Those sequences, like the one with Edmund riding in the sleigh and waving to the cheering crowd, were real-life moments in the 1946 Macy's parade. It was a mad scramble to get all the shots we needed, and we got to do each scene only once. It was bitterly cold that day, and Edmund and I envied Natalie and John Payne, who were watching the parade from a window.

Almost all of the exterior sequences were shot, of course, in New York City, and no city in America does Christmas better. The interiors were shot later in Hollywood on the Fox lot. New York remained bitterly cold that winter—so cold, in fact, that the cameras froze on one occasion and wouldn't turn over. We were shooting the sequence at the end of the film in which Natalie sees the house that she asked Kris Kringle for, and she says, "That's it! Stop! That's it!" Luckily, a very kind woman, Vaughn Mele, lived across the street from where we were filming and offered us her home to thaw out the cameras. We gratefully accepted, and I was happy for the chance to thaw out myself as well. The cameras got the preferred treatment, in front of the fire, and we were all seated in the back, away from its warmth. I consider Vaughn Mele's generosity one of the "miracles" of *Miracle on 34th Street*. I was so grateful for her hospitality that I took her and her husband to dinner at the "21" Club that night. She was so thrilled that she couldn't eat a bite and only drank a glass of milk!

Natalie and John and Edmund—I had a special relationship with each one. I have been the mother to almost forty children in movies, but I have always had a special place in my heart for little Natalie. She always called me Mamma Maureen and I called her Natasha, the name her parents had given her. She loved making little ceramics on the weekends and used to bring me gifts of lovely painted animals and people. Unfortunately, Hurricane Hugo in St. Croix stole them all and I can't find even one. They're up there somewhere in the jet stream watching over me. When Natalie and I shot the scenes in Macy's, we had to do them at night because the store was full of people doing their Christmas shopping during the day. Natalie loved this because it meant she was allowed to stay up late. I remembered all the tricks we pulled as kids in our house, trying to stay up past bedtime, and so I really enjoyed this time with Natalie. We loved to walk through the quiet, closed store and look at all the toys and girls' dresses and shoes. The day she died, I cried shamelessly. It was such a horrible way to go for such a lovely, lovely girl.

When John Payne arrived on the set of *Miracle* each morning, I made sure to greet him with a big, joking smile to make up for the frowns he teased me about on *To the Shores of Tripoli* and *Sentimental Journey*. John really believed in and loved *Miracle on 34th Street*, and always wanted to do a sequel. We talked about it for years, and he eventually even wrote a screenplay sequel. He was going to send it to me, but tragically died before he could get around to it. I never saw it and have often wondered what happened to it.

Each evening, when we were not working, Edmund Gwenn, John, and I went for a walk up Fifth Avenue. Natalie had to go to bed, but we didn't. We stopped and window-shopped at all the stores, which were beautifully decorated for the holidays. Edmund especially loved those nights and acted more like the kid who might be getting the presents instead of the Santa who would be giving them. I got such a big kick out of seeing the expressions of window dressers when they saw Edmund peering in at them—I knew then that he was going to make a big splash as Santa Claus.

But there were so many wonderful actors and performances on *Miracle*. If I only had a dollar for every time someone asked me if that was really R. H. Macy in the picture. No, it wasn't! That was an actor named Harry Antrim. Did you know that *Miracle on 34th Street* was Thelma Ritter's first movie, and her role was uncredited? It was. She had one line and her delivery was so spectacular, such a standout, that it launched her on a remarkable career that earned her six Academy Award nominations.

The picture was finished in February 1947. Zanuck wasn't sure it would be a success, and so he had it released in June, when movie attendance is highest, rather than wait for Christmas. In fact, the publicity campaign barely talked about Christmas at all. The film proved to be a huge success—but then, you already know that. It was nominated for an Academy Award as best picture, but lost to *Gentleman's Agreement*. Edmund won an Oscar for his performance, and Valentine Davies and George Seaton were honored with awards for writing.

Everyone felt the magic on the set and we all knew we were creating something special. I am very proud to have been part of a film that has been continually shown and loved all over the world for nearly sixty years. *Miracle on 34th Street* has endured all this time because of the special relationship of the cast and crew, the uplifting story and its message of hope and love, which steals hearts all over the world every year. I don't think I will ever tire of children asking me, "Are you the lady who knows Santa Claus?" I always answer, "Yes, I am. What would you like me to tell him?"

I arrived back home in Los Angeles in time for Christmas and was riding an emotional high from my experiences in Ireland and New York. The balloon burst when Will completed his tour of duty and was honorably discharged from the United States Marine Corps. Now he was home for good. I was still unpacking from my trip when Will came home and greeted me with another one of his shockers: "I've just bought a house!" I dropped my clothes on the floor when he added, "We're moving in right away."

By the first of February 1947, our car was making its way through the gates of 673 Sienna Way, Bel Air. I looked out the car window in absolute astonishment. It was an enormous, palatial, two-story mansion with five bedrooms, five bathrooms, three powder rooms, dressing rooms, formal dining room, casual dining room, huge gourmet kitchen with separate pantry, living room, linen room, a maid's suite with its own living room and kitchen, and a separate apartment, with its own living room, dining room, and kitchen, attached to the house. Outside was a four-car garage with its own gas station in the basement, an immense covered patio with red bricks polished so that you could dance on them, a pool, and three sprawling acres of manicured gardens.

I could barely squeak out, "My God, Will, why do we need this mansion?" He was offended by the question. "You don't expect me to live in anything less, do you?"

• • •

The financial pressure was mounting. I had to make more money, that much was clear. Even though I was making a very good salary of $2,000 a week, I knew it wouldn't be enough to cover the costs of the new house, nanny, cook, maid, laundress, chauffeur, gardener, pool man, and Will's special talent for blowing money on booze, dames, and the races. I felt the noose tighten around my neck. I had found myself enough trouble to last a lifetime and I was only twenty-six years old.

Lew Wasserman went to work renegotiating my new contract with 20th Century-Fox. At the same time, he was also negotiating a new contract for Tyrone Power. Wasserman was a shrewd, skillful, and fierce negotiator, and he came through for us in a very big way. Ty and I got the very same new contract, a seven-year commitment with no renewal options and a salary increase to $4,000 a week. It was an almost unheard-of deal and a major coup. Studios always had the right to drop you after each year, depending on how well your pictures had done at the box office. Our new contract guaranteed Ty and me employment and an income for seven consecutive years. The only other actor in Hollywood with a better deal was the king of Hollywood himself, Clark Gable.

Will, of course, was ecstatic that more cash was coming in, and it didn't take long for him to come home drunk, with more news. "I've hired a business manager. His name is Bill Duce." Of course, one of the first things Bill Duce did was take care of his pal Will. He told me that since Will and I were married, half of everything I earned was legally his. Duce opened separate bank accounts, one for Will and one for me. Half of my weekly paycheck was then deposited in each of our accounts. Will succeeded in getting his hands on every penny that Lew Wasserman had managed to get me in my new contract. Naturally, all the bills for running the house continued to be paid out of my account, while Will ran around town like a high-rollin' playboy.

Once we moved into the house, Will started throwing parties for all his drinking friends, none of whom I liked very much. Will would get skunk drunk and then go out with them afterward. I don't know where they went or what they did, but I assumed dames were involved. I couldn't deny that Will's drinking was getting much worse. He was passing out around the house and I was finding him unconscious more often than ever before. Bronwyn was getting older and I didn't want her to see her father that way. I also couldn't stand by and watch Will continue to destroy himself. Despite every mean or crazy thing he had done, he was still a human being and in desperate trouble. I was certain that I had to do something before it was too late.

I called my doctor, Dr. Arnold Stevens, at St. John's Hospital, and finally told someone else what I had been living with for the past five years. Dr. Stevens told me to get Will into therapy immediately with a Dr. Sturdevant, and then into a rehabilitation clinic. I was advised to act fast. The next time Will came home and passed out, I sent for an ambulance and had him taken to the clinic that Dr. Stevens had recommended. Thus began a ritual that would become a regular event in our lives: Will is found unconscious; Maureen makes a phone call; Bronwyn is kept upstairs; men in white coats strap Will on a gurney and haul him away in an ambulance.

When he was home, we rarely spoke. At my insistence, he had moved out of the master bedroom and was sleeping on the sofa in his dressing room. No one outside the house, however, knew we were no longer sharing the same bed. We continued to keep up appearances in public whenever we had to, and I kept Will's problem a secret, or thought I did. I'd explain his absences when he was at a rehab clinic or out getting drunk by saying that he was home or somewhere else working on a new script. The press always believed me and I thought I was very clever, until one day my makeup man, Jimmy Barker, whispered into my ear softly, "We know, Maureen. We know."

Sometimes I would have to go with him to parties and other events thrown by his friends in the picture business. One night, I went with him to a party at Jim Hill's home in the San Fernando Valley. Will was smashed in no time and starting to make a scene. I thought, I'd better get him back to the house. I pulled him out of the party and stuffed him into the passenger seat of our car. I got in and started driving over the hill from the valley, back to Los Angeles. He was belligerent and nasty and talking under his breath. In the closeness of the car, I saw the wounded human being he had become, and it was tragic.

I felt empty inside as I made my way down a winding Laurel Canyon Road. Will was now silent, passed out, or so I thought. Then, suddenly, Will opened his eyes and lunged for the steering wheel. He grabbed it tightly and turned it hard to the left. The car swerved sharply toward the edge of the road, toward the cliff and ravine below. I struggled to regain control of the car, but Will wouldn't let go. He kept trying to force the car off the road, while I fought to get us back on it. I kept yelling at him to let go of the wheel, but he wouldn't. The car kept on swerving toward the edge of the road and then back again. I was sure we were going to go over and that the car would roll all the way down the hill. I kept fighting to get control, and finally Will tired. I was panting and my heart was racing as Will slumped back in his seat and slipped into unconsciousness.

In early April 1947, Will's younger brother, Kenny Jr., was finally discharged from the United States Navy. He had served on the U.S.S. *Ticonderoga* and had distinguished himself during the war. Kenny called the house as soon as he was out and naturally wanted to see his brother. Will invited him to stay with us. We had plenty of room, and I was thrilled because I liked Kenny. He was a fine lawyer and had never, ever touched a drop of liquor in his life. I thought, to myself, Wonderful. Help is on the way. I was certain that he would be able to reach Will in ways that I never could. If anyone could help get him on the path to sobriety, surely it was Kenny.

He arrived the following week, and proved to be kind and helpful around the house. Will did slow down on his drinking, and things were looking up. In no time, Bronwyn adored her uncle and so did I. Kenny Jr. was a nice-looking man with a promising legal career and a good set of values. He was also a bachelor, and it didn't take long for him to inquire about one of my friends. Kenny had taken a certain liking to Nancy Gates and she to him, and so I was happy when they started dating. The relationship became quite serious, and before long the two were engaged and headed for the altar.

Then one evening, from out of nowhere, Kenny picked up a bottle of whiskey, emptied it, and never drew a sober breath again.

By the end of May, I had two drunks on my hands. And I had dragged poor Nancy Gates into the nightmare with me. Will and Kenny were toxic together from that moment on. It was like a race to the floor.

By this time, I was filming *The Foxes of Harrow* with Rex Harrison and Victor McLaglen at 20th Century-Fox. Life wasn't any easier on the set. Harrison and I disliked each other from the outset, which wasn't good, because in the film we were playing husband and wife. Hollywood might have called him the greatest perfectionist among actors, but I found him to be rude, vulgar, and arrogant.

During one of our photo sessions together, Harrison and I were standing side by side and he asked me proudly, "You don't like me,

do you?" I raised my nose an inch higher to meet his. "No, I don't."
He pressed on as the camera flashed. "Is it because I'm British?"
An absurd question, to which I replied, "Absolutely not. Why
should I hold you against the entire British population?"

On that set, my gang gave him the nickname "Sexy Rexy" because we thought he was anything but sexy. When he walked by
us, we joked, "Do you think Rex erects?" While we were shooting
our dancing sequences together, Sexy Rexy purposely belched in
my face whenever he was hidden from the camera. Our little nickname for him soon made its way all around the studio lot at Fox.
So the Fox publicity team quickly put a spin on it to protect their
property and created the image that Harrison was a great ladies'
man. The truth is, it was never meant as a compliment.

A few years later, Sexy Rexy was all over the front pages of
the papers in a scandal involving the suicide of actress Carole
Landis. Apparently, Rex did erect and the two were having an affair. The gossip was that Harrison had been with Landis the night
she allegedly took her life as part of a lovers' suicide pact. She
went through with it, but Rex didn't. The studio supposedly destroyed their suicide note, and his contract with Fox was over
shortly after that. His film career was never the same.

By the time I had finished *The Foxes of Harrow*, Kenny Jr. had
joined Will in therapy with Dr. Sturdevant. Kenny was diagnosed
as manic-depressive shortly thereafter and Nancy was called in to
speak with Dr. Sturdevant. He counseled her that she should
break off the engagement because he could not guarantee her
safety. After she broke it off, Nancy shared with me some disturbing things that Kenny had told her when he was drunk. She said,
"Kenny confessed that he only wanted to marry me so that he
could be taken care of and supported by a movie-star wife, just
like his brother."

Kenny's rapid decline did not go unnoticed by his father. Kenny was quickly summoned back to Mississippi. His downward spiral continued, and he eventually underwent shock treatment at New Orleans Hospital. Kenny committed suicide shortly after that by crashing his car into a wall.

Even with all this unpleasantness happening in my life, I managed to make time to work with John Ford in his preparation of *The Quiet Man*. Not even that punch in the chops could derail my commitment to it. By August 1947, nearly three years after we'd started planning the film, we still had no money with which to make it. This caused Duke and me to needle Mr. Ford. "If we don't hurry up and make this picture," I told him, "I'll be so old I'll have to play the old widow and Duke will have to play Red Will."

Progress was being made, but it was going slowly. Mr. Ford had formed Argosy Pictures with Merian C. Cooper, the man who would ultimately produce *The Quiet Man*. Merian C. Cooper was a very serious and highly regarded producer. Before going into business with John Ford, he had been head of production at RKO Pictures and had produced such classics as *King Kong*, *Little Women*, and *The Last Days of Pompeii*. After forming Argosy, Mr. Cooper produced most of Ford's films, including the cavalry trilogy. He received a special Oscar later in his career for his many innovations in the art of filmmaking, including the pioneering of the wide-screen process.

Messrs. Ford and Cooper had begun discussions with famed British producer Alexander Korda as the first potential backer for *The Quiet Man*. Mr. Ford had also communicated with his friend Michael Morris, also known as Lord Killanin. Ford enjoyed rubbing elbows with people who had fancy titles and so he agreed to let Morris act as a liaison with Korda. The deal fell through but Morris continued his friendship with John Ford.

I continued working with Pappy on the *Araner*, taking dictation of script notes in my Pittman shorthand as he chewed and tugged away at his kerchief. Then I'd type them up to be worked into the various drafts of the screenplay. These were the best times I ever spent with Pappy off the set. We were working together on a story about our beloved Ireland, listening to Irish records, speaking with pride of our heritage, oh so happily, happily Irish.

I knew Pappy was fond of me and respected my talent. I didn't know that this fondness would continue to grow over time and change into something far more difficult to explain.

I continued going to Pappy and Mary Ford's dinner parties at their home on Odin Street, and I took Will with me when he was sober enough to attend. Pappy didn't like Will much and neither did Duke. The one person who did take an instant liking to Will was Mary Ford. Mary was a Southern belle from Laurinburg, North Carolina, and Will knew just how to push her Tar Heel buttons. She easily fell for his charms, and in no time they were reveling in their Southern camaraderie, just like Pappy did with me about our Irishness. But the South wasn't all they had in common. Mary had a secret love that I never knew about until she became friends with Will—gambling at the racetrack. Will and Mary started frequenting the racetrack together, and Will used her accompanying him like a papal blessing.

Will went on with the drunken routine of his life. I marched on, day after day, like a good foot soldier in this private battle of ours. I did *Sitting Pretty* with Robert Young and it made a fortune, even winning the Box Office Award for that year. I performed one of my film roles on the Lux Radio Theatre program at Christmas. Even now, much of this period remains hazy to me. As the five-year anniversary of my marriage to Will Price arrived, I couldn't deny the sadness and loneliness that occupied my thoughts. Only

Bronwyn kept me going. She was my whole world and the only true gift Will Price ever gave me. For her sake, I would march on and continue the battle.

The beginning of 1948 had the Hollywood Foreign Correspondents Association wooing me, so I agreed to serve as their master of ceremonies at the fifth annual Hollywood Foreign Press Awards, which later became the Golden Globes. After the awards ceremony was over, I bumped into RKO boss Dore Schary and he asked me to come and see him at his office the next day. I had received the script for *A Woman's Secret* sometime before, and had made no attempt to keep it a secret that I thought the story stank. Schary reminded me that I still had a one-picture-a-year obligation to RKO, so I agreed to be at his office the following day.

I wasted no time when I arrived at Schary's office: "Mr. Schary, the script is terrible and I don't want to do the picture. I have every intention of living up to my end of the bargain with RKO, but this isn't the picture to do it with." Schary knew the script was less than mediocre, but still didn't waver in his commitment to making it. Studio executives had a bit of discretionary leeway to make pictures they wanted to from time to time because they practiced block booking, which meant that RKO would sell its pictures to theater owners in packages, on an all-or-nothing basis. If *A Woman's Secret* didn't turn out well, it would reach theaters anyway, packaged with a few winners, a few that were so-so, and a few more duds.

These were often pictures made as favors, tokens and gifts thrown to stars and starlets for various reasons, but often because one of the top brass was sleeping with someone in the picture. Schary started to bargain with me: "Maureen, I would like to see Gloria Grahame and you make this picture together very, very much. Is there anything that you would like to see as much?" If that was the way he wanted it, there sure as hell was. "Yes, Mr. Schary. I'd like to see my husband, Will Price, with a contract here at RKO to produce and direct movies." Schary reached across his desk with a smile, saying, "Done."

We started shooting *A Woman's Secret* in February and were finished by April. I starred opposite Melvyn Douglas as a frustrated talent manager who shoots her star client (played by Grahame) in a jealous rage. While we were filming, I learned through gossip why Schary so badly wanted the picture made. He was in love with Gloria Grahame. And to provide more real-life drama, Gloria Grahame was also in a relationship with director Nicholas Ray, and was pregnant.

Nicholas Ray and Gloria Grahame were married two months later, in June. Their son was born about six months after that, on November 12. Nicholas Ray told everyone it was a premature birth, but in fact the baby weighed over nine pounds. By that time, Dore Schary had been swept away to MGM where he toppled his nemesis, the legendary and larger-than-life Louis B. Mayer. Grahame and Ray eventually divorced, but the couple drew scandalous headlines eight years later when Grahame married Nicholas Ray's son from a previous marriage. She had married her own stepson after he was all grown up. When asked to justify her behavior, Grahame remarked, "I married Nicholas Ray the director and people yawned. Later on I married his son, and by the reaction in the press, you'd have thought I was committing incest or robbing the cradle!" Grahame's career faded away by the 1960s, but the scandalous story never did.

Luckily, before Dore Schary left RKO, he did make good on his promise to me. Will had himself a movie contract and a picture to direct. The contract with RKO gave Will the opportunity to turn his life around, providing a reason to be sober. I was counting on something within Will that the movie deal would greatly appeal to: his need to be the big shot, to impress, to be somebody. I felt the best chance Will had at sobriety—perhaps his only chance—was if he believed there was something in it for him. He clearly wouldn't get sober for anyone else, but would he do it for himself?

The answer proved to be no. Will cleaned up his act for a few days, but he was unable to sustain it. The discipline and presence of mind required to craft a cohesive story was lacking, as was the clarity of vision. The result of his efforts on *Strange Bargain* was disastrous. Even with the help of seasoned cinematographer Harry Wild, there was not enough usable footage to construct a full-length feature film. Its final-cut running time was just sixty-eight minutes. I had gambled and lost. For their trouble, RKO had nothing to sell.

CHAPTER 12

THE FEISTY REDHEAD:
ENDING THE DECORATIVE YEARS

*D*uring the remainder of 1948 and through 1949, I made five more pictures, one after the other. They were some of the least memorable of my career. *Britannia Mews*, or *The Forbidden Street*, depending on which version you saw (there were two: *Mews* was cut in Britain by Richard Best, and *Street* was cut in Hollywood), was shot in London. The only reasons for you to watch this picture today on television are to see Dana Andrews do a nice job in a dual role, or to watch the fine character actress Sybil Thorndike steal the picture.

Upon returning to the United States, I went right into making *Father Was a Fullback* with Fred MacMurray and my little Natasha (Natalie Wood). It was a comedy stinkeroo that got more yawns than laughs. We shot the picture right around St. Patrick's Day, so I shouldn't have been surprised when I received a very unexpected call on the set from someone I never thought I'd speak to ever again.

"Hello, Maureen, it's Howard Hughes."

"Hello, Mr. Hughes. How can I help you?"

"You know tomorrow is Saint Patrick's Day?"

"I sure do. It's a special day for the Irish."

"Well, it's a big day for me too. There's a new hotel in Houston opening tomorrow called the Shamrock Hotel. I'd like you to be there for the event, with a few others from the industry—to show our support."

I wasn't sure I liked being called from out of the blue and asked for a favor by a man who couldn't speak a single sentence to me over the course of an entire evening. Besides, I still hated flying and only did it when it was absolutely necessary. But who turns down a request from Howard Hughes and gets away with it? Then I realized that I didn't have anything to worry about. I was working on a picture and surely he'd understand. I'd be polite and charming, but still turn him down.

"Oh, Mr. Hughes, thank you so much for thinking of me. It's an honor. I'd love to go for you, but I'm afraid that I'm in the middle of shooting a movie right now, and I can't hold up the picture."

He paused for a moment, and then said simply, "Oh, I see."

"I'm terribly sorry," I added, but Hughes had hung up the phone.

I knew Howard Hughes owned RKO, but I didn't know that he was also a very large private shareholder in 20th Century-Fox. A few minutes after I'd hung up the phone, Lew Schreiber and half of Zanuck's office swarmed down on the set. They closed the picture down immediately and sent me home with an entire team of people from the wardrobe, hair, and makeup departments. My clothes were packed and my hair and makeup were done. It all happened lickety-split, and suddenly I was on my way to the airport. When I boarded the enormous TWA jetliner that would take me to Houston, Texas, I was shocked to see that I was the only passenger on that flight. Hughes made sure to make his point by arranging for my very own four-engine plane with a crew of five to wait on me hand and foot. I conceded, out loud, "Well, I guess Howard Hughes can do anything he damn well wants."

The next film I made was *Bagdad,* an escapist adventure and my first picture with Universal. They called these "tits and sand" pictures. It's one of the films that I point to as part of my decorative years, but audiences loved them. *Bagdad* made Universal a fortune, and Universal purchased part of my contract from Fox as a result of that success. We shot the film on location in the Alabama Hills of Lone Pine, California. A scorpion stung me a few days into the shoot, but other than that, it was an uneventful experience.

My last picture of the decade was *Comanche Territory*, a fairly decent western and the film in which I mastered the American bullwhip. By the time the picture was over, I could snap a cigarette out of someone's mouth.

But one thing was certain as 1949 came to an end: I was growing tired of the course my career had taken. After making twenty-five motion pictures in Hollywood, with the exception of films like *How Green Was My Valley*, *The Hunchback of Notre Dame*, and *Miracle on 34th Street,* many of the characters I had been forced to play lacked enough depth for me to do anything meaningful with the part. The films chosen for me were big moneymakers, making the money that paid for the critically acclaimed art movies that went to other actresses. Lew Schreiber told me that *Sentimental Journey* took 20th Century-Fox out of the red and into the black.

It just wasn't right. Since I was helping pay for the prestige pictures, I wanted the chance to act in a few myself. I wanted a role that I could really sink my teeth into and show my range. I was so frustrated and disappointed for a time that had it not been for the tremendous financial burdens on me, I would have left the picture business and returned to the theater. But a stage career could never support Will's elegant lifestyle. I was in a deep hole, treading water to pay his bills.

With the exception of John Ford, the Hollywood hierarchy didn't seem willing to allow my talent to triumph over my face. I wanted to know why. There were more than enough good roles to go around, weren't there? Was the competition too stiff? Had they assumed I couldn't act because I was pretty? Was I lost in block booking? The answer to most of these questions was yes.

But more than anything, there was a resistance to Maureen O'Hara from studio casting executives. I always felt they resented me. Maybe they thought my acting wasn't worth a hill of beans, but part of me has always blamed the casting couch. I wasn't a whore. I've said over and over, you can have anything you want in life provided you are willing to make the necessary sacrifices for it. I was unwilling to make that kind of sacrifice to get a part in a movie. After the Farrow, Montgomery, and Jessel incidents, Hollywood knew where I stood on the issue.

Changes were required to get my career on the track I wanted, so I made a tough decision. I left MCA and joined the Charles Wendling Agency. Charlie was Claudette Colbert's brother and had promised me better roles if I signed on the dotted line, but the roles weren't coming yet. More important, in my own perform-ances I decided to take the bull by the horns. If I had to continue making pictures that cast me as part of the scenery, I would find a way to break out of the background. I would force myself to the foreground of every scene I was in. Within the confines of these vehicles, I resolved to be such a dominant presence on the screen that I couldn't be ignored.

How I accomplished this feat goes right to the heart of why I became a swashbuckler. I not only brought out the internal strengths of my characters more, I brought out their physical strengths as well. This combination, ultimately, became my trademark: Maureen O'Hara—the fiery, feisty redhead.

One of the first things I did was make it clear on the set that my characters had to be part of the action. They had to let me do all my own stunts and allow me to hold my own on-screen against the men. I had to be able to be their equal as a woman. It was the only way I could deliver a stand-out performance. They reluctantly agreed, and I began to tap into the tomboy who still lived within me. I found and refined that little girl who had dragged the Lombard boy out to the sea at Bray. I found the athlete who loved soccer, boxing, *camogie*, and fencing in school, and I brought parts of both to the screen. One of the first films to showcase the new Maureen O'Hara was RKO's swashbuckler *At Sword's Point*.

The plot of the movie is a little hard to swallow, but it was fun as hell. "One for all and all for one," only this time, it's the sons of the original Musketeers who ride to the rescue, with just one exception. I play Claire, the daughter of Athos, who wields as fine a sword as her father did before her. Former fencing champion Cornel Wilde was cast as my leading man, in the role of D'Artagnan. Cornel was a good actor and a great swashbuckler, as good as Ty Power or Errol Flynn.

I trained rigorously for six weeks with Fred Cavens and his son to perfect my stunt sequences for the picture. Fred Cavens was an outstanding Belgian military fencing master and had trained all the great swashbucklers in Hollywood. He taught me intricate attacks and parries, envelopments, disengagements, and coupes. Physically, I've never worked harder for a role. My efforts won me the admiration and affection of the stuntmen, but drew only sneers from the film's director, Lewis Allen. He said it was a joke that the studio was letting a woman fence. I was livid and determined to make him eat his words. Fred Cavens and the stuntmen, who now considered me *their* girl, and one of them, all came to me and said, "By God, when you do your first fencing scene, fence the bleedin' hell out of it. Just go at it. We'll watch out for you. Make that son of a bitch look like a horse's ass so he'll eat his words."

The first action sequence was shot in Hollywood at Sherwood Forest, a canyon area rich in foliage within Griffith Park. Cameramen in the picture business used the old saying, "A tree is a tree; a rock is a rock; so shoot it in Griffith Park." In the sequence, I'm in a horse-driven coach coming around a corner and have to jump out and start fencing with several guards of the rebellion.

When Lewis called, "Action," and that coach rounded the corner, I leaped out and started fencing like a son of a bitch. I lunged and attacked. I parried and counterparried with first this stuntman and then that one. I rotated my foil with such finesse it was as if I were holding a bird in my hand. I killed this one, disarmed that one, and each of my opponents fell one at a time. When it was over and Lewis finally called, "Cut," the stuntmen all burst into applause. Lewis was sitting in his chair, dumbfounded, with his mouth wide open, as I strolled past him to my chair. I knew then that I had tapped into something very powerful. Hollywood snobs might have sneered at these pictures, but audiences never did. They loved them. The studios sure made a lot of money off their stuntgirl.

But my patience had long run out at home. A few months earlier, Will had come home and announced once again, "I've bought a new house." We were back on Stone Canyon Road in a bigger house than we'd had when we lived there before. Then, in February 1950, during bouts of sobriety, Will, along with L. B. "Doc" Merman, formed a production company, Price-Merman Productions. It was a bit of a miracle really because Doc Merman worked with Pine Thomas Productions, a big independent production company in Hollywood. He could make things happen. Doc Merman knew everyone in the picture business. How Will was able to convince a man like Doc Merman to go into business with him I still don't know, although Will had the ability to get people's attention in Hollywood. He lived in a fancy mansion and was seen around town in a chauffeur-driven car. With half my paycheck in his pocket, he could buy a lot of dinners and drinks—not to mention a dame or two, if that's what someone wanted. And Will was a braggart. He didn't think twice about dropping the names of John Ford, George Cukor, and Olivia de Havilland.

With Price-Merman in place, Will had a purpose and a reason to drink less. He announced that he was leaving for San Francisco to write the script for the first picture the company was planning to produce. Will would be directing the picture and they were expecting to borrow me from Fox to play the leading role. I agreed to play the role if they could get permission from Fox for me to make the film. I was hopeful that this venture would be a success for Will. With his own success would come the means to be a high roller on his own terms. I hoped that if he could do that, he might let Bronwyn and me go without an ugly fight.

The day he left for San Francisco to write *Tripoli,* I took Bronwyn to Mass and prayed to God to keep Will sober long enough to complete the film. Bronwyn followed my lead and knelt down beside me with her hands together.

A few days later, a box was delivered to the house. It was from the hotel where Will was staying in San Francisco. It was addressed to our home at 662 Stone Canyon Road, but had Will's secretary's name on it. I opened it anyway. Will had bought her the most beautiful lingerie you have ever seen, but mistakenly had it sent to his own address. (I learned later that whenever I went on location to make a movie, Will moved her, and others, into my house and my bedroom. Our staff even served them breakfast in my bed every morning. I was never saddened by these incidents. Instead, I felt angry, insulted, and hopelessly trapped.)

Meanwhile, God answered our prayers and Will returned from San Francisco with a finished script. Doc Merman worked with William Pine and William Thomas in securing the green light from Paramount Pictures to proceed with production. By the middle of March, I had gone to work on *Tripoli* with Will directing me. *Tripoli* was a service picture with all the formulaic elements that made them favorites of the moviegoing public. The story was set in the early 1800s and followed heroic marines as, to raise the American flag, they battled the pirates of Tripoli.

Every favor that could be called in to make this picture a success was called in. John Ford permitted the use of his Ford stock company. William Pine backed up Will's lack of directing experience as assistant director, in addition to his role as producer of the film. John Payne was cast as Lieutenant O'Bannion, leveraging our box-office successes from *Miracle on 34th Street*, *Sentimental Journey*, and *To the Shores of Tripoli*. I was even willing to play the Countess D'Arneau to see this picture succeed. To be fair, Will did a credible job of directing the picture. He managed to stay sober during the production. The film was in the can on time and within budget. I went out as part of the publicity and raved to the press about how brilliant a director Will was. I presented the Prices as the ideal married couple, doing big things together. Paramount made a lot of money on the picture and so did Price-Merman. Once again, Will had within his grasp a real opportunity to save himself.

And once again, he grabbed the bottle instead of the brass ring. Will fell off the wagon and was back in rehab shortly after that. This time, however, there was something different. Will came to me one night and said, "I know I have to stay sober, Maureen. I don't want to blow this opportunity with Doc." I was stunned. It was the first time Will had ever admitted the severity of his problem. "That's good, Will," I began, "I want this to work out for you too."

"I don't like the place you send me to. They aren't helping me." I was floored that we were having the conversation. It was the first time we had really talked in longer than I could remember. "It's where Dr. Stevens sent you," I explained. "He says Dr. Sturdevant is the best there is."

"But I don't like him," Will continued. "I've found another doctor. I want him instead."

Will's new doctor was at a very private psychiatric hospital specializing in the treatment of alcoholism and drug addiction. It was expensive, but I agreed to send Will there and pay for it because he wanted to go. For the very first time, he was seeking help on his own. I wasn't about to do anything to interrupt that progress. Will checked himself into the hospital in May 1950, and was there when another bit of good news reached me.

Every major studio had already turned down *The Quiet Man* more than once. They all called it a "silly, stupid little Irish story that will never make a penny." So Duke convinced John Ford that he had nothing to lose and to let him take the script to "Old Man Yates" at Republic. Herbert J. Yates had been a Wall Street man before becoming head of Republic. He was a numbers guy and not an artist. Yates read the script and his reaction was the same as every other studio boss: "It's a silly little story that won't make any money." But Yates was a shrewd businessman who knew the value of having a director like John Ford on his lot, and that's when he said the magic words. "But," he continued, "I'll finance the picture if you make me a western first, with the same director, same producer, same cast and crew, same everybody, to make up for the money I'm going to lose on *The Quiet Man*." And with another handshake in May 1950, six years after I had first shaken hands with John Ford on the set of *The Spanish Main*, we finally had the go-ahead to make *The Quiet Man*.

In the middle of June 1950, the Ford stock company, myself included, arrived in Moab, Utah, to make *Rio Grande*. The picture was the final installment of John Ford's cavalry trilogy, based on three short stories by James Warner Bellah that Ford had read in the *Saturday Evening Post*. The trilogy also included *Fort Apache* and *She Wore a Yellow Ribbon*, both of which also starred Duke. Again, with a few exceptions, cast and crew were all members of the Ford stock company.

Rio Grande is the story of cavalry officer Kirby Yorke (played by John Wayne), who commands an outpost on the bank of the Rio Grande where new recruits are trained to fight the Apache Indians. Lieutenant Colonel Yorke is forced to confront his past when his son (played by young Claude Jarman Jr.) arrives as a new enlistee. I played Kathleen Yorke, Lieutenant Yorke's estranged wife who shows up hell-bent on taking her only son back home and away from the military life that destroyed their family. In the end, the boy proves himself to his father, and Kirby and Kathleen reconcile.

Neither John Ford nor Duke really wanted to make this picture. To them it was just a path to *The Quiet Man*. It was understood by all of us that this was the only reason we were doing it. Without that commitment from Yates, *Rio Grande* would never have been made—at least not by John Ford and his company. Duke almost backed out in the beginning. He was having trouble with Yates on a back-salary problem, but Mr. Ford stepped in and settled the matter. Of course, he was only playing the diplomat to soften up Old Man Yates for later, when he would ask for the budget to shoot *The Quiet Man* in Technicolor. We all took less money than usual to accommodate Yates and to accommodate the budget of $1.2 million that Mr. Ford asked for and got to make *Rio Grande*. I, quite frankly, was happy to be working with Mr. Ford again, and to be working with John Wayne. They paid me $75,000 for the picture, but I'd have done it for less if it would have helped us make *The Quiet Man*.

For me, the most special part about making *Rio Grande* was that it was the first time that Duke and I worked together. We were very friendly, but not yet the closest of friends. The seeds of that deep friendship were planted on *Rio Grande* and grew naturally over time, and while making four more pictures together. We loved working with each other. From our very first scenes together, working with John Wayne was comfortable for me. We looked like a couple who belonged together. We both had an inner core of strength, and we were both gutsy! Did I know we had that special erotic chemistry together that would be so magical on-screen while filming *Rio Grande?* No I did not; neither of us did. There were no kinetic sparks from which to duck. But when we saw ourselves together on-screen for the first time—oh yes, we knew.

One thing you could always count on while making a picture with John Ford was having a lot of stuntmen on location with you. *Rio Grande* had numerous horse-riding stunts as well as battle sequences with Apache Indians. Ben Johnson, Dobe Carey, and Claude Jarman all performed their own stunt work on the picture, including the standing double-horse Roman rides. Ben was a former rodeo star and was widely considered the best horseman in Hollywood, and he taught the others how to perfect that very dangerous stunt in less than three weeks. Tragically, two stuntmen lost their lives filming *Rio Grande*, though it was never made public. I was told that they had fallen while crossing the river during a scene and had drowned in the heavy river mud. Everyone always said, "The river was too thick to drink and too thin to plow." The crew couldn't see them when they fell because the mud was so thick. They figured their bodies would go farther downriver and they'd find them, but each day they didn't. To the best of my knowledge, their bodies were never recovered.

Two new members joined the Ford stock company stunt crew on *Rio Grande*. Chuck Roberson was a young, gruff, and handsome wrangler with an eye for and a way with the ladies. His overactive libido on the picture earned him the nickname "Bad Chuck." He was to be Duke's stuntman for almost thirty years. Chuck Hayward, on the other hand, was always a very good boy on location. We called him "Good Chuck." Bad Chuck and Good Chuck and I would work together many times over the years, and they would teach me how to do some of my most dangerous stunts.

I loved being out on location with the Ford stock company. There was such a sense of family to it. We all stayed at the same motel and were driven to and from the set together. The entire cast and crew always ate meals together. Mr. Ford loved to be entertained at the end of a hard day's work. During dinner, Mr. Ford would tell you what he wanted you to do. As usual, he would always have me get up and sing Irish songs. He'd have Duke sing too, but for Mr. Ford, Duke always had to sing off-key. Duke could, in fact, sing—he had a surprisingly nice voice—but he always accommodated Mr. Ford with an awful rendition of the song so that Mr. Ford could laugh and make fun of him. The stuntmen sang cowboy songs with the Sons of the Pioneers, a western group Mr. Ford frequently used in his pictures. Victor McLaglen performed comedy sketches that he had performed for audiences as a young actor. These endeavors were far more than performances at the palace for the king. Mr. Ford wanted a family life on the set. And in the end, the picture was always better because of it.

Despite all of this, to me there was something noticeably different on this set, as compared to when I had made *How Green Was My Valley* with John Ford ten years earlier. I could see that Mr. Ford himself, his behavior, had changed. While we were shooting *Rio Grande*, I clearly saw the darker side of John Ford, the mean and abusive side. It caused me to reevaluate him. I had already had a glimpse of it once, but had long since forgotten that punch he'd given me at his home, dismissing it as a moment of drunken misfortune. On *Rio Grande*, however, my feelings about John Ford started to change. He was no longer a god to me; I saw cracks in his armor. The things he did were usually confusing, at times frightening, but almost always made me angry.

One minute he was my best friend on the set and the next he was insulting me. First, we were two happy fellow Irishmen. He'd pretend that he could speak Gaelic—which he could not; he knew only some words and phrases—and made me have mock conversations in Gaelic with him. He would say something to me in fake Gaelic and I would answer affirmatively, *"Seadh. Seadh,"* while nodding my head. Everyone on the set thought we were speaking Gaelic with each other the entire time we shot *Rio Grande,* but we weren't—it was mostly just gibberish. He seemed to revel in his trickery, and was pleased that I did not expose him.

Then thirty minutes later, after making him look good and Irish in front of the crew, he'd ridicule me under his breath while I was performing. He'd mutter, "Why don't you lift your goddamned head up a little more and get it right? Can you manage that?" They were small things, but he did them in a mean and nasty way, needling me instead of just asking me to do it the way he wanted. Usually, when Mr. Ford criticized you, he did it by muttering his insult or order under his breath but always loud enough for all to hear. It was very frustrating and grated on me.

On the picture, I watched him alienate himself from Ben

Johnson. At one of our evening dinners, Ben was talking with Dobe Carey and made a comment about one of the scenes we had shot that day. Mr. Ford overheard the conversation and took Ben's comment as a criticism of how he had directed the scene. He gave Ben an awful tongue-lashing in front of the entire cast and crew, and then started calling him "Stupid" as though it was his name. Ben was a total professional on the set and quietly excused himself from the dining hall, but there was a very cool atmosphere between them for the remainder of the film. Ben didn't work with John Ford again for almost fifteen years. He later went on to win an Academy Award, without John Ford, for his performance in *The Last Picture Show.*

But more than anything, it was Mr. Ford's vicious treatment of John Wayne that changed my feelings. He was extremely severe and cruel to Duke on the set. It was horrible treatment, unlike anything I had ever seen. He repeatedly belittled and insulted him in front of the entire cast and crew. Duke would just stand there with his head lowered, hat in hand, while Mr. Ford tried to reduce Duke to a miniature version of the man he was. I kept silent, while screaming in my head, "Punch him, Duke. Knock him on his ass. Do something!" But Duke was too much a professional, so he took it—all of it. It made me sick to my stomach and more than once I had to excuse myself from the set so I could go to the bathroom and vomit.

We shot *Rio Grande* in less than six weeks, and were now at long last clear to go on and make our pet project together. But as I left location and made my way to Hollywood, I was deeply troubled by what I had experienced. All I could wonder was, Why had he treated us that way? He should have been thrilled because he had the money to make *The Quiet Man.* Was he so insecure that he could like himself only by being something he was not, and destroying everyone else around him? While making *Rio Grande,*

I never lost respect for John Ford's gifts as a director; the artistic mastery could not be denied. Yet, I was beginning to find him very strange and complicated and confusing, as a man, and I was deeply worried. I could never have predicted just how valid this concern would prove to be.

CHAPTER 13

HERSELF

As we readied to make *The Quiet Man*, I had a window through which to peer. I was discovering things about Ford that gave me insights into his motivation and his creative process. John Ford understood the hearts and souls of men better than anyone else I had ever known. He knew our motivations, our desires, and, most of all, our fears. He knew how to elicit reactions of his choosing. His was a unique fascination with the events of life as they unfolded around him— simple or grand moments, it made little difference because all revealed something about the human condition. It was a pure and genuine, God-given fascination.

Ford could spot an old fisherman sitting on a bench stitching holes in his net and be captivated for hours. He'd study every weathered line on the man's face and every crack in his chapped hands. They'd tell him a thousand stories. He could see the old man's love of the sea. He could taste the salt in the air and feel the cool spray of the ocean against his face. He'd remember the day the man taught his young son how to tie his first Turle knot and perfect loop. He knew the good and loving wife waiting for him at home with a hot and hearty supper, just as she had every night for more than forty years, never complaining of their simple life, still loving that old hat he had brought home on her birthday years before. Ford knew the significance of the holes in that net—there would be little caught that day, fewer fish sold to merchants and scarcely enough to feed every family in the village. Somewhere a young lad would have no dinner that night. The boy would lie awake with nothing but anger burning in his belly, swearing to leave one day to make a life for himself, swearing that he'd never go hungry again.

John Ford walked through life setting stories in motion regardless of whether he ever captured them on film. Ford lived his creative process every single moment of his life. I think he sought refuge there. He told stories and lies. Lies and stories—they were one and the same to him because he was a congenital fibber. The need to lie was already within him while he slept peacefully in his mother's womb. Many people were taken aback or even infuriated by this side of his personality. They thought him a damn liar. But they missed the relevance of it and its importance to his genius. John Ford was the world's greatest storyteller because he was the world's most convincing liar. He rarely told the truth and he rarely lived the truth. John Ford was always shooting a script, no matter what he was doing.

I came to understand this about him in the most unexpected way during the several months that preceded filming on *The Quiet Man*. Ford was now completely immersed in the picture. With *Rio Grande* behind him, he was working feverishly on the story for *The Quiet Man*, and had already asked *How Green Was My Valley* author Richard Llewellyn to write the first draft of the screenplay. It became an obsession, and I believe Ford himself started living the story of *The Quiet Man*. In September 1950, Ford went to Ireland to start laying the foundation for shooting the following June, and to get in deeper touch with his Irish roots.

He already knew my family, having visited them while he was in London during the war, sometime around VE Day. Naturally, Daddy and Mammy invited him to stay with them during this visit. Ford fell in love with my family; he took them as his own. The FitzSimons clan was so much of what Ford had always pretended and longed to be—born and raised Irish, in the Emerald Isle. He sat up for hours trading Irish stories with Daddy, breaking his cigar in half and sharing it. He spoke to Mammy about making designer clothes for Mary and Barbara. He took an interest in the acting careers of Charlie and Jimmy. He walked under the Nine Arches to Milltown and visited the Dropping Well. By the time Ford had returned to Hollywood, he wished more than anything that he could be part of the FitzSimons clan.

I was getting ready to leave for Australia to make a western for 20th Century-Fox. Though my life was in turmoil, I was still eager to go and make *Kangaroo*. I loved the script and asked Darryl Zanuck to cast me in the picture. But things at home had reached a breaking point with Will. His condition had worsened since he'd started treatment with his new doctor. He was blacking out more than ever. Bronwyn saw her father completely unconscious many times. He began urinating on the walls and draperies in our home. I couldn't live like this anymore. More important, I couldn't continue exposing Bronwyn to it. She was getting older and I knew I wouldn't be able to make excuses for her father's condition much longer.

I had been too frightened of the consequences of leaving him, but had finally become more frightened of staying. In November 1950, I finally made the difficult decision to file for divorce before I left for Australia. But before I could file, I received an unexpected call from Pappy and Mary Ford asking me to come and see them. They somehow knew that I was planning to divorce Will and they wanted to talk with me about it. I don't know how they knew. Was it so obvious that I wanted out of the marriage? Had Will sensed that the end was near and called his gambling friend Mary for help? I needed support and encouragement from trusted friends. I needed the strength to go through with it, but that was not the advice the Fords gave me.

"Don't rush into anything before you go to Australia," Pappy and Mary began. "Take more time to think about it while you are away. You might change your mind."

I couldn't possibly conceive of changing my mind, but I continued to listen as Mary chimed in, "You can always go through with it when you get back, if you still want to. We don't want to see you make a terrible mistake." I was expecting support, but instead had the wind taken out of my sails. John and Mary Ford had talked me out of filing, and had persuaded me to give Will more time.

Two days later, on November 17, 1950, I left Los Angeles and began my journey to Australia. At the Fords' insistence, Will went with me on the first leg of the flight, to Honolulu, Hawaii, where we stayed for a few days. I was also in Honolulu at the request of John Ford's trusted aide, Mark Armstead. Mark had arranged for me to meet with high-ranking members of the U.S. Navy to voice my support for a movement that was under way to secure for John Ford an increase in rank, to rear admiral. I played the good and loyal foot soldier and praised Pappy as a great American highly deserving of a new commission. But inside, I was still hurt by his advice on Will. I couldn't understand why Pappy would make such an effort to keep me in a marriage in which I was so miserable. My confusion only deepened when a strange letter from John Ford arrived for me at the Honolulu Royal Hotel. It was postmarked November 19, 1950, and had been written by Ford while he was on his way back to Ireland. It was addressed to "Herself" and read:

En route to Eire (again)

All rite! All rite! All rite!!

So American Air service is better! I always said you were smarter than me—My only casualty was y'da's pencil—(Charlie Fitz's Xmas pencil-don't make any wise cracks) It got bent like a pretzel (y'da's pencil I mean).

You know-agra-being Irish & fey—(did y'not know I was Irish? I am—from good Spiddal stock—good solid ~~peasant~~ *shopkeeper stock). And as I was saying, being Irish & fey . . . I had a hunch about our trips-you west-me east.*

An' thank God it happened to me for if anything happened to you-I would die. For I love you so much my darling—a million words couldn't tell—and them in Gaelic—

It's twenty-two hours now since I saw you & my heart is breaking already-but then again it swells & mends when I think of you-not your beauty-intelligence-talent or even your lovely eyes-but for you as a person.

I worship you-for yourself.

Believe me! my love—

(we are flying over Palm Springs—and I kissed you!)

Do you like Honolulu? It's nice but not for us—

I hope Elmer & the boys played sweetly for you. The sun smiled on you & that palm leaves waved at you as you drove to the Royal and that you found this note when you got there-

(Which is higher-O'Connell Bridge or the Cliffs of Moher?)

*Arrah Maisín ma chree how much happiness you have given me &
how little I've given you-but girleen I love you so much—*
    As this letter might go astray
    I won't sign except as

                              Séan Aloysius O'Feeney
                              John Ford
                              Who claims he's your fella-

"*I see in you perfected-All that's wrong in Me*"

I couldn't believe my eyes. I read the letter over again, challenging my brain to prove that the words were really there on the
page. My first thoughts were, Why the hell is Pappy writing stuff
like this to me? Where is this coming from? Then I answered my
own questions: He must have been drunk. I knew John Ford was a
periodic alcoholic. I had been told it, had had it confirmed by
Duke and others, even Mary had said so, but I had never, with my
own eyes, seen him drunk. I had been told how Pappy could be
sober for weeks or months, not touching a single drop, and then go
off on a hell-raising two-week bender on the *Araner.* According to
the stories, when Pappy was drunk, he made Will's episodes look
like serene moments at a Transcendental Meditation seminar. I
dismissed the letter as drunken nonsense, put it in my suitcase,
and didn't give it another thought. I left Will in Honolulu a few
days later and flew off to Australia to make *Kangaroo.*

When I arrived in Sydney, Australia, I was looking forward to getting to work on the picture. *Kangaroo* was the first film by a major
American studio to ever be made in Australia. It was very important to the country, and the publicity around the picture was
remarkable. The Australians were so excited to have us there and

were one of the most gracious people I have ever encountered on location.

The plot of the picture involves an Irish immigrant, Michael McGuire (portrayed by Scottish vaudevillian Finlay Currie), and his daughter, Dell (guess who?), who are Australian cattle ranchers but face poverty and death during the devastating drought of 1900. Their problems worsen when two gentlemen of fortune befriend McGuire and scheme to steal both his daughter and his fortune. Fox borrowed MGM star Peter Lawford (or "Peter Awful" as everyone called him) to play my love interest, and a hoofer from the New York stage, Richard Boone, was cast as the heavy. The first script I read in Hollywood was wonderful. It was the reason I asked Zanuck to cast me in the role. He had already cast his then current girlfriend in the part, but dropped her from the picture as soon as I asked for the part. I was heartbroken when I was given the revised shooting script in Sydney and saw how it had been ruined. The film's director, Lewis Milestone, had rewritten Martin Berkeley's story and made it about a man and his conscience struggling with the question, "Are you a sinner if you only think about sinning, or do you have to actually commit the sin to be guilty?" It was the worst piece of rubbish I had ever read.

He had destroyed a good, straightforward western. I called my attorney, Lloyd Wright, back in America, and asked him to get me out of the picture. I tried to quit, but was told it was impossible, that I had to stay and make the movie. There was far too much riding on *Kangaroo*—for the studio, for Australia, and for the United States. International commerce issues were in play. I was told that I would be creating a huge political incident if I walked off the picture. I had no choice but to do it or be in serious trouble. So I went ahead and made the picture.

Though I hated every minute of the work, I absolutely loved Australia and the Australian people. One quarter of the entire

Australian population was Irish, after all. Every time I left my hotel and went anywhere, a bagpipe band followed me. It was lovely, but a bit too much.

Unfortunately, Peter Lawford and Richard Boone were not having the same kind of luck with the public and press that I was. Lawford and Boone were rude and disrespectful to many Australians and the press as a whole, and the Australians came to dislike them both with a passion. While we were still in Sydney, the press set out to get them and tailed Lawford and Boone everywhere they went, waiting for the chance to pounce. The press sure gave it to them when they caught Lawford and Boone in a brothel full of beautiful boys. The press couldn't wait to break the story. I got a panicked late-night call from the publicity head of 20th Century-Fox Australia, Sydney Albright, saying, "Maureen, you've got to help us kill this story! The people and the press here love you, and if you don't, it will kill the picture."

The next morning I went to a secret meeting with the press that had been hastily arranged by the studio. I told them, "Listen, this is the first Hollywood movie ever to be made in Australia. It is very important. If you break this story, you're not just going to hurt Peter Lawford and Richard Boone, you're going to hurt me, the whole cast and crew, your own country and the people of Australia, because the studio will shut down this picture. Australia will suffer much more than those two will." I knew it would make them reconsider. In the early 1950s, Australia was a far cry from the tourist mecca it has become since Paul Hogan first bid us "g'day." Cattle still outnumbered people by a two to one margin. So they killed the story. I was never thanked by 20th Century-Fox, but I gained many friends in Australia.

The Lawford-and-Boone incident only confirmed that I was in for a long location and that it was going to be hell. I couldn't help but wonder, Why is everything in my life so crazy? With the exception of Bronwyn, nothing about my life made any sense to me. Then another letter from John Ford arrived. This one was post-marked December 5, 1950, and again, it was for "Herself." He was in Dublin now and staying with Daddy and Mammy. Again, it was full of romanticized notions about me, referring to the moments of happiness that I had given him. It was short but potent:

> *Upstairs*
> *13 Churchtown*

> *Oh my loved one. I miss you so much! Every time I think of you a poniard goes thru' my heart-*
> *Again a million thanks for the hours of happiness you've given me-*
> *D'ya know you're awful sweet, loyal, talented & so goddamn BEAUTIFUL?*
> *So I close-*
> *Blessing you & loving you*

>> *Séan*
>> *You've never called me by my name-*
>> *But I prefer the above.*
>> *S.A.K.OF.*

I didn't know what the hell he was talking about. What moments of happiness? I assumed he meant the times we'd spent on the *Araner* working on script notes for *The Quiet Man*. Did he mean the sharing of our Irishness? This time I showed the letter to Jimmy Barker and Faye Smyth. We all knew how notoriously eccentric John Ford was, and so with Faye's and Jimmy's advice, I decided to dismiss the letter. The last thing I wanted was a problem with Ford, so I put the significance of the letter out of my mind.

The fact is, we were all so damn miserable on *Kangaroo* that we were thrilled to just hear from Pappy. We were unhappy with the director and all agreed on how wonderful it would be if John Ford showed up to rescue us and save the picture. All three of us wrote Pappy a few letters over the next few days. We told him how much we missed him and wished he were there with us. "Oh, Pappy, we'd be so thrilled to look up and see you walking down the avenue," I wrote. Then we bundled them all up and mailed them off together.

I was in Australia for months and the situation on the film was getting worse with each passing day. I cried, many nights. Lawford and Boone were horrible to me even though I had saved both their hides. And though a few scenes were shot in Sydney during the first weeks, the script called for drought conditions, so we were soon on location in the outback. Sydney was so lush that year that most of the film was shot a thousand miles west, in the desert near Port Augusta. The Australian government built a colony of cabins there for us and called it "Zanuckville," but it was obvious that we were out in the wild. It was very primitive, and blistering hot—105 degrees and more on most days. There were fans in the dining tent, but I still had to fight off a swarm of flies for every mouthful of food. I was even clawed something awful by a cuddly little koala bear during a scheduled photo shoot.

As Christmas and New Year's came and went, with me away from home and without much to celebrate, my spirits continued to fall. Then another Ford letter arrived. This one was postmarked January 10, 1951, and had been sent airmail from Korea. Ford had left Ireland and gone to Korea to make a fifty-minute documentary for Republic studios called *This Is Korea!* His letters to Herself were becoming stranger and stranger, and this one made me wonder out loud, "Is he going mad?"

Korea

My darlin' my loved one my heart- Maisín!

Oh God-at last-at long last-I hear from you! And such lovely letters (Oh thank you my heart) the last dated Jan 6. And here I was moping like a gossoon-about my last & only love—Irish like-an' all the time you were writing regularly! And thru' it all I got the impression you were still fond of me. Darling-you've made me so happy! I looked at the letters for a whole day—afraid to open them—then I said, "I'll read one a day." Then like a drunk & his bottle I read them all-word for word-inflection for inflection-I thought I would have a heart attack-frankly, I damn near fainted several times. I've read them over a hundred times, each time they're different. Again my love thanks. You've made me so happy!!! I love you-I love you-I love you! I kiss you a million times! I'm delirious with happiness.

Oh Maisín agrad, why can't we just chuck it & go back to our lovely Isle-the three of us? Life is so different there-the people-our people-are nicer. We can social climb a bit and say we're peasants.

Did you like the "houseen"? It's at Ballyconnelly (Hell-I already told you) but it's lovely & lovely-so beautiful—

Brian Hurst and I have paid two years rent on Michael Kil-lanin's church cottage (church of Ireland ol' dear) in Spiddal. Nice fishing-bathing-plain but comfortable-but too near my relations-Ballyconnelly is away up in Connemara-near Ballylahunch-

(Gawd what am I raving about! And me old enough to be your grandfather!) But a guy can dream can't he? And I'm in love-for once. Ireland was so pretty my darling-oh how I love it-and you.

I hope this letter makes sense. I'm writing by candlelight out in the boondocks. (I think I'll knock off a while and rest my eyes & hands & re-read your letters a couple of times-I feel sensual-all aglow & warm with love-I can feel your arms around me-and your lips pressed to mine and your red hair-oh my love).

Sleep tight my sweet. I hope I'm still y'fella-think kindly of me my love for I love you with all my heart & soul.

Séan

I hadn't been overly concerned about these letters up to this point, but now I was. Over the next several weeks, more letters arrived for Herself. By the end of February, I had received a stack of them. I couldn't keep dismissing them as John Ford eccentricities or as harmless whims during a drunken stupor. I could no longer deny that, for whatever reason, John Ford was sending me love letters. Something was driving his bizarre and shocking behavior, but I didn't yet know what it was. It scared me, and I didn't know what I should do. Should I save them and show them to Mary? Was their marriage in trouble too? I hadn't a clue, but I sure as hell didn't want to be the cause of any trouble between them—even if it was all in John Ford's head. Should I confront him about them myself? I knew all too well that one never fared well when challenging Ford on anything. And I didn't want to do anything that would jeopardize my making *The Quiet Man.*

Then a lightbulb went off in my head. That's it, I thought. That's what this is all about—it's all about *The Quiet Man.* That crazy, brilliant, old son of a bitch is still writing his script. I remembered one of the last letters he had sent Herself. By that time, I had stopped reading them, only skimmed them, then packed them away. There was something in it about *The Quiet Man*, something telling that I had seen, I was sure of it. I searched through the letters again until I found it and began to read it—but carefully this time.

"At long last" as one of <u>your</u> rulers said not so long ago-I hear from you! From Sydney-a short note but it was balm to my tortured soul-after six weeks—Gawd! That mail service between here and there is <u>really</u> lousy—or—as Charlie Fitz says= "You write often but don't mail them"

BUT—I aint complaining—any little word to know you are still on this little planet-to know my darlin' cailín ruagh is living-singing-breathing-that her eyes are still speckled with gold flecks-and to know a flash of emerald on the horizon will throw her mind back to our beloved Eire—(& who knows-maybe a little of that stardust will blow off onto me)

I just re-read the above. It sounds like a lament but really it isn't-perhaps it's the eternal keening of the Wandering Celt-something hereditary from our Irish mother's womb calling to her loved ones far from the land-the Mother Cry-which is so a part of Irish home life-a cry to the far flung corners of the Earth—

Churchtown Road-Spiddal-Sheridan St.-Stone Canyon-wherever they live-I should write this to you-my darlin' -who knows or feels it more than mí Maisín? I guess the answer is I love you so much & miss you so goddamn terribly-

(Darling Maisín-I have a great need of you-a great physical urge-not the bay but the heart-if I could only see you just to hear you laugh)

I'm sorry about the mail business-the distance makes things tough but I'm not expecting much-you've a job to do-that comes first-you know my dear-that whatever you feel like doing is O.K. with me. I'm so grateful for the few weeks of happiness you've given me (few weeks! It was a lifetime!) You're still my darling loyal girl-come hell or high water-I'll always love-revere you-please think kindly of me-not much-a little bit.

<u>BUSINESS</u>=I think honestly we're getting a great story-the girl's part is simply terrific! It's the best part I've read for a -

gal-dramatic-comedic-wistful-pathetic-yet full of hell & fire-passionate & sweet-

 For goodness sake & your family's sake-bend every effort to do it-this is my farewell to movies & I want it good-It will only be great if you play it for I've written it-guided it-slanted it for you. As my last picture-if the shootin' war holds off. I can only force myself to enthusiasm if you & Duke are present-

 Frankly-before I pass on-I want to see you established as a great actress (which you are) with a great performance to your credit-Our personal friendship past or present doesn't enter into it. Altho' I'm selfishly professional in my attitude and you can't blame me on my last pro. effort-I still feel as tho' you're part of me-the things I love & I couldn't or wouldn't do it with anyone else. Something would be missing-They say "There's no fool like an old fool" & I'm in love for the first time-and proud as all bloody hell about it—So you can see-Maisín ma chree-how important you are to the picture (and how important you are to me-will you laugh! Please laugh-I can hear you).

 Darlin' Maisín-carry on-you're a great great actress & don't let anyone tell you differently-stick it out-fight on & please keep that forehead & that little place in your heart for me-

      On account of I love ya
      Séan

I've kept these letters from John Ford secret for over fifty years. With the exception of Jimmy Barker, Faye Smyth, and my brother Charlie, until now I've never shared them with anyone. For years, I didn't know why I kept them. I realize as I write this now that I must have known, deep in my heart, of their significance in understanding how John Ford made his masterpiece— *The Quiet Man.* They show us how this remarkable filmmaker actually lived the *Quiet Man* story while he was creating his art. If they were only love letters from John Ford to Maureen O'Hara, I would have kept them private and destroyed them. I believe these are love letters from John Ford to Mary Kate Danaher. I am sharing them with you, dear reader, because the film is so beloved all over the world, and I am the last of its principal players who can add something meaningful to how it was made.

I don't believe it's a coincidence that for the movie John Ford changed the names of the three main characters in the published story "The Quiet Man." The names he chose are very telling. The last name of Duke's character was changed from Sean Kelvin to Sean Thornton. The Thorntons were a John Ford family relation in Ireland. Sean was also John Ford's Irish name and the same one he signed in the letters to Herself. He did it also for Mary Kate Danaher. Ford always loved the story about how I was named, and of the argument that had occurred between Mammy and Daddy. He made them tell it to him over and over, every time he saw them. He changed the name of my character from Ellen O'Grady to Mary Kate, two of the names suggested for me. It's long been said that Ford named Mary Kate Danaher for the two women he loved most over the course of his life, his wife, Mary, and Katharine Hepburn, but that is not true. He even changed the name of the villain, the one who controlled Mary Kate, from Liam O'Grady to Red Will, after my husband Will, which infuriated me at the time.

I have often said that *The Quiet Man* is my personal favorite of all the pictures I have made during my career. It is the one I am most proud of, and I tend to be very protective of it. I want its historical record to be factual and truthful. So as I continue and get deeper into it, here's fair warning—I am about to set the record straight, let a few people have it, and in the process shatter some myths. Hopefully, I will also do justice to the truly joyful and wondrous experience we all shared in the land of Ireland while making this magical picture.

I returned home to Hollywood in March 1951, after five months on location in Australia. I was looking forward to resting before leaving for Ireland in June, wishfully thinking that the problems I had left behind had magically worked themselves out while I was away. I was about to find out that they were much worse than even I knew. A few days after I got home, Bill Duce's secretary came to the house to see me. Duce had been handling our financial matters, at Will's insistence, for quite some time now, and without a lot of overseeing by me. That was a catastrophic mistake. His secretary dropped a bombshell on me, saying, "Maureen, I just can't stand it anymore and had to come here to tell you the truth. You're broke." My heart started to race. "What do you mean, I'm broke?" I asked. "How can that be? I have several hundred thousand dollars in the bank!" She was on the verge of tears. "No, you don't. You don't have a penny. Bill Duce and your husband have spent every cent you had. It's all gone, Maureen . . . all of it."

I called the bank and verified that my accounts had indeed been cleaned out. After starring in over thirty motion pictures, I was stone-cold broke. Thank God I still had my weekly paycheck or Bronwyn and I would have been out in the street. There was nothing I could do about it, of course. My husband had spent the money. Technically, no laws had been broken, there was no theft. There wasn't any point in yelling about it. It's impossible to argue with a drunk. The money was gone and there wasn't a damn thing I could do about it.

I decided to go and see Will's doctor. I wanted to know just what the hell he was doing out there for all the money I was paying him. I made arrangements to attend a presentation that the doctor was giving for the family members of his alcohol- and substance-abuse patients. I sat there and watched in disbelief as this man drew circles and triangles and squares on a chalkboard. He connected and intersected them with lines and told us that this explained addiction and how he was going to cure our loved ones. It was the biggest bunch of rubbish I had ever heard. I stood up and blew my stack, saying, "All that stuff you're doing up there is a whole heap of rubbish! It's nothing but bloody nonsense!" I stormed out of the place and swore that I would get to the bottom of what was really going on.

What I discovered was shocking. Will's treatment center was supposed to be a very exclusive rehabilitation hospital catering to a clientele of substantial means. I suspected, however, that his doctor wasn't really interested in curing anybody. The hospital proved to be far less a treatment center than an expensive country-club resort, where they were secretly providing patients with prostitutes, booze, and prescription pills. It appeared that he was keeping patients there for weeks and then sending the bills to the families. Whenever he thought he had kept a patient there as long as he could, he'd give him shock treatment and send him home.

I had had enough and stopped paying them, but shortly after I did, Will showed up at the house with his doctor, who informed me, "Miss O'Hara, I have reviewed your husband's case thoroughly and am convinced the cause of his problem is *you*. I believe you have a serious medical condition and would like you to urinate in this bottle for analysis." I told them both to forget it but they kept nagging me and nagging me until I almost had a migraine. So I did it!

A few days later, Will's doctor showed up at the house. This time he said, "Miss O'Hara, the lab results have confirmed my suspicions. You have a very serious growth on your kidney, and unless it is removed immediately, your body will begin to resemble a man's. I have a car here to take you to the hospital. We must go now." I wasn't getting in that car with anyone. I excused myself and went upstairs to call my own doctor at St. John's Hospital. Dr. Stevens said, "Maureen, get out of that house right now and come straight here."

I left the doctor in my living room and rushed right over to St. John's Hospital. Dr. Stevens had me admitted and arranged for a renowned specialist from UCLA to examine me. I was there for days and had every test you can name. After they were over, the doctor gave me his official diagnosis. It absolutely floored me. He said, "Miss O'Hara, you are perhaps the healthiest woman I have ever examined. The operation your husband and his doctor want you to have has one of the highest fatality rates of any surgical procedure. It is my professional medical opinion that you should seek a divorce immediately."

You didn't have to think for too long to figure out what was planned for me. But how is someone supposed to react to the news that another person has just tried to arrange her demise? I couldn't accept the ramifications of it. I was afraid to be in the house with Will, but still did nothing to initiate divorce proceedings. I don't know why. I knew he had guns in the house, he had owned them ever since he'd gotten back from the war. I found them and hid them within a wall. Though I now kept a baseball bat next to my bed, I often had a sleepless night if Will was home.

In early April, a call came from Universal informing me that I had been cast as a Tunisian princess in *Flame of Araby*. I wasn't up to making another lousy picture and wanted to save myself for a great performance in *The Quiet Man*. But Universal made their intentions known right away: Make the movie or be suspended. I had no choice but to make it or I wouldn't have been allowed to make *The Quiet Man.* I did all the wardrobe fittings for *The Quiet Man* during my lunch breaks on *Flame of Araby.* We wrapped the picture on June 2, and Bronwyn and I were on a plane the following day, heading home to Ireland.

CHAPTER 14

THE QUIET MAN

The cares of the world seemed to vanish overnight and a feeling of peace and serenity took me over as my plane reached the coast of Ireland and closed in on Shannon Airport. If you have never had the chance to visit her in the summertime, then you must. She is simply glorious. Tiny bumps rose on my arms as I peered out of my airplane window and looked down upon the deep blue sea that surrounds her golden coastline. Bronwyn and I tried to spot one of her hidden harbors, nestled tightly within. I even tingled as I gazed upon her dramatic cliffs one more time, and I am still inspired by the cliffs of Moher no matter how many times I see them. I felt warm and safe, as one always does at home, when I saw her sprawling central plain again, surrounded by mountainous hues that varied from lush emerald green to the deep purple of heather to the solemn richness of her dark black bogs. I have never seen her more majestic than she was that summer of 1951. This would be the first time she was ever captured in Technicolor, and I knew before our wheels ever touched the ground that the real star of *The Quiet Man* would be Ireland herself.

Excitement was everywhere when we arrived. It felt as if all of Ireland knew we were coming. Daddy and Mammy met us at Shannon Airport, but they were far less interested in the picture I was about to make than in seeing their seven-year-old granddaughter, who had just made her first Holy Communion. You have to imagine the electricity that was in the air that day as all of us arrived to make this picture. We had waited patiently for seven long years, and now we knew the cameras would be rolling in just a matter of days. We were like children eager to begin a wondrous journey together—giddy, glowing, and positively agog!

The Quiet Man is a simple and funny love story. Sean Thornton (John Wayne) is an American boxer who has returned to the village of Innisfree hoping to rebuild his life after killing an opponent in the ring. His dream of a quiet and peaceful life is threatened when he purchases White O'Morn, the small cottage where he was born. Red Will Danaher (Victor McLaglen) is the village bully, and he wants the land because it rests next to the home of the widow Tillane (Mildred Natwick), whom he hopes to marry.

Fireworks begin when Sean meets and falls in love with the feisty redheaded Mary Kate (me), who just happens to be Red Will's only sister. With a little trickery from Father Lonergan (Ward Bond) and the ever thirsty matchmaker Michaeleen (Barry Fitzgerald), Sean wins White O'Morn and Mary Kate's hand without having to fight Red Will.

When Red Will discovers that he was tricked, he refuses to pay Mary Kate's dowry. The villagers are hoping a fight between the two men is about to begin, but Sean still avoids it. Mary Kate believes she hasn't been properly wed without her dowry, so she uses the ultimate weapon of persuasion—no dowry, no lovemaking. Of course, the pressure builds, Sean ultimately snaps, and one of the greatest fights in movie history begins.

The story has interesting roots. On February 11, 1933, John Ford read a story in the *Saturday Evening Post* titled "The Quiet Man" and fell madly in love with it. It had been written by an unknown author, Maurice Walsh, an Irishman born and raised in the small village of Ballydonoghue, in the north of County Kerry, an area well known for its storytellers and poets. Ford purchased the motion-picture rights to the story from Walsh in 1936 for only $10. Walsh was paid another $2,500 when Ford sold the idea to Republic, and also received a final payment of $3,750 when the picture was finally made.

John Ford spent the next fifteen years working on developing the story into a screenplay that he could get financed. By the time he had finally acquired the movie rights, Walsh had already changed the story quite a bit and made it part of his novel *Green Rushes*. The "Quiet Man" chapter in the novel focuses on the IRA's struggle against the Black and Tans. Richard Llewellyn's draft of the script closely followed the *Green Rushes* version, but John Ford knew this would never play to either Hollywood studio bosses or American audiences. Most of the work we did on the *Araner* involved removing the politics from the story and focusing it on romance and comedy. It was screenwriter Frank Nugent who later masterfully fleshed out the plot and characters with Mr. Ford, and who brought to the film its whimsical humor.

John Ford's dream was to shoot a breathtaking Technicolor epic all over Ireland, with a special focus on the small village of Spiddal, in County Galway, the place of his ancestral roots. He had spent a great deal of time in Spiddal during his earlier visits to Ireland in 1950, but ruled it out for logistical reasons. At a loss, he needed local assistance and commissioned my brother Charlie

FitzSimons (Charlie Fitz from here on) to work with Argosy unit manager Lee Lukather to scour the countryside looking for alternative locations. Based on their research, John Ford chose the lovely little village of Cong, in County Mayo, as the village of Innisfree. All of the exterior sequences for *The Quiet Man* were filmed in Cong, surrounding areas within County Mayo, and a few in nearby County Galway and County Clare.

One of the many fallacies surrounding *The Quiet Man* involves how these locations came to be used for the picture and who was involved in their selection. Let me set the record straight right now. Every location used in the picture was selected by John Ford himself. Charlie Fitz and Lee Lukather found location options that Mr. Ford ultimately approved or threw out. No one ever told John Ford what he should do in his movies. You never made concrete suggestions, with strong opinions about them, to him because he would immediately dismiss them and do the exact opposite of what you had suggested. John Ford didn't need anyone to tell him what was best for his pictures; he knew the minute he saw it.

But the biggest fallacy about *The Quiet Man* that I feel I must correct once and for all involves the role of Lord Killanin. In book after book which I read about *The Quiet Man* or John Ford, Michael Killanin is named as being instrumental in selecting locations for the picture. He was not. He may have offered a few location suggestions to Ford along the way, but the job of recommending location options to Mr. Ford was assigned to and completed by Charlie Fitz and Lee Lukather, period. But what has truly astounded me over the years is that Lord Killanin is also named as an uncredited producer of *The Quiet Man.* It is not only absolute rubbish, but also shameful. There was only one producer of *The Quiet Man,* and that was Merian C. Cooper. Herb Yates received credit as executive producer because he was head of Republic and paid for the movie.

Michael Killanin was John Ford's friend. The only thing he did while we were shooting the picture was visit the set from time to time and join Mr. Ford at public appearances. He did not participate in the making of *The Quiet Man.* If he had, he would have received credit for it. There were and still are union laws that govern this. There would also be payroll records for the time he spent working on the picture and detailed documents that show his involvement in the day-to-day making of a motion picture. There aren't any because they don't exist. And they don't exist because it never happened. The only documentation that does exist are letters between Lord Killanin and John Ford that have more to do with their personal friendship than anything else. There was an early suggestion that he act as liaison for John Ford with Alexander Korda, but that deal fell through and Korda ultimately had nothing to do with the picture. I never, EVER, heard John Ford refer to Killanin as anything other than a friend.

John Ford loved to manipulate and use people. He'd tell you whatever you wanted to hear, or flatter you, if he thought it served him well. You couldn't trust anything that he wrote or said to you. Any credit John Ford might have given Lord Killanin after the picture was finished was given to please himself. Lord Killanin's friendship appealed to Ford's ego. John Ford always saw himself as a descendant of peasants, and loved nobility and fancy titles, surrounding himself with important people whenever he could. He was impressed by them and felt they legitimized him. Even his own tombstone reads "Admiral John Ford." It doesn't read "Director John Ford."

Michael Killanin used the Ford letters to associate himself with the success of *The Quiet Man.* I know people have written about my assertions on this point and have politely inferred that I am confused and underestimate the important role he actually played. They've also suggested that I'm just trying to give my own brother more credit. Ludicrous, all of it. I only want the historical record of the film to be accurate, and the people who truly worked hard on it to receive the credit they deserve.

The day I arrived at Shannon, Bronwyn and I went straight to Dublin with Daddy and Mammy. I hadn't been there five minutes when the phone call came from Meta Sterne, in Cong: "Mr. Ford wants you on the set tomorrow." I arrived in and left Dublin the same day. I was sure the old man thought, Well, I'm not going to let her stay there. He would have loved being with Daddy and Mammy more than anything, and he wasn't about to let me have that pleasure to myself. I joined most of the cast and crew in Cong, at Ashford Castle, where we stayed while filming. It is a magnificent seven-hundred-year-old castle, situated at the water's edge on the Lough Corrib. Other members of the crew stayed at local bed-and-breakfasts, guesthouses, and inns.

We started shooting the very next day, on June 7, 1951. All of the outdoor scenes were shot on location in Ireland. The inside scenes were filmed toward the end of July at Republic, in Hollywood. Of course, the principal players in the picture were Duke, myself, Victor McLaglen, Mildred Natwick, Ward Bond, Francis Ford, and Barry Fitzgerald. We were the only Hollywood actors who filmed in Ireland. The other characters credited in the film as the "Irish Players" were cast from local Irish talent, and many of them were members of the Abbey Theatre. Back in Hollywood, Mr. Ford completed the cast with members of the Ford stock company.

One of the most special things about making *The Quiet Man* is that it truly was a family affair. Many family members of the principal cast and crew were a part of this picture. Both of my brothers were actors in it. In addition to helping Mr. Ford with finding locations, hiring local talent, and handling legal matters, barrister Charlie Fitz also played Hugh Forbes in the film. Our younger brother Jimmy played the role of Father Paul, under his stage name James Lilburn. Even Daddy and Mammy's driver, Kevin Lawlor, was in the movie, playing the fireman on the train. The Ford family was well represented as well. Francis Ford played Dan Tobin, the sick old man with the long beard who ran down the road and wouldn't die. Mr. Ford's other brother, Edward O'Fearna, was a second assistant director on the picture. Mary Ford's brother, Wingate Smith, was first assistant director. Young Pat Ford doubled for Victor McLaglen during the fight sequence in which Red Will falls into the river. That was Pat who fell into the water and not Victor. Barbara Ford stayed home in Hollywood and worked with the editors cutting the picture. Ken Curtis played Dermot Fahy, and became John Ford's son-in-law a year later when Barbara and he were married.

Duke brought his second wife, Chata, and four of his kids—Michael, Patrick, Toni, and Melinda—to Ireland. Duke's kids were all on the cart with me during the scene at the Innisfree horse race where Mary Kate's bonnet is left on the pole. Victor McLaglen's son Andrew was another second assistant director. The Reverend Cyril Playfair was played by Arthur Shields, Barry Fitzgerald's younger brother. Even my hairdresser, Faye Smyth, had her sister, Neva Bourne, on this picture in charge of women's wardrobe. I could keep naming relatives, there were so many.

The excitement on the set was matched by the excitement of the people of Cong when we arrived. *The Quiet Man* was the biggest thing to ever happen in that village, and it brought about many wonderful changes that benefited the local townsfolk there. Until we made the movie, Cong had no electricity. In addition to electricity, telephone service to Cong was extended because of the movie. And Mr. Ford wanted the entire community to be a part of his film, so he used many locals as extras.

Obviously, I was eager to see how John Ford was going to act toward me on and off the set. His letters had me confused and curious, but not overly concerned. I wanted to know if he was still playing this *Quiet Man* romance-fantasy of me in his head. I was relieved to see that he was no different from how he had always been. He never mentioned the letters to me, and it was strange, as if they had never existed. On the set, he was the typical Mr. Ford—happy at times, irritated at others, sometimes insulting, at times abusive, acerbic with his wit, a bastard, but always in control—and so I felt everything was normal. I later learned, after the picture was finished, that he was still clinging to these fantasies about me. But while we were making the movie, he managed to hide that from me.

With that said, let me get this out of the way once and for all: I did not have an affair with John Ford while we were making *The Quiet Man*, or at any other time. The man was old enough to be my father! I've heard the rumors that have been thrown around. These stories and assumptions are spewed out in interviews and end up printed in books about John Ford as though they are fact. I'm sorry, guys, but you have it wrong. You should have asked me. Ford did not assign me to a room at Ashford Castle that was adjacent to his, as one person alleged. What Ford did do, however, was deliberately assign me to a room that was very beat up, with holes in the worn-out carpet and wallpaper peeling off the walls. Duke, on the other hand, had a gorgeous suite. I thought, Oh, that old bastard. He did this on purpose, just so I'll make a fuss and complain. But I never said a word. I would never have given him the satisfaction.

While I'm at it, let me kill another story. It has been written that toward the middle of filming, Mr. Ford was unable to continue shooting the picture, overcome with grief and depression because I had turned him down the night before. That's tantalizing and juicy gossip, but it's utter rubbish. It is true that Duke, Ward Bond, Wingate Smith, Charlie Fitz, and I were summoned one morning to Mr. Ford's room, where we found him lying in bed. He said, "I can't do it. I don't want to work today." We all stayed there with him, discussing what we should do, and Mr. Ford made me keep heating up a hot-water bottle for him to put on his stomach. The other men in the room had turned away from him for a moment, continuing the conversation, and he said to me softly, "Maureen, don't let me out of this bed. I want to get drunk."

Duke, Ward, and Wingate had seen him drunk before and knew that a John Ford drinking binge could jeopardize finishing the picture. Wingate Smith offered a possible solution: "Well, if he's sick and stays in bed, then Pat Ford can take over and direct the picture." All of our jaws fell open and Ward Bond said what most of us were thinking, "No way. If Pat Ford takes over, I'm leaving." We had to get the old man through it, so we stayed with him and saw to it that he remained in bed. The next day, Mr. Ford was back on his feet, as if nothing had happened, and went on directing the picture. The episode had passed and a catastrophe had been averted. Shooting had been stopped for only one day. Rumors range from Duke having directed the rest of the picture, to Lord Killanin having directed the rest of the picture. *The Quiet Man* had only one director—and that was John Ford.

But enough of the gossip. I want to share more with you about shooting the movie. First, the weather couldn't have been better while we were filming. We had so much sun that we used to ask cameramen Winton Hoch and Archie Stout if they were putting sunshine pills in the camera. Many books refer to a great deal of rain during the shoot, but that wasn't true, and came from John Ford. If you said to John Ford in an interview, "Oh, I understand the rain was awful on *The Quiet Man*," he'd say, "Who the hell told you that shit? It was blazing sun and we could hardly stand the clothes on our back." If they asked him about the beautiful summer conditions, he would say, "What the hell are you talking about? It rained so much I almost stopped shooting the picture." Whenever you asked Ford a question, he would beat it down and say it was the opposite. But the weather was so wonderful that I used to take naps in the tall grass.

The single day that it did rain was just when Mr. Ford needed it. Right after the scene where Duke and I kiss in the windy cottage and I hit him, there is the sequence in which I run from the cottage, cross a stream, and then fall as the rain and wind storm about me. That was real rain in the scene. The rest of the rain in the picture came from rain machines. The wind actually blew me down in that scene, but I kept going because Mr. Ford always made it clear to his actors that "You do not stop acting no matter what happens in a scene until I say cut. I am the director."

I loved Mary Kate Danaher. I loved the hell and fire in her. She was a terrific dame, tough, and didn't let herself get walked on. As I readied to begin playing her, I believed that my most important scene in the picture, the one that I had to get just right, was when Mary Kate is in the field herding the sheep and Sean Thornton sees her for the very first time. There is no dialogue between them. It's a moment captured in time, and it's love at first sight. I felt very strongly that if the audience believed it was love at first sight, then we would have lightning in a bottle. But if they didn't, we would have just another lovely romantic comedy on our hands. It had to be perfect, and the script provided me with a little inspiration, but not enough. Sean's line to Michaeleen—"Hey, is that real? She couldn't be"—didn't quite give me what I needed. I found a passage in Walsh's story that hit the mark, and I used it as motivation for how I would play the scene:

And there leaning on a wall was the woman. No ghost woman.
Flesh and blood or I have no eyes to see. The sun shining on her red
hair and her scarf green as grass on her shoulders. She was not look-
ing at me. She was looking over my head at the far side of the pool.
I only saw her over my shoulder but she was fit to sit with the Mona
Lisa *amongst the rocks. More beautiful by fire and no less wicked. A*
woman I never saw before, yet a woman strangely familiar.

The scene comes off so beautifully. Mr. Ford brilliantly kept
the camera stationary and had me walk slowly down and out of the
frame instead of following me as I walked away. It's one of my
favorite shots in the movie, and, if you have never noticed it before, it's worth watching the movie again just to see it.

Of course, the scene that everyone always asks me about is the
scene with Duke and me in the cemetery. Most of the Quiet Mani-
acs, those who keep the film in its cult-classic status, tell me that
this is their favorite scene. It's the sequence on the bicycle when
Sean and Mary Kate escape Michaeleen's watchful eye. We run into
the cemetery and it begins to rain. As thunder chases me under the
arch, Duke takes his coat off and wraps it around me to keep me dry
and warm. The rain drenches us and his white shirt clings to his
body and becomes translucent. In that moment, we are truly together in each other's arms, and we kiss. It is sensual, passionate,
and more than any other scene we ever did together displays the
on-screen eroticism of the Wayne and O'Hara combination.

There were two parts to that scene. The first part we had to get
in one take or Mr. Ford would have strung us up by our toes. It's
everything that happens right up to the embrace and kiss. We had
to get it in one take because our clothes were sopping wet when
we finished. If we missed it, then our costumes would have to be
cleaned, dried, and ironed. Our hair would have to be washed,
dried, and reset. Makeup would have to be reapplied. These

things take hours and hours to do and cost thousands and thousands of dollars for each take. We got it in one.

Once we were drenched and part one was in the can, we could focus on the kiss. But Mr. Ford rarely allowed more than a couple of takes, and I think we got that one in two. Why is the scene so erotic? Why were Duke and I so electric in our love scenes together? I was the only leading lady big enough and tough enough for John Wayne. Duke's presence was so strong that when audiences saw him finally meet a woman of equal hell and fire, it was exciting and thrilling. Other actresses looked as though they would cower and break if Duke raised a hand or even hollered. Not me. I always gave as good as I got, and it was believable. So during those moments of tenderness, when the lovemaking was about to begin, audiences saw for a half second that he had finally tamed me—but only for that half second.

Mr. Ford did not make Duke perform the kiss over and over, as I've read. The suggestion has been that Mr. Ford was living, through Duke, the experience of kissing me. Not in this scene, although I do believe John Ford longed to be every hero he ever brought to the screen. He would have loved to live every role John Wayne played. He would have loved to be Sean Thornton. His vivid stories—of riding with Pancho Villa or his longing to be a great naval hero or an Irish rebel—were all fantasies of being men John Ford could never be in life, yet desperately wanted and needed to be. He was a real-life Walter Mitty years before Thurber gave Mitty literary life.

Visually, there are so many magnificent sequences in the film, like the windy kiss in White O'Morn when Mary Kate is caught cleaning the cottage. That scene was shot in Hollywood, and Mr. Ford used two large wind machines to blow our clothes and my hair for the effect. These were two large airplane propellers on a stand that Mr. Ford controlled by sending hand signals to an operator. Once again, it was a scene tailor-made for Duke and me. He pulls me away from the door and kisses me as I struggle to break free. He tames me for that half second, and I kiss him back, but then follow up with a hard blow across the face for the offense.

Now let me tell you what really happened with that slap. That day on the set, I was mad as hell at Duke and Mr. Ford for something they had done earlier in the day. My plan was to sock Duke in the jaw and really let him have it. But Duke was no fool, and he saw it coming, he saw it in my face. So he put his hand up to shield his chin, and my hand hit the top of his fingers and snapped back. My plan backfired and my hand hurt like hell. I knew I had really hurt it and tried to hide it in the red petticoat I was wearing. Duke came over and said, "Let me see that hand. You nearly broke my jaw." He lifted it out of hiding; each one of my fingers had blown up like a sausage. I was taken off the set and sent to the local hospital where it was X-rayed. I had a hairline fracture in one of the bones in my wrist, but in the end got no sympathy. I was taken back to the set and put to work.

While one is working on a motion picture, it's natural to get mad at the others from time to time. I almost found myself in John Ford's barrel while we were shooting the Innisfree horse-race sequence down on the beach. The scene again required the use of wind machines during one of my close-ups. But instead of the wind machine blowing my hair away from my face, Mr. Ford put the machine behind me and blew my hair forward. Well, at that time I had hair like wire. It snapped and snapped against my face. The wind was blowing my hair forward and the hair was lashing my eyeballs. It hurt, and I kept blinking. Mr. Ford started yelling at me and insulting me under his breath: "Keep your goddamn eyes open. Why can't you get it right?"

He kept yelling at me and I was getting madder and madder. I finally blew my lid. I put my two hands down on the side of the cart and yelled, "What would a baldheaded old son of a bitch like you know about hair lashing across your eyeballs?"

The words had no sooner left my mouth than I was nearly knocked off my feet by the sound of a collective gasp on the set. No one spoke to John Ford that way. There was absolute silence. No one dared move, speak, or even breathe. I don't know why I did it. He made me mad and I just blew my stack. Immediately, I thought, Oh my God. Why didn't I keep my bloody mouth shut? He's going to throw me off the picture. After years of waiting to make *The Quiet Man*, I was sure I was about to be tossed off the set. I waited for his explosion. I waited without moving a muscle and watched as Mr. Ford cased the entire set with his eyes. He looked at every person—every actor, every crew member, every stuntman—and he did it fast as lightning. I could see the wheels in his head turning. The old man was deciding whether he was going to kill me or laugh and let me off the hook. I didn't know which way it would go until the very moment that he broke into laughter. Everyone on the set collapsed with relief and finally exhaled. They followed Mr. Ford's lead and laughed for ten minutes—out of sheer relief that I was safe. Then we went on and shot the scene.

But in the end the old man got the last laugh. He and Duke agreed to play a joke on me. To do it, they chose the sequence where Duke drags me across town and through the fields. I bet you didn't know that sheep dung has the worst odor you have ever smelled in your life. Well, it does. Mr. Ford and Duke kicked all of the sheep dung they could find onto the hill where I was to be dragged, facedown, on my stomach. Of course, I saw them doing it, and so when they kicked the dung onto the field, Faye, Jimmy, and I kicked it right back off. They'd kick it in, and we'd kick it out. It went on and on, and finally, right before the scene was shot, they won, getting in the last kick. There was no way to kick it out.

The camera began to roll, and Duke had the time of his life dragging me through it. It was bloody awful. After the scene was over, Mr. Ford had given instructions that I was not to be brought a bucket of water or a towel. He made me keep it on for the rest of the day. I was mad as hell, but I had to laugh too. Isn't showbiz glamorous?

And the sequence itself is perfect for Duke and me. I fight him the entire way, but he won't have it. I take a swing at him, so he kicks me in the rear. In the end, he tosses me at the feet of Red Will and wins my dowry, and I concede. But the audience knows that he only *thinks* he has tamed me for good.

One thing I have always loved about John Ford pictures is the fact that they are full of music. Whether it's the Sons of the Pioneers or the Welsh Singers, you know that eventually someone is going to sing in the movie. I was thrilled on *The Quiet Man* because it was finally my turn. I sang "Young May Moon" in the scene with Barry Fitzgerald, and, of course, "The Isle of Innisfree." I first heard that melody when played by Victor Young at John Ford's home in 1950, and I thought it was beautiful. When we returned from Ireland, John Ford, Charlie Fitz, and I wrote the words that I sang in the movie.

We finished filming in Ireland in early July, and returned to Hollywood to complete the interiors. Half the picture was shot there. Naturally, some of the "Irish Players" had to come back with us, and I was blessed that Charlie and Jimmy were among them. I now had my two brothers living with me in America. The interiors were completed at the end of August, and Mr. Ford went right to work editing his movie. When I went in to see the film at Argosy, Duke was there, having just seen it. I walked into the office and he ran over to me, picked me up, and spun me around. He said, "It's wonderful, and you're wonderful." But Herbert Yates of

Republic had a different reaction. He wanted *The Quiet Man* to be no more than a certain length. Ford's version was more than a few minutes over that, and Yates told him to cut the picture further.

But Ford was far too smart for him. When *The Quiet Man* was previewed to distributors and theater operators at Republic, Mr. Ford instructed the projection operator to stop the projector at the precise length that Yates had requested. Of course, Ford hadn't cut the film at all, and so the screen went black right in the middle of the fight-sequence finale. The audience went wild and demanded that the projector be turned back on. Mr. Ford cued the operator and the fight sequence continued. The audience rose to their feet and cheered when it was over. Old Man Yates wasn't about to touch it after that, and Mr. Ford was allowed to keep his extra minutes.

There is only one fitting way to end our discussion of *The Quiet Man*, and that's with a whisper. No matter what part of the world I'm in, the question I am always asked is: "What did you whisper into John Wayne's ear at the end of *The Quiet Man*?" It was John Ford's idea; it was the ending he wanted. I was told by Mr. Ford exactly what I was to say. At first I refused. I said, "No. I can't. I can't say that to Duke." But Mr. Ford wanted a very shocked reaction from Duke, and he said, "I'm telling you, you *are* to say it." I had no choice, and so I agreed, but with a catch: "I'll say it on one condition—that it is never ever repeated or revealed to anyone." So we made a deal. After the scene was over, we told Duke about our agreement and the three of us made a pact. There are those who claim that they were told and know what I said. They don't and are lying. John Ford took it to his grave—so did Duke—and the answer will die with me. Curiosity about the whisper has become a great part of *The Quiet Man* legend. I have no doubt that as long as the film endures, so will the speculation. *The Quiet Man* meant so much to John Ford, John Wayne, and myself. I know it was their favorite picture too. It bonded us as artists and friends in a way that happens but once in a career. That little piece of *The Quiet Man* belongs to just us, and so I hope you'll understand as I answer:

I'll never tell.

CHAPTER 15

HOLA, ENRIQUE

I was invited to the Mexican Film Festival to receive an award. I had been away from home for most of 1951 and wasn't quite sure I wanted to attend, but Will talked me into going. He had written a new script with Pat Ford called *Mark of the Whip,* and the story was set in Mexico. He and Doc Merman wanted me to accompany them to the festival to help pursue financial backers for the picture. I was still willing to do anything that might help Will have a career and success on his own, so I agreed to go.

We arrived in Mexico City the first week in December, and within hours of checking in at the hotel, Will went looking for a bottle. He disappeared, and I didn't see him again until days later, when the festival was over. His vanishing act left me in the precarious position of attending the festival with his business partners while I tried to save the opportunity for him. I knew all of them from having worked together on *Tripoli*. Doc Merman was with his wife, and Pine-Thomas Productions also came along. We went to the festival without Will, and I smiled and shook hands with everyone they introduced me to. Toward the end of the first day, I received my award at a long presentation ceremony in a theater.

Afterward, we were invited to one of the elegant dinner parties that are always given at these affairs, but we didn't go. Doc, his wife, and I decided to have a quiet dinner at a nice restaurant instead. It was a decision that changed my life forever and began my emotional metamorphosis. During dinner I noticed a man, at a table in the corner of the room, staring at us. I assumed I had been spotted and flashed him one of my warm "star" smiles. He rose and made his way to our table. As he got closer, I realized that I had met the man before, in Hollywood, at another industry event.

He was Miguelito Aleman, the son of Mexican president Miguel Aleman. "Maureen, Maureen, it's nice to see you." I greeted him with the few words I had picked up at the festival: "*Buenos noches,* Miguelito."

We chatted for a bit and I introduced him to Doc and his wife. Then we went over to his table and met a few of his friends. We were all shaking hands with each other when Miguelito said, "Maureen, this is Enrique Parra Hernandez." The gentleman rose and took my hand, holding it warmly. He had a strong yet gracious presence and he looked me squarely in the eye. Enrique Parra made a very favorable first impression. We made small talk and Miguelito played translator and then said, "We're going to a nightclub now. Why don't you join us?" I wasn't up to it, and insisted, "Oh no. I'm so tired. I've got to get to bed." Then Doc said, "Oh, come on. Let's go. Let's get out and see a bit of Mexico." So I caved in and we all went to the nightclub. It was a lovely evening, full of dancing. I got an instant energy burst as soon as I heard the

Latin music, and found myself on the dance floor with Enrique Parra for most of the night.

Later on, I learned from Miguelito that I had spent most of the evening with one of Mexico's most important men. Enrique Parra was a member of President Aleman's most trusted inner circle and held the reins to the nation's banking in his hands. I had danced the night away with Mexico's banking czar.

The next day, Will still hadn't shown up, and we couldn't find him. I was invited to a dinner for the industry that night at Enrique Parra's home and I again went with Doc and Mrs. Merman. It was an eclectic gathering of people, about thirty guests in all, talking about the artistry of the films shown at the festival that year. They discussed every nuance of each performance, the different directing techniques, the best new writers, until I could barely keep my eyes open because of the long day.

Enrique Parra was watching me from his seat with an amused expression as I tried to fight off a narcoleptic episode. He finally came to my rescue and brought with him his friend who owned one of the finest restaurants in all of Mexico City. I was grateful for having been saved, but then found myself in an interesting dilemma: Enrique only spoke Spanish and I only spoke English. We couldn't communicate without help, and so his friend acted as our translator. It was a very different and fun way to get acquainted, because someone else was privy to the entire conversation. Enrique and I really hadn't had much of a conversation the night before, at the nightclub. So we chatted about this and that, our backgrounds, and we eventually got to the subject of religion. I was shocked to find a person who was even more devout a Catholic than I was! Despite Enrique's position in life, his wealth and political power, he was a very down-to-earth man. He was, like me, comfortable in his own skin, and still very much in touch with his roots. His background was Chichimeca Indian. On my way back to the hotel after the evening was over, I tried to recall the last time I had had a more genuine and pleasant conversation with someone. I couldn't remember, it had been so long.

Will finally showed up at the hotel the night before we left and passed out in his room. We returned to Hollywood the following day, where he continued his free fall. His little disappearing act in Mexico had cost him dearly. Price-Merman was over and done with. Despite my best efforts at covering for him at the festival, Doc and William Pine moved quickly to distance themselves from Will as soon as they were back.

Christmas came and I did my best to make it special for Bronwyn, but her father's condition was impossible to conceal. I tried to be jolly and festive, walking through every holiday tradition like a smiling zombie on automatic pilot. My unhappiness was smothering me. Will never showed up that Christmas Day. We waited and waited for him before making the turkey dinner. Charlie Fitz and I finally put the turkey in the oven, but we burned it. Bronwyn was sick to her stomach with the flu. The whole day was awful for everyone. The marriage was over. Four days later, on December 29, 1951—the day of our ten-year wedding anniversary—Will staggered out the front door with a suitcase in his hand, and never came back to live there.

I knew what made him leave. The party was over and Will knew it. His world had changed and was very different once I returned from Ireland. Charlie Fitz and Jimmy were at the house all the time now, and he wouldn't dare treat me the way he had before in front of them. Frankly, I don't believe Will had the guts to face them on a daily basis. When my brothers first moved to Hollywood, I continued to cover for Will and make excuses, as I always had to friends and colleagues. I was embarrassed and afraid of letting my family down. But it was impossible for me to deceive them for long. They knew me far too well, and, given Will's behavior, it was impossible to explain away everything they saw. As I opened up and was truthful with them, I received the support I had not only hoped for, but desperately needed. I should have trusted my family sooner. Charlie and Jimmy were very quick to say, "Get out of this marriage. You can't put up with this. You can't put Bronwyn through this."

That was all I needed. Once I knew my family was behind me, I was committed to divorcing Will. I quickly initiated discussions with my attorney, Lloyd Wright, on how to end the marriage. There were many things to consider, and so I didn't want to rush it. The most important of those issues was custody of Bronwyn and what to offer Will. There were financial issues: How much debt was he in? What were my liabilities? What about alimony? By the first week in January, the plans for my exit were well under way.

That wasn't the only thing in my life that was moving in a positive direction. So was my friendship with Enrique Parra. Shortly after I returned from Mexico, I received a telephone call from a woman who said, "Miss O'Hara, I have Licenciado Parra calling from Mexico City. I'll be your interpreter during the call. Will you accept?" One is always announced by professional title in Mexico and Enrique was a prominent lawyer as well as a politician. I didn't know how he'd found my telephone number, but imagined that with the resources of an entire government at his disposal, it hadn't been difficult. I accepted his call and we had another warm and friendly conversation. Then he called again and then again. Soon we were talking on a weekly basis. I liked talking with Enrique. He was genuinely kind, intelligent, and considerate. It had been so long since a man had shown me attention in such a respectful and gracious way. By the end of January, we were making plans to see each other during his upcoming visit to California in February. I was working on a new picture for Universal and invited him to visit me on the set. His answer surprised me. "That would be great. My son and his friend will be with me and they would love it." I hadn't known he was married. So was I—even though I wouldn't be for long. We were friends and that was great. "Sure," I said. "Bring them along. I'll introduce them to Errol Flynn."

It had been almost ten years since Errol Flynn had made his great under-the-table escape and waved his wicked good-bye to me from the exit. He had been such an awful, naughty scoundrel that night. But by the time we neared wrapping up *Against All Flags*, he had won me over. I respected him professionally and was quite fond of him personally. Father Time was slowly calming his wicked, wicked ways, and deep within that devilish rogue, I found a kind and fragile soul. It was inevitable that Errol and I would work together. He was the undisputed king of the swash-bucklers, still is to this day, and I was their queen.

In *Against All Flags*, set in the 1700s, Errol is once again the danger-loving hero, only now he's trying to infiltrate a pirate stronghold on the island of Madagascar. I'm Spitfire Stevens, the hot-tempered pirate captain who'd rather blow a man's head off than let him get fresh with her. But Flynn's charms make Spitfire swoon, and I help him defeat the ruthless pirate lord played by Tony Quinn.

I enjoyed working with Errol because he was a pro. He always came to work prepared. He rehearsed hard and practiced his fencing sequences very meticulously with Fred Cavens. As you might expect, Flynn was an excellent fencer. He also knew his lines, something I greatly respect in an actor.

Of course, there was one glaring inconsistency with his professionalism. Errol also drank on the set, something I greatly disliked. You couldn't stop him; Errol did whatever he liked. If the director prohibited alcohol on the set, then Errol would inject oranges with booze and eat them during breaks. We worked around his drinking. Everything good that we got on film was shot early in the day. He started gulping his "water" early in the morning and by four P.M. was in no shape to continue filming. It was hard to watch him, very frustrating, but you forgave him because what he had given you earlier in the day had been so terrific. I performed all my romantic close-ups (shot at the end of each day) to an X marked on a black flag that was supposed to be Errol Flynn. A script girl read his lines in a dead, expressionless monotone. It was very difficult to react to her delivery and pretend the flag was Errol Flynn.

Against All Flags made a pot of money for the studio when it was released, and satiated the appetites of hungry swashbuckler fans all over the world. For me, I was flattered when critics said that I had outfenced Errol Flynn!

The day Enrique and his son Quico came to the set, Errol was still in good form and every bit the dashing hero for the boys. With an introduction to Errol, I was in like Flynn with Quico and his friend. Later that night, I joined them for dinner, and thank God the kids spoke English or we would all have spent the evening smiling and nodding. Enrique was marvelous to watch with his son, and Quico adored him. I couldn't help but feel sorry that Bronwyn hadn't been so lucky with her father. I had such a good time that night with Enrique that I almost forgot I was still married. It had been six weeks since I had last heard from Will.

Will had never disappeared without any word for so long, and I was concerned; I had good reason to be. At the end of February, Lloyd Wright delivered the bad news. Will had borrowed heavily from the bank. An entire portfolio of bad investments had put him $300,000 in debt. To make matters worse, these loans had all been taken out in my name. I was advised to end the marriage fast, before he did anything else that was reckless and for which I could be held liable. The papers were being drafted so I could file for divorce in April, but those plans were put on hold when sad news came from Will's father in Mississippi. Will's mother had passed away unexpectedly. Despite all he had put Bronwyn and me through, I couldn't file for divorce. I didn't feel it was right to serve him with divorce papers while he was grieving over the loss of his mother. She was Bronwyn's grandmother and had always been very kind to me. I decided to wait a short but reasonable period of time.

A bit of good news finally came in May when *The Quiet Man* was released in the United States. It was a smash hit. The picture was already doing magnificently abroad, and American audiences loved it so much, you could barely get into the theaters. The critics raved about it, loving everything. I was even getting good reviews, and for my performance! (Though one critic, the bloody bastard, did say that it took the likes of John Ford to drag a good performance out of me.) I was being congratulated everywhere I went, and for the first time in my career, Oscar talk was in the air. It was a very exciting time.

Unfortunately, I was already working on another western stink-eroo called *The Redhead from Wyoming,* for Universal. It was disappointing to be working on such a lousy picture while I was receiving praise for such a highly regarded piece of filmmaking. Then I was injured on the set when an extra fired a prop gun too close to me during a gunfight scene. I had powder burns on my neck and shoulders and under my arm. I was rushed to the studio hospital for first aid and to scrub the chemical powder off so it didn't permanently stain my skin.

I was sent home early that day and had an eerie feeling the minute I entered the house. It was one of those natural-instinct moments that tells you something isn't right or as it should be. Worry washed over me. Something told me to go upstairs and check the secret closet that was hidden within my large closet in the master suite. I used it as a safe for my favorite jewelry and most important documents. I had just been in it that morning and knew that everything was as it should be. Now, something had changed. I knew it.

I rushed upstairs and unlocked the door that led to my bedroom. I went to the master closet and unlocked its door. I opened it, turned on the light, and unlocked the door to my small hidden closet. As I opened it and peered inside, what I saw chilled me to the bone. A piece of paper had been placed, clearly in sight, for me to find. It was what was on the page that freaked me out—shamrocks doodled in green pencil. I had seen shamrocks like these once before. I knew their source immediately. I had seen them doodled in the same green pencil on the bottom of some of the letters sent to Herself by John Ford. Somehow John Ford had been in my house that day. He had been in my bedroom and in my most private and secret place. How could he get into my home without being seen? How could he get through the locks? Easy. Rear Admiral John Ford knew plenty of men who could get him in anywhere. It not only gave me the creeps, it positively terrified me.

I never confronted Ford with it. I never confronted him about anything. I was afraid to. I never knew what he might do or what the repercussions might be. I also didn't want to give him the satisfaction of seeing me react to the manipulative things he did to me. I always felt that saying nothing would drive him absolutely crazy, and that was consolation enough. But I had noticed a change in the way Ford acted toward me after we returned home from Ireland and finished *The Quiet Man*. He was more distant, and started giving me the mean and nasty treatment he usually reserved for others. The bonds of our Irishness seemed to be melting away, and I could sense an odd sort of resentment.

I decided to go see him and share with him the good cheer surrounding the success of *The Quiet Man.* I wanted to assess the situation. When I arrived a few days later at Argosy, on the Republic lot, the first thing I did was ask Meta Sterne, "How's the old man doing today?" Meta was frank, as usual. "I don't think you should go in there, Maureen," she began. "Himself is mad as hell with you. Has been for weeks now. What did you do?" I couldn't answer her. I hadn't a clue. We had been on good terms the last time I'd seen him. "I don't know, but you know Pappy, it could be anything or nothing at all. I guess I'm about to find out."

Meta put up the warning sign. "I don't know if I would go in there if I were you. He might just throw you out." This was silly. I had to get in to see if the rift was real. "I know what I'll do," I began. "I'll open the door to his office and toss my hat inside. If he throws it back out, I'll know I'm really in the barrel. If he doesn't, then I'll go in and see him." Meta liked the idea, so I slowly opened his door and tossed my hat into his office. I waited ten seconds and then twenty, thirty, forty, all the way up to a minute. It didn't come back out, so I opened the door and entered.

Pappy was sitting behind his desk with his back to me, talking on the phone. It was Mary, and they were discussing wedding plans. He waved me in without turning to me. On May 31, Ford's daughter, Barbara, was about to marry Ken Curtis, one of the Sons of the Pioneers, and I knew Pappy wasn't thrilled about it. I had been with them on the *Araner* the day Ford refused to let Ken aboard. Pappy was being awful to him and Mary pleaded with me, "You go and talk to him. Please. Barbara really likes Ken and I don't want Jack to spoil things for her." Of course I couldn't say no to Mary, so I spoke to Ford. He hemmed and hawed but finally acquiesced. Mary later gave me a beautiful gold Virgin of Guadalupe medallion for persuading him to be nice to Ken.

My eyes surveyed Pappy's office while he continued speaking

with Mary. My attention turned to the many photographs Pappy had displayed on his wall, people he had worked with and admired—Duke, Cagney, Fonda, and others. Then I realized that out of the dozen or so that were there, one picture had been turned around to face the wall, as if banished. I peered over while his back was still to me and looked at whose picture it was. My jaw fell; it was a photograph of me.

Pappy slammed the phone down and finally turned to me. He studied me for a moment, assessing my demeanor. I remained poised and he leaned back in his chair. "This wedding thing for Barbara is turning into a goddamn circus. You coming?" I nodded. "Well, I hope the damn thing works out for her this time," he added. Barbara had already been married once, to actor Robert Walker, but it lasted only a few months. "Not like that capon son of a bitch. He can't do anything right." I knew Ford was referring unkindly to his son, Pat. He always called him that and it always bothered me. A capon is a castrated cock—what a horrible thing to say about his own son. Pappy was still furious about Pat's divorce because there were kids involved. To John Ford, a real man does what he has to do and lives up to his responsibilities. I didn't respond to his remark and changed the conversation.

"The reviews are great. Looks like we have a shot at some Oscars." Ford rolled his eyes, signaling indifference. "I don't give a shit about that. Listen, I'm lining up a picture in London with Brian Hurst and Michael Killanin. It's for you and Duke, *The Demi Gods*. I'm looking to start around October, so keep that open." I nodded, but didn't commit. Meta buzzed him; it was Mary again and so I said good-bye and left.

On my way back from the office, I was troubled by the whole experience. Why was my picture turned around? I knew then that my read on the whole situation in Ireland might have been wrong. Was he still harboring some fantasies about me, and was he now angry that nothing had come of it? Or was this also part of his creative process? The separation and detachment from his Mary Kate now that the film was done and his story had been told? I didn't know which it was, but I suspected that the issue wasn't behind me. I knew that when angered, whether for a real reason or in his own head, John Ford could hold a mean and nasty grudge. I didn't know then, but I was soon to learn just how miserable and spiteful that experience could be.

Despite my concerns about Ford, I was happy. The truth is, I was happier than I had been in over a decade. I had been spending a great deal of time with Enrique Parra. My friendship with him was blossoming into something very beautiful and serious. Neither of us had set out to fall in love with each other when we met, but fate was leading us there. My falling in love with Enrique Parra happened over time, as I came to know and care about him in a more intimate way. I think at first I was just so happy to be included in his life and have him show a sincere interest in mine. Will and I might have shared the same house, but we lived completely separate lives our entire marriage. When I was with Enrique, we were inseparable. It felt so good to be cared about and fussed over by a man I was attracted to and truly interested in. For the first time in so very long, I felt alive again.

Enrique came to visit me often in Hollywood and became friends with my brothers and sisters. Margo and Florrie were now living in North America with their husbands. They all liked and respected Enrique. I had become friends with President Aleman and had even hosted a party in my Bel Air home in his honor when he and Enrique were in Hollywood on business. Still, I was navigating in uncharted waters. I was in a relationship with a married man, and legally I was still a married woman.

I decided to hire a private detective to make sure that what

Enrique had told me about his wife was true. He had assured me that they were no longer in love—hadn't been for years—and that she had a boyfriend of her own. I believed him, but had to be certain. I could never have continued with the relationship if they were happily married, especially when there were children involved. Everything checked out. My detective followed Enrique's wife all around Mexico and told me that she had a boyfriend who was a bullfighter. Enrique and his wife's marriage was one of financial convenience and nothing more.

We decided to move carefully and discreetly until both of us could get free. There were other people involved, spouses and children, whose feelings deserved to be carefully considered. We also decided not to comment publicly about our relationship, so I remained quiet. There was no question as to what the outcome would be, however. We agreed that when the right time came, Enrique and I would be married.

At the end of June, I placed two transatlantic telephone calls. The first was to Will, in London. I told him I was leaving him and agreed, on the advice of my lawyer, to pay off the $300,000 debt he owed. He agreed to the divorce. The second call was to Daddy and Mammy, in Dublin. It was the conversation I had feared and dreaded for ten years. I told them the truth about everything, and they showered me with their love. All they wanted for me was my happiness and what was best for Bronwyn. I not only had their permission, they felt leaving Will was the right thing to do. On July 1, 1952, I legally filed for divorce from William Houston Price on grounds of incompatibility, and sought full custody of our daughter. I issued the following brief statement to the press:

Today I have filed for divorce from my husband, Will Price. He will be better off without me. He wants to make pictures and has a chance in England. He is an excellent director and I wouldn't hesitate to work for him.

The divorce was final one month later, on August 5. As part of a private settlement, I received full custody of Bronwyn and Will agreed to pay $50 a month in child support. I got the house, two cars, a few municipal bonds, and the life insurance policy, all of which I had paid for. I also agreed to pay him alimony. All I really wanted was Bronwyn's happiness and safety. I would have walked away from everything else if I had to in order to be free. And I was free at last. My ten-year nightmare had finally come to an end . . . or so I thought.

By October, I was going to Mexico City on a regular basis to be with Enrique. I would usually spend anywhere from one to three weeks at a time there, and I was quickly learning the language. In the beginning, Bronwyn and I stayed at the Hotel Continental, but very soon in the relationship, we moved into one of Enrique's homes in the Paseo de la Reforma, close to the statue of Independence. It was a lovely three-story home with the formal Mexico City architecture that I love so much. Enrique still maintained a large home with his wife, though they had separate quarters, and whenever I was in Mexico City, he stayed with me.

I always took Bronwyn with me to Mexico. She was in school now, so I made arrangements with an American school there for her to attend whenever we were in Mexico City. She started making friends there and was soon enjoying her new life, exploring a wonderful foreign culture.

The truth is, everyone in Mexico City knew about us. Enrique was well known and so was I. We were accepted and recognized as the loving couple that we were. After several months together, I was even invited to meet Enrique's mother. He took Bronwyn and me to her home and the entire Parra family was there. Enrique's mother was quite ill, and we all gathered around her bed and spoke to her. She was warm, charming like her son, and kind. After a while together, she asked me to kneel and then blessed me and my relationship with her son. From that moment on, Bronwyn and I were family.

My life with Enrique was a simple one. Enrique and I spent our time together playing golf every day, though I wasn't very good, and having lovely meals together afterward. We walked to the local shops, holding hands, and talking to the people we knew on the streets. I started doing the things for him that all wives do for their husbands: making his doctors' appointments, making sure his suits were cleaned, taking Quico and his friends here and there. I think what I loved most about my life with Enrique was that he made me feel needed. He came to rely on me as part of his daily life, not as a meal ticket, like Will had made me feel. Everyone who knew Enrique had always relied on him. I think I was the first person in his life whom Enrique felt he could rely on.

We were very happy together, but Enrique was experiencing difficulty in ending his marriage. There was a lot at stake financially, but there was more to it than that. In addition to a son, Enrique also had a daughter, Negrita, and she was the apple of his eye. Negrita did not approve of me or of my relationship with her father. In all the years I was with Enrique, I never met her. She was very close to her mother. Complicating the matter, Negrita was very ill with diabetes and frequently slipped into diabetic comas. Enrique was frantic, and always seemed to be rushing to and from the hospital. Though he never said it to me, I am certain that Enrique was fearful of what a divorce might do to Negrita and to her health.

Despite the frustration of not being able to get married right away, everything was going smoothly until John and Mary Ford rattled the hornet's nest. While they were in London, they had had dinner with Will and told him that Bronwyn and I had moved to Mexico and that I was living in sin with Enrique. Will accused me of trying to keep him away from his daughter, in violation of our divorce agreement. He said he was happy that I had met someone, but then dropped a possible threat by mentioning Ingrid Bergman and the Pia Lindström scandal. In 1949, Ingrid had gone to Italy to film *Stromboli* with director Roberto Rossellini. She fell in love with Rossellini and left her husband for him. Unfortunately, she also left her daughter, Pia. The public was outraged at what she had done, and so was Hollywood. The scandal hurt Bergman's career for years, and it never fully recovered from it. Will was suggesting that he might be willing to cause the same kind of trouble for me.

In February 1953, I was making a second picture with Jeff Chandler, one called *War Arrow*. Jeff was a real sweetheart, but acting with him was like acting with a broomstick. Meanwhile, Oscar buzz was everywhere. The Academy was getting ready to make their formal nominations for the previous year (1952). Many of my friends and colleagues seemed to think I had a real shot at being nominated for my work in *The Quiet Man*.

The night the Academy committee was meeting to make the formal nominations, I had a set of ears in the meeting. Anne Baxter was a friend and a fellow client of my publicity agent, Jean Pettibone. Anne was a member of the Academy committee and promised Jean and me that she would call us when the nominations had been made. We waited anxiously by the phone all night. Imagine our excitement when Anne finally called and said, "Maureen, you're in. You've been nominated." We were so thrilled that we stayed up the rest of the night so we could get the first edition of the newspaper to read about my nomination. But when the paper hit the streets that morning, I was surprised and disappointed to see that I hadn't been nominated.

Jean placed a call to Anne right away and asked her what had happened. She told me, "Maureen, you were genuinely nominated. I don't know how or who knocked you out of the box. I had to leave about a half hour before the meeting was over." *The Quiet Man* had been nominated for a total of seven Academy Awards, but my name was not among them. I was heartbroken but never told anyone what Anne had told us. A month later, at the twenty-fifth annual Academy Awards, John Ford won his fifth Oscar as best director, for *The Quiet Man.* Winton Hoch and Archie Stout also won for best cinematography. A few days after the awards ceremony, Meta Sterne called. The old man wanted to see me. As I entered his office, Ford threw a small white box with a ribbon on it at me and said, "Here! That's for what they stole from you." I opened it to find a gold bracelet inside. Hanging from it was a little gold Oscar statuette. I knew instantly that if what Anne Baxter had told me was true, it had been John Ford himself who had knocked me out of the box.

For the remainder of 1953, I was a woman on the move. Enrique and I were splitting our time pretty evenly between Hollywood and Mexico City. I sold the big house on Stone Canyon Road and bought a far lovelier and more sensible home on Somma Way for Bronwyn and me. Life was full of change, but we were at peace. As the end of the year approached, I boarded a plane and flew to Spain to make another escapist picture, *Fire over Africa*, for Columbia Pictures. We shot all the exteriors there and the interiors in London. But very soon, the industry tabloid *Confidential* magazine would claim that I was somewhere else altogether, and I would find myself at the center of one of the most important and publicized scandals in Hollywood history.

CHAPTER 16

THE LONG GRAY LINE

hatever you do, stay away from the old man after dark. Stay with us." That's what the stuntmen in the Ford stock company told my brother Jimmy when I was making The Long Gray Line in early 1954. If there was one thing you could predict when working with John Ford, it was that he would be completely unpredictable on a picture.

The Long Gray Line is the true story of an athletic trainer at West Point who spends fifty years molding that long, gray line of cadets. The picture was originally cast with Duke in the leading role of Marty Maher, but Columbia recast it when he was held up shooting another movie. Mr. Ford was reviewing his casting options when I dropped discreet hints that Tyrone Power would be perfect for the role. Ty was eventually cast, with me playing his wife, Mary O'Donnell. Donald Crisp, Ward Bond, Robert Francis, Harry Carey Jr., and Betsy Palmer rounded out the cast. My brother Jimmy played a young cadet. All the exteriors were shot on location at West Point and the interiors were filmed in Hollywood on the Columbia lot.

This was the fourth picture I'd made with John Ford, and it was by far the most difficult. I knew the dos and don'ts. I knew about being in the barrel. I expected some unpleasantness that he would surely throw my way, but I never—EVER—expected his cruelty and the grief he was about to put me through. Our relationship had changed. There was anger toward me and it was revealing itself in all its ugliness.

Mr. Ford greeted me out loud every day on the set with, "Well, did Herself have a good shit this morning?" Then he would ask the crew, "How is Herself's mood today?" If they said, "Oh, she's in a great mood," he would respond, "Hell, then we're going to have a horrible day." If they said, "She's in an awful, bad mood," he would say, "Wonderful. Today is going to be great." He would do it in front of the entire cast and crew, including me, as if I weren't there at all.

Between takes and scenes, Mr. Ford hurried me along by shouting, "Come on! Move that big ass of yours." He was delighted with insulting me in front of everybody.

He had never before treated me so consistently rudely on a picture. It was a constant barrage of degrading insults and snide remarks. I found myself in the barrel from day one and didn't know why. Usually, if you were in the barrel, you eventually got out to make room for someone else who had rubbed him the wrong way. Not on this picture. The barrel was mine and mine alone.

In the past, anything that Mr. Ford dished out I had always taken on the chin, without flinching. I prided myself on not letting him know he had gotten to me. I lost my cool on *The Quiet Man*, but even that was done in a humorous way, and I was really more frustrated than anything else. On *The Long Gray Line*, I was angry, and no matter how hard I tried to hide it, I'm sure Mr. Ford knew I was at my breaking point. He caused me to snap the day Duke came to visit the set.

Mr. Ford refused to allow Duke and me to talk to each other, even though we were only a few feet apart. We couldn't say a single word to each other. He forbade it and told us, "You are not to talk. You are not to speak." So we had to sit there and maintain this incredibly awkward silence while Mr. Ford chewed and tugged on his kerchief, relishing being such a bastard.

It was the last straw. I thought, That's it, I've had it. I'm not taking any more of this. I was going to walk off the picture. The only reason I didn't walk right there and then was because there was a scene I had wanted to play from the moment I'd read the script, and it hadn't been shot yet. It was the very next scene we were scheduled to shoot. I'd be damned if the old bastard was going to drive me off the picture before I played that scene. It's fitting that it was my death scene. I had been agonizing over how I was going to play it, and I worried about it for weeks. Then it came to me the night before I was scheduled to do it. I thought, Well, I'll just die. That's all. I won't do anything. I'll just go in there and die. So I wanted to perform that death scene very much.

I did the scene just as I'd planned. I just closed my eyes and died. When I was finished and Mr. Ford yelled, "Cut," Ty broke down sobbing and I knew I had nailed it. I was very satisfied with it and ready to now walk off the picture. I felt bad for Ty, but I couldn't put up with any more of Mr. Ford's cruelty. But the old man was a master at monitoring the vital signs on his set. He knew he had pushed me too far. He knew I was going to walk off the picture. And he was ready for it. Right after my death scene was over, Mr. Ford stood up and demanded the attention of the entire cast and crew. He called them from every corner. Everyone was standing around the set now. It was all very serious. Mr. Ford never did this. It made me wonder, What is he up to now? It was vintage Ford dramatics. Raising his hands for effect, Ford said, "Ladies and gentlemen, if you want better acting than that . . . find it." And then he walked off the set as the entire crew burst into applause. I bought it and thought, Aw, isn't he sweet and kind? What a remarkable compliment. And so I stayed and finished the picture. The old son of a bitch had won again.

I had a few theories about why he was such a bastard on that picture, but all of them led to one simple conclusion: John Ford was punishing me. I wanted to know why. What had I done? Was it for not having the same feelings that he had expressed to me in all of those letters? Was he jealous of my friendship with Duke? Angry that I divorced Will, against his advice? Was it because of Enrique?

Ford himself had given me all the clues I needed in his office at Columbia weeks before we'd started shooting *The Long Gray Line.* It started gradually. The first clue came the day I went in to discuss my costume tests. As I walked in and stood at his desk, Ford was drawing on a pad in front of him while he spoke. Penises. He was drawing hundreds of penises on the pad, in front of me. Big ones and small ones. Thin ones and fat ones. Penises of every size and shape. It was a curious preoccupation that started to make me feel uncomfortable because he was being so precise and diligent. I refused to look down at them, pretending to take no notice. I knew he wanted me to look at them, but I just stood there and kept my eyes up and forward while he spoke and continued to draw. It must have burned him up that I refused to acknowledge what he was doing. I thought it was strange, but dismissed his odd behavior as an attempt to shock me. We finished our conversation and then I left him there to continue with his doodling.

What I saw a few days later couldn't be dismissed that easily. I went to Ford's office to show him the revised sketches for my wardrobe. My arms full of the sketches, I walked into his office without knocking and could hardly believe my eyes. Ford had his arms around another man and was kissing him. I was shocked and speechless. I quickly dropped the sketches on the floor, then knelt down to pick them up. I fumbled around slowly and kept my head down. I took my time so they could part and compose themselves. They were on opposite sides of the room in a flash. The gentleman Ford was with was one of the most famous leading men in the picture business. He addressed a few pleasantries to me, which were forced and awkward, then quickly left. Ford and I went on with our business. Not a word was said, and I played it out as if I hadn't seen a thing.

Later, that actor approached me and asked, "Why didn't you tell me John Ford was homosexual?" I answered, "How could I tell you something I knew nothing about?"

John Ford's sexuality wasn't any of my business. What I saw did surprise me, though. By this time, I thought of him as part of John and Mary Ford the married unit. I knew there were warts and blemishes on the surface of their relationship, but down deep, at the core, I thought they were content and even happy. Yet there were signals I'd never bothered to think too much about: the separate bedrooms, his insulting her, the periodic drinking, and the lack of outward affection they showed to each other. I now believe there was a conflict within Ford and that it caused him great pain and turmoil.

These kinds of desires were something John Ford could readily accept in others, but never in himself. He saw himself as a man's man. He was a military hero and the compadre of rugged stuntmen. He was also too immersed in the teachings of Catholicism. He would have seen it as a terrible sin.

Feelings for another man were something he would never be able to embrace. I recalled one of the letters he had sent to me while I was in Australia. There was a passage or a prayer in one that at the time confused me, but now seems much clearer. He wrote:

> *Father—I love my man dearly*
> *I love him above my own life*
> *But, Father—my soul hurts me—*
> *I've never been in the same bed with him—*
> *And I want him heaven knows—*
> *Father, dear—what shall I do—*
> *Oh what shall I do?*

I wonder if John Ford was struggling with conflicts within himself. These conflicts were manifested as anger toward me, his family, his friends, his heroes, and most of all, himself. His fantasies and crushes on women like me, Kate Hepburn, Anna Lee, and Murph Doyle—all of whom he professed love for at one time or another—were just balm for this wound. He hoped each of us could save him from these conflicted feelings, but was later forced to accept that none of us could. I believe this ultimately led to my punishment and his downward spiral into an increased reliance on alcohol.

I obviously wasn't the only one who figured this out, or the stuntmen wouldn't have given Jimmy that cautionary warning. Something had obviously happened in the past and they knew what it was, but they could never betray him.

I also believe that this is why Ford advised me to stay with Will. His fantasies were more real to him if he thought I was an unhappy woman trapped in an awful marriage. Once I was free and had fallen in love with Enrique, that was all shattered, and his anger and resentment surfaced. Ford even started picking apart my friendship with Duke. He began implying that there might be some kind of romantic interest between us. From out of nowhere he said to me, "Oh, you don't want to have anything to do with Duke. He's got a penis this big," and then lifted his little finger. I replied, "Pappy, I'm not interested in Duke that way and he's not interested in me. You know that." As that friendship grew, Ford seemed to feel more and more threatened by it.

But one of the most telling signs of Ford's growing anger came during a meeting at Columbia Pictures shortly after we finished filming *The Long Gray Line*. I was not in attendance, but my brother Charlie Fitz was. Charlie was now working for Ford and Merian C. Cooper at Argosy. The meeting included production head Jerry Wald and the publicity staff. They were discussing publicity for the picture and my participation in it when Ford said to Charlie, "Well, if that whore sister of yours can pull herself away from that Mexican long enough to do a little publicity for us, the film might have a chance at some decent returns."

Charlie was outraged and stood up in the middle of the meeting to take Ford on. "You take that back," he warned. "You don't say things like that about my sister." The meeting grew very uncomfortable, but Charlie wouldn't back down. He stood up for me until he forced Ford to apologize. That's the kind of man Charlie was. There aren't many in the picture business who would risk their entire careers by confronting a giant like John Ford, even by defending their sister's honor.

Ford knew he had been outclassed and that he was wrong. A few days later, his Buick pulled up in front of the house. When Charlie Fitz opened the door, Ford said, "Charlie, I've come here to shake the hand of the only honest man I know." The two shook hands and Ford climbed back in his car and left.

Still, John and Mary Ford made it no secret that they did not approve of Enrique. In all the years we were together, they never once invited him to their house for dinner, nor were they even willing to meet him. When I went to have my hair done at the Westmore Beauty Salon, the manager told me that Mary Ford had been there a few days before. When he asked her if she had seen me and how I was doing, her answer shocked him. She said, "Oh her? She's living with a black man now."

It was clear that John Ford was going through changes and that they were terrible ones. They would continue to damage our relationship in the years ahead in ways that could never be fully repaired. In the beginning, while making *How Green Was My Valley,* our relationship seemed like a bright and rosy path leading to wondrous things. In many ways, it did. But as it started to unravel, it grew ugly, and I realized that we were traveling down a long gray line of our own.

I made two more pictures in 1954, but neither was great. I made *Lady Godiva* for Universal. Though the studio enjoyed the publicity benefits of closing the set during the famous horseback ride, I was not in the nude, as the studio claimed to the press. I wore a full-length body leotard and underwear that was concealed by my long tresses. An unexpected pleasure on the film was watching a promising young actor named Clint Eastwood cut his teeth on it. I knew he'd go far. Critics hit the film hard. At the end of the year, I was back in Mexico making *The Magnificent Matador* with Tony Quinn for 20th Century-Fox. Critics disliked it also, and found it dull. I wasn't surprised. Even the people of Mexico seemed bored while we were filming. A bullfight sequence was shot and they booed it because the matadors didn't actually kill the bulls. Of course we didn't. We would have had to kill a bull for every take. It was a ludicrous criticism.

For several years, I had been bouncing from studio to studio, and I hated it. In December, I negotiated a five-picture contract, at $85,000 per movie, at Columbia Pictures with studio boss

Harry Cohn. Cohn was known as a tough and hard-nosed businessman, a man without a heart, but I didn't think that at all. I'll never forget the day Cohn sent for me to come to the studio. I wondered, What have I done now? Is he mad at me? When I walked into his office, he greeted me with "Sit down," which I did. "I'd like you to stay with me this afternoon." I agreed in a way that asked what I really wanted to know, which was "Why?" Then Cohn told me, "Maureen, you're one of the few people I know who understands Judaism and Catholicism, how a Jew thinks and how a Catholic thinks. I'd like you to stay with me because you will know what this means to me as a Jew." I listened intently because I could see and hear how serious he was. "Today, my wife and sons are converting to Catholicism. Please stay with me." Cohn loved Judaism as much as I love Catholicism. I knew he was heartbroken and I was very touched that he wanted to share this personal moment with me. I sat with him and looked on as he kept checking his watch. Then tears started rolling down his cheeks. Finally he said softly, "Well, it's over now. It's done. You can go." Cohn kissed me on both cheeks and thanked me. I've never forgotten it.

As 1955 rolled in, I was once again asked to be emcee at the Hollywood Foreign Press Awards, being held in Coconut Grove. That year, Marlon Brando was also nominated for an Academy Award for his performance in *On the Waterfront*. Marlon wasn't Hollywood's favorite, not by a long shot. Hollywood disliked him, disliked his character, his attitude, everything about him. Their dislike was so vitriolic and nasty. Hollywood was going to make sure he didn't win the Oscar. It made me mad as hell. I thought, Wait a minute. The Academy Award is supposed to be for excellence in performance. It is not a popularity contest. I couldn't keep my mouth shut. After I handed out the awards, I spoke to an audience full of the most influential people in the picture business. I said:

Ladies and gentlemen, now that the awards have been presented this evening, there is something I feel very strongly about and that I would like to share with you. It has always been my understanding that the Academy Awards are for acting ability and not for one's popularity. This year, there is a young man up for the best actor Oscar and the vitriol against him is so horrible that he hasn't got a chance of winning if it is only about who likes whom best in this business. Frankly, I think this young man has given the most remarkable performance of the year and that he deserves it. I hope when you're voting this year you remember that.

Marlon won the Hollywood Foreign Press Award that night and the Oscar a few months later. Lew Wasserman and MCA were thrilled, because they represented him. Lew said, "You got Marlon the Academy Award." I didn't, of course; Marlon's performance earned him the award. But I might have given the voters the right push when they needed it. Shortly after the Academy Awards ceremony, the most beautiful potted roses arrived at the house. They were from Marlon and his representatives at MCA. I planted them in front of the house and each one took. I called them the Marlon Brando roses. Most of them are still there and doing well.

I was also still walking a long gray line with Will. He was back in Hollywood, wanting to spend time with Bronwyn. The terms of our divorce allowed him to see her on a regular basis, but he was inconsistent at best. He'd often show up late to pick her up or not show up at all. He rarely called to speak with her. She was very confused. His drinking was the reason, of course, but his alcoholism had never before put her in harm's way. That changed the day Will agreed to pick up Bronwyn and a friend from school. I received a distressed phone call from the Fords. Will had dropped the girls off there and I needed to come and get them right away because they were terrified.

They were supposed to spend a nice day together, but Will had shown up at the school very drunk. He put the two girls in the car and then got behind the wheel, heading for John Ford's house. The trip was reportedly more hair-raising than a roller coaster ride. He swerved across the lines, nearly veered off the road, and almost bashed into a large tram. Bronwyn was so traumatized that she had to be put in Barbara Ford's bed to calm down. By the time I got there, she had wet the bed in fright.

Without the financial support I had provided for years, Will was becoming more and more unstable and desperate. One evening, he showed up at the house very late and drunk as a skunk. Bronwyn and I were in Mexico, but Charlie Fitz was there and showed him the door.

Before he left, though, Will did express his dissatisfaction with the fact that Bronwyn was spending so much time in Mexico City with Enrique and me. If our ten years together had taught me anything, it was that Will would be willing to use Bronwyn as a pawn in any way necessary to get what he wanted.

CHAPTER 17

SCANDALOUS

On June 20, 1955, Will filed a petition in the Superior Court of Los Angeles suing me for custody of Bronwyn. In his petition, he charged that I was openly consorting and living with Enrique Parra, that I was immoral and no longer a fit and proper person to have custody of our daughter. Three days later, I filed a countersuit asking the court to prevent Will from seeing Bronwyn unless it was under strict court supervision. I charged that he had been grossly intoxicated in front of her and had endangered her health, safety, and life. It was an awful mess. Will said he wanted Bronwyn, but I knew he really wanted money. I wanted Bronwyn safe, so I dug my heels in and got ready for the fight.

It got very ugly and nasty and was all over the papers. There is nothing worse than having your personal problems become somebody else's entertainment. I received a great deal of support from so many, including one very courageous man whom I have never forgotten. I was in a market near Schwab's Drug Store on Sunset Boulevard when he approached me.

"Excuse me, Miss O'Hara. There's something I think you need to know. It's about your ex-husband."

"Yes, what is it?" I asked.

"We know all about him and what he does. We don't want that cocksucking bastard to get your child."

That was an expression I had never heard before and hoped I would never hear again. The man was a very obvious homosexual and was telling me that he knew Will had been with men. I later had it confirmed from a trusted friend that Will and Brian Desmond Hurst were more than just friends.

I was in a state of shock as the man continued. "We know him. We know what he is and are willing to testify to it in court for you."

That was a remarkably kind offer. In the 1950s, homosexuality was still hidden deep in one's closet.

I asked him, "But don't you know that testifying could put you in jeopardy?"

"We don't care," he went on. "We think so much of you that we want to stop this man from hurting you and your daughter."

I've never forgotten the generosity of his offer, but I couldn't let him do it. I settled with Will one year later. He received no money, but I got a retraction of his charges. I settled because if I had continued with it, Bronwyn would have been the only one to suffer. I was willing to face the papers and the fire, but I couldn't put her through it.

Shortly after that, I received a call from Darryl Zanuck: "Maureen, I've just cast you as Anna in the film version of *The King and I*." I could hardly see straight. I had dreamed of singing in a serious musical from the time I started in motion pictures. As I told Zanuck how great a job I intended to do in the picture, he slowed me down. "Wait a minute. I'm sending Lew Schreiber to New York to see Rodgers and Hammerstein tomorrow with some sample records of your voice," he continued. "They have final casting approval, but it should just be a formality." Lew called me from the airport and asked me to wish him luck, which I did repeatedly. But Rodgers and Hammerstein refused to listen to my records. I was told when Lew returned to Hollywood that when Rodgers and Hammerstein heard my name pass his lips, they exclaimed, "Our Anna . . . played by a pirate queen? Never!" Rodgers and Hammerstein called me a pirate queen! Ouch—it still hurts. I was out and Deborah Kerr was in. Studio songbird Marni Nixon dubbed her singing voice in the film.

In December, I made my only picture of 1955. *Lisbon* was a Republic melodrama full of mystery, international intrigue, and murder. For the first time in my career, I got to play the villain, and Bette Davis was right—bitches *are* fun to play. Welsh-born Oscar winner Ray Milland not only starred in the picture, but directed and produced it as well. *Lisbon* was the first Hollywood picture ever filmed in Portugal and we took just thirty days to shoot it in CinemaScope. The plot involves an adventure operator (Milland) who has been using his powerboat as a vehicle for smuggling. He is hired by a crooked international financier (played by Claude Rains) to rescue an American held for ransom behind the Iron Curtain. I play the American's scheming wife who wants him back—but dead—so she can get her hands on his fortune.

Before we got started, Herb Yates and Milland thought filming in Portugal was going to be a cakewalk. They were wrong; it was nothing but trouble. Still, we did manage to finish the film in thirty days, and I was back home by the middle of January. I went right into costume testing for my next picture. *Friendly*

Persuasion was to star me opposite Gary Cooper and was the story of a family of Indiana Quakers in the 1800s who are forced to choose between their peaceful ways and fighting Southern troops to save their town. I couldn't wait to work with Cooper because he was my kind of tough leading man. I knew our chemistry together on-screen could be real dynamite, but unfortunately I never got to make the picture.

The day before we were set to begin shooting, I went to see John Ford about a film he wanted me to make with Duke, in August. When I arrived at his office, I told Meta Sterne how excited I was to be working with Cooper. She knew Ford's attitude toward me had changed and warned me, "Whatever you do, don't say a word about it to the old man. Don't tell him a thing about anything you are going to do. Don't discuss it, and keep your mouth shut." I thought, Well, I've already shot the wardrobe and hair tests and we're going to start actual shooting tomorrow, so what does it matter? So I walked into Ford's office and stupidly told him about the picture.

When I got back home from his office, the phone was already ringing. It was my agent. He was in a panic and demanded to know, "Maureen, what happened? You're out of the movie." I was stunned. I said, "I don't know. Everything was fine when I was at the studio." I was devastated and called Meta at Ford's office to see what she knew. She said, "Maureen, I warned you and begged you to keep your mouth shut and not tell the old man, and now look what you've done." Ford had picked up the telephone as soon as I left his office and torpedoed me. I was out and Dorothy McGuire was in.

My consolation prize was a lousy comedy for Universal with John Forsythe called *Everything But the Truth.* The story is about a fourth-grade schoolboy (Tim Hovey) who, after learning a lesson in class about truth and honesty, reveals to the public that his uncle paid a kickback to the mayor. The truth is, the movie was so bad our own families didn't see it, and neither did I.

John was wonderful to work with, though, and every bit the dashing gentleman he still is today. Little Tim Hovey, on the other hand, was a monster. He terrorized everyone on the set nonstop, all day long. By the end of the first week, my nerves were so shot that I finally snapped when the little bastard sneaked up behind me and jabbed a long, sharp hatpin into my rear end. I chased that kid all over the set until I caught him. I threw him over my knee and gave him the spanking of his life. His mother was on the set and rushed over in a panic, but I turned to her with fire in my eyes and said, "Don't you say a word, because I'm not stopping!" She backed away slowly, with a faint smile on her face, and watched me give him the licking that she secretly wanted to give him herself.

Despite all the horrible things John Ford had done to me, I reported happily to the set of *The Wings of Eagles* in August 1956. I was working with Duke, Ward Bond, and that mean old son of a bitch, and it was good to be home again. The film was the true story of an old friend of John Ford, Frank "Spig" Wead, a naval aviator who later became a Hollywood screenwriter after breaking his back in a nasty fall. Duke played Spig and I played his wife, Millie. In a comic turn, Ward Bond played the cantankerous director John Dodge, a spoof on John Ford himself. The picture gave Duke and me some wonderful dramatic scenes, although much of my best work was left on the cutting-room floor. Millie Wead had slipped into alcoholism later in life, but, at the request of her children, Mr. Ford cut that wonderfully dramatic footage out of the picture. The edited picture was good, but not vintage Ford. Something was missing. Perhaps that old magic—the Ford-Wayne-O'Hara fire—was hard to recapture given all that had happened among us. I never worked with John Ford again.

• • •

Charles Laughton told me early in my career, "They are going to say a lot of untrue things about you, so never forget, today's newspaper is tomorrow's toilet paper." He knew from experience that the pursuit of stars by the media is a practice as old as movies themselves. Fans are drawn to stars by images of us attending spectacular events, dressed in beautiful clothes and expensive jewelry, stepping out of limousines, posing in front of flashing cameras. Well, of course we don't live our lives like that. In the days of the studios, such appearances were carefully orchestrated to pack a glamorous wallop. Yet, in a strange way, these images kept fans and stars apart. I believe that on some level there is the need for fans to see evidence that stars are actual flesh and bone, and no different than anybody else.

In the golden days of Hollywood, there were many who understood this need and provided it for fans. Hedda Hopper and Louella Parsons certainly did. Walter Winchell did, perhaps better than anyone else, and was a founding father of tabloid journalism. By invading our lives and revealing our secrets, they brought stars to heel and humanized us. Winchell appealed to working-class people who were fascinated by the rich and famous, but also eager to see them fall—or at least stumble in a big way.

But in the 1950s, there was no tabloid more popular and more destructive than *Confidential* magazine. *Confidential* was devoted exclusively to the misadventures of Hollywood movie stars and other celebrities. It was sold at newsstands and in supermarkets all over the country. More than ten million readers clamored to get each issue every month. Naturally, there had been things printed about me in movie magazines from time to time, but the stories had been fairly harmless, and so I took Laughton's advice and paid them no heed. That all changed when *Confidential* magazine's March 1957 headline read:

IT WAS THE HOTTEST SHOW IN TOWN WHEN . . .
MAUREEN O'HARA
<u>Cuddled</u> IN ROW 35

The tabloid printed a story claiming that during a showing of *Ben-Hur* to a packed house at Hollywood's Grauman's Chinese Theatre, I was busy having a steamy interlude in the back row of the theater with a Latin lover. Of course, the story was an outrageous lie. It never happened. I had been seriously libeled in the most offensive way. The descriptions of our alleged behavior were so lewd and obscene that they were talked about all over Hollywood. To make matters worse, my daughter could read it, as could my parents (who had joined their children in America a few years earlier), siblings, friends, and everyone else I knew. I was outraged.

The story claimed that when the usher in charge of aisle C turned his flashlight on us he discovered a torrid, eye-popping sight. I was supposedly found spread across three seats with my blouse open. The story claimed that the usher had coughed and broken us up, but had later come back with his flashlight. This time, I was allegedly sitting in the man's lap facing the *back* of the theater with the Latin man unable to see through me. The story concluded with our being thrown out of the theater.

The year when *Confidential* magazine lost all sense of decency was 1957. I wasn't the only star targeted in such a malicious way. The July issue featured an article entitled "Why Liberace's Theme Song Should Be 'Mad About the Boy.' " That same year, Dorothy Dandridge filed suit against the magazine when it claimed that she'd had a passionate outdoor encounter with a bandleader at a Lake Tahoe resort. Dorothy countered that the story was ludicrous because in the 1950s "Negroes were not permitted that freedom."

The entire industry was outraged. Throughout Hollywood,

studio bosses, stars, and politicians were organizing and readying themselves to take on *Confidential* magazine. All they needed was a lightning rod, a front person, to lead the charge. The call came from George Murphy in late May. I was recuperating from surgery after the removal of a ruptured disk in my spine, a war wound from the dragging sequence in *The Quiet Man*. Murphy was a well-regarded hoofer turned actor who later became president of the Screen Actors Guild. He had been given an honorary Oscar for his public-relations work promoting the motion-picture industry, and often served as its mouthpiece on matters of public policy. He later left Hollywood and became a United States senator from California.

Murphy said to me, "Maureen, we need someone to pioneer the case against *Confidential* magazine and we have picked you. We've had the FBI on your tail and you're clean and clear. No one can hurt you . . . so will you lead the charge for us?" This added sense of responsibility and purpose fueled my already burning desire to bury the rag. I felt like I was Joan of Arc, responsible for saving the motion-picture industry, and so I said yes.

On July 9, 1957, I initiated my now famous legal case against *Confidential* magazine and sued for damages in excess of one million dollars. I later increased my demand for damages to five million. In the suit, I charged that *Confidential* had printed a story that was knowingly false and maliciously degrading to me without any regard to my reputation. In the beginning, I had the entire industry behind me and I was their heroine.

It got very nasty, very fast. Right away, two FBI agents were brought in to live with me when they found out that *Confidential* was planning to break into my house. Bronwyn had to sleep with me in my bed because the magazine was going to have a nude man with them and photograph him there in the house to use as proof that I was promiscuous. They never did break in,

32

Errol Flynn and I
ham it up for
photographers during
the filming of *Against
all Flags*, 1952.

Dining with Enrique Parra

33

Swashbuckling in *At Sword's Point*, 1952. The studio thought I was crazy to perform all of my own fencing stunts, but I loved it.

Bronwyn plays for the camera at seven.

Posing as Lady Godiva, 1957

37

Posing in London during the
filming of *Fire Over Africa*, 1954

hottest show in town when.

MAUREEN O'HARA
Cuddled in ROW 35

By R. E. McDONALD

ALMOST ANYONE who's ever been to the movies knows about Hollywood's famous Grauman's Chinese Theater. That's where the stars go to get their footprints recorded in cement. That's where they stage some of movieland's gaudiest premieres.

But you'd have to be an usher to get the real low-down on what goes on in this celebrated movie house. Garbed in your flashy uniform and equipped with your tiny flashlight, you'd discover something to make your eyes pop. Because Grauman's is also the theater where the stars go—not to watch the movie but to bundle in the balcony. And the show that goes on in the back seats often beats anything that's flickering on the screen.

No one can predict when an act along the aisle is going to produce more steam than the advertised attraction. For instance, a gentlemanly assistant

when the usher in charge of aisle "C" came rushing out to report that there was a couple heating up the back of the theater as though it were mid-January. Easing down the aisle, he saw the entwined twosome. It was Maureen and her south-of-the-border sweetie.

His eyes accustomed to the darkness, he saw even more than that. Maureen had entered Grauman's wearing a white silk blouse neatly buttoned. Now it wasn't. The guy had come in wearing a spruce blue suit. Now he wasn't. The coat was off, his collar was open and his tie was hanging limply at half mast in the steam.

Maureen Made Movie-Viewing History

Moreover, Maureen had taken the darndest position to watch a movie in the whole history of the theater. She was spread across three seats—with the happy Latin American in the middle seat.

This is going to the movies?

The assistant manager coughed. Then he coughed again. For all the reaction he got from Maureen and

I found myself in a highly publicized
scandal when *Confidential* magazine
printed this untrue story about
me in its March 1957 issue.
I filed suit three months later.

Left to right: Prosecutor William Ritzi, me, Charlie Fitz, and Jimmy as we leave the
courthouse during a recess. My date-stamped passport later proved I was out of the
country the night I was supposedly in Grauman's Chinese Theater.
I won the suit and put *Confidential* out of business.

Performing a song during "The Fabulous Fordies" episode on *The Tennessee Ernie Ford Show*. Television variety shows helped my career rebound after the *Confidential* scandal. They also showed audiences that I could sing.

My first album was *Love Letters from Maureen O'Hara*, a compilation of pop songs that I recorded for RCA Victor. I later recorded *Maureen O'Hara Sings Her Favorite Irish Songs* and *Christine*.

After twenty years making films, I finally returned to the theater in 1960 when I starred in the Broadway musical *Christine*. Sadly, the show closed after just one week.

Alec Guinness chats with Fidel Castro while I speak with other visitors on the set of *Our Man in Havana*, 1960.

With Hayley Mills. This is my favorite shot in *The Parent Trap*, 1961. The film gave my career another boost starring in family comedies.

Tough Brian Keith crumbles after I sock him in the eye during a scene in *The Parent Trap*. He was a natural at comedy.

Jimmy Stewart and I dance the twist
in *Mr. Hobbs Takes a Vacation.*

Mammy was a wonderful actress.
Look how she brought this character
to life with her eyes.

Henry Fonda gives me a spanking during a scene in *Spencer's Mountain*, 1963.

Duke does the same during a scene in *McLintock!* I was black and blue for days.

Duke and I bust up after finishing the mud pit scene in *McLintock!*
He was my best friend for forty years.

51

Duke supervises as I am hauled up during a very dangerous stunt in *McLintock!*
In the background, Red Morgan is telling me to get down before I kill myself.

52

With my gang on the set of *McLintock!* Left to right in back: Lucille House, Rosemary
Odell, me, Jimmy Barker. Left to right, front: Adele Palmer and Faye Smyth

Daddy and I meet the pope at the Vatican while I was there filming *The Battle of Villa Fiorita*, 1965.

With Rossano Brazzi and his friends on the set of *The Battle of Villa Fiorita*, 1965

Charlie Blair receives the coveted Harmon Aviation Trophy from President Harry S. Truman during a ceremony at the White House, 1951.

With Charlie Blair on his Farewell Tour Around the World as he retired from Pan Am

Jackie Gleason welcomes me back to the set of *How Do I Love Thee?* in 1970.

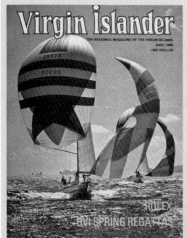

After I married Charlie Blair and moved to St. Croix, I became publisher of *Virgin Islander*. Charlie bought the magazine so I would be too busy to make movies.

Posing for a photographer with Charlie in our garden

Posing in front of this quarter-scale model of Charlie's P-51.
The model is part of the memorial honoring Charlie that is on top of the
Queen's Building at London's Heathrow Airport.

Observing the Congressional
Gold Medal awarded to Duke
in 1979. I asked Congress to
strike on the medal just three
words: John Wayne, American.

John Candy and I
share a private moment
on *Only the Lonely*, 1991.

My grandson, Conor Beau FitzSimons

Leading the St.
Patrick's Day Parade
as Grand Marshal in
New York City, 1999

but one night a car showed up at the house to pick me up. I was told the car had been sent by my lawyer to take me to his office. Naturally, I called, and it wasn't true at all. He hadn't sent the car and he rushed right over. The car took off as soon as he arrived.

Then all of a sudden, Liberace and Dandridge dropped their cases and settled with the magazine. Without any warning, George Murphy called me and said, "Maureen, these lousy bastard sons of bitches. The industry is no longer supporting you on this. You're on your own. I'm sorry, and may God help you." He then hung up the phone. My own industry had thrown me to the wolves. I never knew why they backed out, but always wondered if there had been some behind-closed-doors blackmailing going on. I always wondered what *Confidential* might have had in their files to make so many people buckle.

Still, help or no help, I wasn't about to give up. I decided to go forward with my suit and take on *Confidential* magazine alone, if need be. There was no way that I was going to let them break me now.

The trial was very theatrical and was played out all over the papers. The jury was taken to the theater to see the exact seat where the alleged act was supposedly committed. I was the star witness. After my testimony, I faced a throng of reporters and issued a statement from the courthouse steps:

My testimony, I will stand by it. It is the same as always. This incident never occurred in Grauman's Chinese or any other theater.

The dramatic courtroom climax came when *Confidential* testified, on the record, and gave the precise date and time the incident in the theater supposedly occurred. That proved fatal for them and we were ready for it. In a moment of great drama, I promptly whipped out my passport and showed it to the judge. The official, dated stamps proved that I could not have been in the theater that night because I wasn't in the United States of America then. I was in Spain making *Fire over Africa* for Columbia Pictures. (No one connected with the picture ever came forward in my defense.) The courtroom broke into applause and the judge had to quiet it. My passport proved my innocence. *Confidential* magazine was found guilty of conspiring to publish obscenity and libel. My victory was the first time a movie star had won against an industry tabloid. *Confidential* magazine would never survive the loss in court and shortly thereafter passed into history.

CHAPTER 18

THE DAME CAN SING!

If the 1930s and 1940s were Hollywood's golden age of cinema, then the 1950s belonged to television. More than half the homes in America were now equipped with television, and people were enjoying hours in front of their sets. It was a time of Lucy and Desi, Milton Berle, Jack Benny, Sid Caesar, Jackie Gleason, and Ed Sullivan. There were sitcoms and dramas and westerns—but more than anything, variety shows were the crown jewel of prime time. Variety shows were wonderful because they brought vaudeville into the home. They had opening monologues, comedy sketches, song-and-dance numbers, and, most thrilling of all, they were performed in front of a live audience.

At the risk of sounding uppity, I didn't want to do television at first. I was a movie star. But my film career hadn't yet recovered from the *Confidential* magazine scandal, and I hadn't made a movie in over two years. I needed to make a move.

I had wanted to sing from the time I was a little girl in Dublin. The small amount of singing I had done in films had been when my character sang a song as part of the story. I had already asked every studio boss I ever worked for to cast me in a musical. So when I was asked to appear for the first time on *The Dinah Shore Show* in 1958, I had reason to agree. Large television audiences would hear my voice and say, "The dame can sing." So would studio bosses, directors, and producers. Performing on television would also get me back to work.

The Dinah Shore Show launched me as a musical guest star. I sang a solo and then joined Dinah and Shirley MacLaine in a song-and-dance number. Television producers took notice after that, and it marked another turning point in my career. I spent the next few years making the rounds on every top variety show. I appeared many times on *The Perry Como Show*, *The Andy Williams Show*, *The Garry Moore Show*, *The Bob Hope Show*, the *Hallmark Hall of Fame*, and *The Ed Sullivan Show*, to name a few. My favorite performance was singing songs from the 1940s on *The Tennessee Ernie Ford Show*. The episode was called "The Fabulous Fordies."

My appearances on these variety shows also paid off in a big way professionally. In May 1958, I signed a three-year agreement with RCA Victor to join the label and make record albums. I envisioned a whole new avenue of my career opening up if this was a success. *Love Letters from Maureen O'Hara* was a compilation of pop songs selected by the label for me to record. The album sold for $3.98 when it was released and did well, especially overseas, but I was never paid for it. Personally, I didn't like the album because pop is not my kind of music. I like opera, Irish folk songs, and German lieder. It didn't quite knock Rosemary Clooney off the charts, but it was a respectable recording-artist debut.

My guest appearances also led to offers for my own television show. Most of the premises were wrong for me, but I made pilots for two of them, neither of which aired. One was terrific and the other was awful. I was very excited about *The Woman in the Case*, a dramatic anthology series created by Quinn Martin and based on Edgar Lustgarten's book. I agreed to star in one third of the stories and to introduce other top female stars for the other episodes. CBS production head William Dozier was at the helm of the project, but then CBS went through a reorganization and Bill Dozier was out; so was every project he was connected with. The second series was a half-hour sitcom called *Daphne,* and was loosely based on *Auntie Mame.* It was so bad they couldn't find a sponsor to back the show after the pilot was finished.

Then, in early 1959, Ingo Preminger, highly regarded director Otto Preminger's brother, approached me to star in a Broadway musical called *Christine.* It was a golden opportunity. I was still a theater snob deep down, and had always dreamed of returning to the stage in a musical. But I also didn't want to rush into it. If I was finally going to Broadway, then the show had to be good. A one-week run would be a disaster, and would kill any chance at all of establishing myself as a bankable Broadway leading lady. I told Ingo I was interested but needed to hear the music and read the script. I also had to get permission from Columbia Pictures.

It had been three years since I'd made *The Wings of Eagles* with John Ford at MGM. I hadn't made a picture for Columbia under the six-year exclusive contract studio boss Harry Cohn had signed with me after I made *The Long Gray Line.* Cohn died of a heart attack after the ink was dry. Had he lived I would have worked more for Columbia. He always told me, "You're the only one in Hollywood with the guts to come into my office, sit down, look me in the eye, and say no."

I changed agents again and went back to MCA, where I had more success. My new agents, Jack Bolton and Harry Friedman, quickly went to work getting the okay from Columbia for me to do the play. Columbia was in a bind and wanted to make a deal. Lauren Bacall wasn't free to shoot a picture they wanted her in and they needed a replacement. Columbia agreed to let me go to Broadway, but only if I stepped in and made *Our Man in Havana* for them first. After a very long dry spell, I was finally back in front of the movie cameras again.

When we arrived in Havana on April 15, 1959, Cuba was a country experiencing revolutionary change. Only four months before, Fidel Castro and his supporters had toppled Fulgencio Batista, who had ruled Cuba for over twenty-five years. My sister Florrie had come with me to Cuba and stayed the entire time I was there. The Cuban people greeted us warmly and appreciated that I now spoke Spanish. We could feel their excitement as they readied for a new way of life. It was a time of great hope.

Based on writer Graham Greene's screenplay from his novel, *Our Man in Havana* is a comedic twist on the James Bond story. A vacuum-cleaner salesman (played by Alec Guinness) accepts a part-time job as a British secret agent in Batista's Cuba. Of course, he has no idea how to be a secret agent and so he starts inventing make-believe stories of espionage. I played Beatrice, another secret agent whom London has sent to help Guinness. Acclaimed British director Sir Carol Reed directed the film. Actors Burl Ives, Noël Coward, Ernie Kovacs, and Jo Morrow were also in the picture.

It took a while to figure out the ways of the new Cuban government. At first, officials in the interior ministry were offended that the studio asked for permission to film in the capital. The ministry responded by saying, "Giving written permission would look like the Batista days, when everybody needed permission for everything." But as soon as we started shooting, the interior minister demanded a copy of the script and had it translated into Spanish. He didn't like the way the script portrayed the revolution. The new government wanted a few changes. Graham Greene was forced to add more to glorify the fight against Batista. Lines that were the least bit sympathetic to Batista were cut or changed.

We worked a rigorous six-day schedule. All the exteriors were filmed in Havana and the interiors were filmed later at Shepperton Studios, in London. Nearly all of the dialogue shot in Cuba had to be dubbed later, in the studio, because the streets of Havana were so noisy. Castro did come to the set once during filming to meet the cast. He whispered softly the whole time, so I couldn't hear a word he said. He did not ask me on a date as was reported, nor was he romancing Jo Morrow during the making of the film. The publicity department made that up.

Enrique came to visit for a week and we enjoyed some of the sights on my day off. After he left, I spent my time off with members of the cast. Occasionally, I had dinner with Burl Ives and Alec Guinness. Alec was wonderful to work with. I respected his work a great deal and so I was very pleased when he paid me a compliment, saying, "You know, Maureen, I never thought you—being Irish—could do an English accent, but you have and it's wonderful." He was a Catholic too, and so we went to Mass together during the picture, but if I was one second late, he wouldn't wait for me. He was a stickler for punctuality and professionalism on and off the set. It was wonderful to work with him because I'm tarred with the same brush in that way.

Most nights, I stayed close to the Capri Hotel, our home base. You would meet everyone important in the revolution there sooner or later because it was a popular place to go for dinner or coffee or to smoke a cigar. I enjoyed interesting conversations with Che Guevara there. I had met Ernesto "Che" Guevara very soon after arriving in Cuba. How could I not meet Che? He was one of the great heroes of Latin America. Che was often at the Capri Hotel. I would see him in the restaurant and he'd come to my table to say hello and eventually would sit down and join me. Che would talk about Ireland and all the guerrilla warfare that had taken place there. He knew every battle in Ireland and all of its history. Che knew more about Ireland than John Ford did. I couldn't believe it, and finally asked, "Che, you know so much about Ireland and talk constantly about it. How do you know so much?" The Argentine mercenary and former doctor surprised me with his answer. He said, "Well, my grandmother's name was Lynch and I learned everything I know about Ireland at her knee." He was Che Guevara Lynch! That famous cap he wore was an Irish rebel's cap.

I spent a great deal of time with Che Guevara while I was in Havana. I believe he was far less a mercenary than he was a freedom fighter. I think he was a product of his grandmother and her teachings. I look back on how young and idealistic Che was when I made that picture. It's hard to believe that he had already helped to topple a dictator and liberate a nation. Today he is a symbol for freedom fighters wherever they are in the world and I think he is a good one. When word came of his capture and execution, I was deeply saddened. I have no doubt he had no regrets as he faced his assassin and spoke his final words: "I know you've come to kill me. Shoot. You are only going to kill a man."

Toward the end of filming, I received word through a member of the crew that an old friend had sent his regards. Errol Flynn was in the country making a low-budget film called *Cuban Rebel Girls* and was hoping we might see each other while I was there. Errol wasn't doing well. Hollywood had forgotten the icon they'd once called "the Baron," and his health was failing. Errol often said, "They've great respect for the dead in Hollywood, but none for the living." I didn't go to see him and have always regretted it. He died just a short time later of a heart attack. Like Che, his very last words were true to form: "I've had a hell of a lot of fun and I've enjoyed every minute of it."

We finished filming in Havana by the middle of May. I left Cuba and went back to New York. Enrique met me there and we enjoyed an extended weekend together at the Waldorf before I went on to London to shoot the interiors for the picture. While I was in New York, I also met with the creative team for *Christine* and began initial discussions on the contracts. I met author and playwright Pearl Buck to discuss the character, as well as the musical team of Sammy Fain and Paul Francis Webster to discuss the songs. We were all auditioning each other, of course, and by the time I left for London, we had a deal.

Our Man in Havana wrapped in London at the end of July and I decided to spend another month traveling through Europe. Enrique joined me in Madrid and then again in Paris. I finally fulfilled my dream of attending Mass at the cathedral of Notre-Dame de Paris. Afterward, I climbed the famous bell tower and was photographed by many tourists who were happy to see Esmeralda back where she belonged. Everything was precisely as it had been on the set of *The Hunchback*. Enrique and I spent my thirty-ninth birthday in Paris buying French perfume and eating gorgeously rich food at the Marquis. The next day, we flew to Geneva and then went on to Rome. I was blessed in meeting the Holy Father, Pope John XXIII, and kissed his ring. He is the only man I have ever bent my knee to.

The month we spent together in Europe was one of my favorite times ever spent with Enrique. I was very happy and ready to begin my Broadway adventure in New York. On January 1, 1960, it was announced in the press that I had officially accepted the title role in *Christine*, and would be performing in the play at the Forty-sixth Street Theater. April 20 was scheduled as opening night and rehearsals were set to begin in early February.

Before that, though, I did the Christmas and New Year's Eve shows for Perry Como and also performed in *Mrs. Miniver*, on the *David Susskind* show. I got wonderful reviews for *Mrs. Miniver*, but I have never been able to get a copy of the show. I would love one and maybe someone will come up with it.

In February, *Our Man in Havana* hit theaters across the country and was a smashing success. I received very favorable reviews for that performance too, but I share the credit with Alec Guinness and America's fascination with Fidel Castro. After three years in movie exile, I had a hit on my hands. My telephone was ringing off the hook again and I was off to Broadway.

Christine was a racy story for 1960, and it caused a lot of talk. Christine, the widow of a British baronet, goes to India to visit her daughter, who has married a Hindu doctor and is about to give birth to her first child. When she gets there, however, she finds that her daughter and the baby have both died. Only her son-in-law is left, and according to Indian custom, she is considered his mother, and it's her duty to nominate and choose a new wife for him. But over time, they fall in love, and she must choose between herself and another woman for him. There you have it: a mother-in-law who falls in love with her son-in-law, set to music. It was cocktail-party chatter run amok. I loved its controversial nature and proclaimed in the press, "Mothers-in-law have heard jokes about themselves for years. Now their time is coming."

Christine had all the makings of a Broadway hit. It had a strong story written by an acclaimed author who had received both the Pulitzer and Nobel prizes. It also had the two-time Academy Award-winning team of Sammy Fain and Paul Francis Webster behind the music. They were responsible for countless favorite pop songs, including "Love Is a Many Splendored Thing" and "Friendly Persuasion." The director, Jerome Chodorov, was one of Broadway's most successful playwrights and directors.

I moved to New York in early February and brought my musical accompanist, Elaine Parkey, with me. The rigorous work leading up to opening night was no surprise to me. My acting roots were in the theater and the Abbey had taught me well. Rehearsals for a play are always long and tiring. Musicals have singing, dancing, and acting in them, and each discipline requires its own separate training and preparation. You start at nine A.M. sharp and work until the late hours of the night on scenes and blocking the songs and dances. As April neared, I was confident that we had a good show.

One of the most important steps in the process of bringing a play to Broadway is the tryout stage. This is where the producers try the production out in cities other than New York to see how audiences receive it. It gives them the chance to make changes based on feedback and audience reaction, or it gives them the confidence to go with what they have. We took *Christine* to Boston and Philadelphia for three weeks and the reviews scared the hell out of our producers. They were hoping for the kind of audience reaction received by *Bye Bye Birdie*, the latest musical success on Broadway. We didn't get it, nor should we have.

I thought the producers were panicking. Being compared to *Bye Bye Birdie* was unrealistic and inappropriate. *Bye Bye Birdie* was a musical based on rock 'n' roll; we were bringing to the stage a classic musical along the lines of *The King and I* or *The Sound of Music*. *Bye Bye Birdie* was about America in the late 1950s as Elvis Presley went into the service and rock 'n' roll widened the generation gap. *Christine* was about exploring a marvelous foreign culture and comparing its customs to our own.

It was clear to me that our producers didn't have confidence in their own musical. They started cutting the songs, changing the script, and even changing the costuming. By the time they had finished hacking the production to bits, it was ruined. We had a boring romance and no memorable songs, which is a killer on Broadway. No matter what, at the end of the night, the audience has to find at least one song memorable for a musical to make it.

I knew the show was in serious trouble. Director Mitch Leisen called and offered to take over. He had directed Ginger Rogers in *Lady in the Dark*, and offered to step in and save the production. His idea was to keep us out of New York and tour the country until everything was perfect. It was precisely the right thing to do, but they turned him down.

We were taken back to New York and the press started reporting that *Christine* was having problems getting ready for opening night. Author Pearl Buck then went public and demanded sole writing credit for the play instead of sharing billing with a writer who had participated in a script rewrite. The feud between the two of them was played out in the papers and soon everyone knew the production was in disarray. The producers, Chodorov, and Buck were all upset with each other. On April 12, they announced that opening night was being delayed a week for further rehearsals and changes.

I went to the producers, my heart aching. I was very honest and told them flat out, "The changes you have made have destroyed this play. I was born and raised in the theater, and let me tell you, you've got a flop on your hands." They were insulted and took my honesty as a stab in the back. For the remainder of my tenure with the play, they never again spoke directly to me. When I looked in their direction, they simply turned from me as if I didn't exist. It was all so childish. By opening night, even director Jerome Chodorov had dropped out of the production and demanded that his name be removed from the credits. In the program, no director was credited for *Christine*.

Christine opened on Broadway on April 28. Mammy came in from Hollywood, and we had a full house that night. The surprising thing was that *Christine* played every performance to a packed house. We were sold out every night, and the reviews were much better than anyone expected. Critics were taking it easy on us, and my notices were absolutely wonderful. Despite the show's terrible problems, audiences seemed to enjoy it. So I was surprised when the producers informed me that they were shutting down the show for good on May 7, just one week after we opened. Something was fishy about the whole thing. I never knew why they closed it—we were selling tickets. I left New York and, sadly, never starred in a Broadway production again.

Though my Broadway experience was a major disappointment for me, Hollywood was eagerly awaiting my return. The show was no sooner over than the call came from my agents. Walt Disney wanted me for his next big movie. It was a family picture and, quite to my surprise, would start one of the most successful periods of my career. At an age when many leading ladies see their careers begin to slow, mine was about to skyrocket all over again.

CHAPTER 19

THE PARENT TRAP

There's a terrible truth for many women in the picture business: Aging typically takes its toll and means fewer and less desirable roles. I was lucky. The phone was ringing and offers were still coming in. As the 1960s began, a new breed of Hollywood leading lady was emerging. She was elegant, international, and wonderfully comedic. Audrey Hepburn was the quintessential cosmopolitan girl in *Breakfast at Tiffany's*. Sophia Loren won our hearts in *Houseboat*. Even Natalie Wood had grown up and was making *Splendor in the Grass*.

And then, of course, there was still Marilyn. A few years earlier, Marilyn had called and asked me to play a joke on her husband, Joe DiMaggio. Apparently, Joe was a fan of mine and always teased Marilyn about how attracted to me he was. She was sick and tired of hearing her husband talk about me and I don't blame her. She asked me if I would mind being wrapped in a big box with a ribbon tied in a bow around it, to be her gift to Joe on his birthday. The huge box would be on a large table, and right before he opened it, she was going to say, "Now, Joe, after I give you this, I don't ever want to hear about Maureen O'Hara again." Then as he pulled the bow and ribbon off, I was supposed to pop out of the box while the crowd shouted, "Surprise!" I thought it would be great fun, but, sadly, they separated just before it could be done.

As an actress, I don't think I was always elegant, but I was certainly international and comedic. The early 1960s were very much a time for Walt Disney fare and family comedies in general. All the studios were making them, and audiences were forsaking their TVs to see them. Walt Disney's offer couldn't have been better timed. He wanted me to play the mother of twin sisters, both of whom were to be played by child star Hayley Mills, in a film called *The Parent Trap*. Some leading ladies resist playing mothers because they don't want to be viewed as matronly. Not me. I never minded playing mothers. I always judged a role by the qualities of the character and her contribution to the story.

I never played boring, stereotypical mothers, and I foiled stodgy notions of what mothers should look like on-screen. Hollywood could go right ahead casting me as a mother all it wanted, because I was going to make her the toughest and hippest mamma audiences had ever seen.

I fell in love with the script for *The Parent Trap* as soon as I read it. It was wonderful, and I knew families with children would relate to it on many different levels. It's the story of a separated family, wife and one daughter in Boston, husband and other daughter in California. The girls are twins who meet each other at summer camp, switch identities, and hatch a plan to bring their parents back together.

Mr. Disney's story editor, Bill Dover, had found a novella titled *Das Doppelte Lottchen*, written by Erich Kästner, and the studio purchased it. Disney hired David Swift, who had directed Hayley in *Pollyanna*, to write and direct.

Since Hayley was still a relative newcomer, Disney wanted known stars to play the parents. I was offered the role of Maggie, with my usual star billing, which was fine, but the money was horrible. My minimum asking price for a movie was $75,000, and Disney was only offering me one third of that. I loved the script and the part but couldn't make the picture for that amount of money. It was going to break my heart, but I'd have to turn it down.

I told Jack Bolton, "I can't do it. I know what I'm worth and I can't undervalue myself like this. Tell Mr. Disney thank you, but, if he wants O'Hara, it's seventy-five thousand or nothing." Jack thought I was making a huge mistake and pleaded with me to change my mind. "Maureen, you're crazy. This is a great role in a very big movie and it will get us over the hump. We're just crawling out of the woods from the whole *Confidential* mess. You won't get it. Disney doesn't budge." I held my ground. "No, Jack, I'm sure about this. I'd rather sell shoes at Saks Fifth Avenue than work for that kind of money. Please deliver my message."

Jack called back a short time later, ecstatic. "Maureen, I can't believe it, but Disney went for it. You're in!" It was a wonderful moment of triumph and I was pleased that I hadn't sold myself out.

The Parent Trap is one of my most popular films. It is particularly special to women and girls who come from broken homes. They relate to it so strongly because they had many of the same feelings and hopes for their own parents to get back together. Children watched it over and over, believing that it was possible for their family too. Every now and again, someone tells me how the film helped them through hard times, and that makes me feel wonderful.

The Parent Trap is a comedy, and let me tell you, comedy is difficult, especially slapstick. The trick is to have fun while performing it, and to convey that sense of fun to the audience without coming off as corny. The film was successful because we didn't make that major mistake, and because of its strong script from David Swift, his solid direction, the chemistry among the cast, and the tremendous amount of creative freedom given to us by Walt Disney. We began filming *The Parent Trap* in July 1960, and filming lasted until the end of September.

I don't think we could have hoped for a better director for the picture than David Swift. He was a comedy writer in radio and television before Walt Disney gave him his big break behind the camera. He had created the popular sitcom *Mr. Peepers*, with Wally Cox, and this background gave him a great touch with comedic scenes and a sense of timing in the delivery of funny lines. His direction was significant in maintaining the rhythm of the comedy. He claimed to have "just hired the best actors and then kept out of their way," but he did much more than that.

The film was so well cast and the story had so many wonderful and funny characters. It was very much to Swift's credit that he cast Brian Keith to play the part of my ex-husband. Brian had never done comedy before *The Parent Trap* and it was a real change for him. He had always played tough and gruff characters before that, which made him my kind of leading man. He was big and strong and burly, and Swift always called him "Mr. Masculine" on the set.

Brian was a natural at comedy. His delivery always came with a warm twinkle in his eye that defused his menacing size. We see this best in the sequence between Brian and me where we quarrel, and I eventually punch him in the eye. Instead of this big and tough man showing her who's boss, he falls to pieces like a little boy crying for his mommy and the audience falls in love with him.

One of my favorite scenes in the picture is when Brian finds my brassiere hanging in the bathroom. He doesn't know I'm at the ranch yet and assumes it belongs to Hayley. The size of the cups throws him for a loop and he wonders, How could I have never noticed that before? Daddy's little girl is changing, and he tells us how painful it is for him without a single word of dialogue. Great stuff. Interestingly, none of us was sure Mr. Disney would spare the scene and not cut it from the picture. This was the first time a brassiere had ever been shown in a Disney movie, and we feared it might be too racy for him. But Mr. Disney loved what Brian had done with it and allowed the scene to stay.

Of course, *The Parent Trap* wouldn't have been as special without the remarkable performances by Hayley Mills. I use the plural here because she really did bring two different girls to life in the movie. Sharon and Susan were so believable that I'd sometimes forget myself and look for the other one when Hayley and I were standing around the set. It got quite confusing, and even Hayley knew which girl she was playing only by which wig she was wearing. She hated wearing those wigs and thought the short one made her look like Laurence Olivier in *Hamlet.*

Showing twin sisters together on-screen at the same time was no small task in 1960. They used a few different methods to achieve the effect. The easiest and most common way was by filming a series of over-the-shoulder shots. These shots had Hayley facing the camera in the background while her double, Susan Henning, was in the foreground. The back of Susan's head was turned to the camera, so we could never see her face.

The other method was more complicated. When the twins were shown side by side, with their faces visible, then the scene had to be shot using a split screen. Half of the lens was covered as Hayley played Sharon, in Sharon's clothing. That same scene was then shot again with the other side of the lens. Hayley now played Susan, in Susan's clothes, and that side of the film was then exposed. The images were brought together later in the lab, creating the effect of both twins standing side by side.

It's no wonder that Hayley and I got along well. Her family and upbringing were ensconced in the arts just like mine had been. (She is the daughter of John Mills, one of Britain's finest actors, and her mother is novelist Mary Hayley Bell.) I enjoyed playing her mother and she worked bloody hard on the picture. Hayley is British and was playing an American, which meant she had to use an accent. I watched her practice for hours slowing down her speech to get it just right. I was impressed by her discipline.

It didn't take us long to figure out that Hayley, who was fourteen when we shot the picture, was going through adolescence. Most young girls get to experience that in the privacy of their homes and don't have to struggle through it on a movie set. Starring in a movie, and with her hormones going crazy, the poor girl did get a bit emotional once in a while. There were a few times when David Swift was tough on her about her accent and she burst into tears and ran to her mother like a little girl. Then on other days I would see her stiffen and grow distant when her mother arrived on the set. The young lady wanted her independence. One day she asked me, "Maureen, did you ever feel like you didn't like your mother when you were my age?" I had to force myself not to smile, and assured her, "Your mother loves you and just wants to make sure you're not getting into trouble. It takes time for mothers to stop worrying. They never really do. It will pass and you'll love each other just the same as you always have." It was very sweet.

The shoot really was wonderful and went without a hitch, and Walt Disney deserves tremendous credit for it. He really gave us creative carte blanche while we were filming, and that's a luxury. He complimented our work enthusiastically and always told us how wonderful we were and how pleased he was. We were thrilled and listened to his praise, believing every word of it.

After filming ended, I was excited, anticipating its release. I knew the movie was funny and that families would love it. Everything was going great leading up to the premiere. But it all hit the fan when Disney released the picture's early promotional ads in the newspapers. I was shocked and angry when I saw that the credits for the picture read:

WALT DISNEY
Presents
HAYLEY MILLS and HAYLEY MILLS
in
THE PARENT TRAP
Starring MAUREEN O'HARA and BRIAN KEITH

My agreement with Walt Disney had been tossed out the window. I had a contract that was quite clear. I was the leading lady of the picture, and I was to receive top billing. Now Disney wanted the extra publicity of promoting Hayley in a dual role. I was livid, but it was not a case of movie-star ego. This was business, and Disney and I had an agreement. My contract stated that no other actress in the picture could have her name appear before mine in the credits—period. It wasn't Hayley's fault. Walt Disney made that decision himself.

I called my agents at MCA and told them, "The credits for *The Parent Trap* have to be corrected and those ads stopped. A deal's a deal, and I have a contract!" Jack Bolton agreed with me and then called Disney. We were diplomatically told to go screw ourselves. That made me even madder. MCA legal was brought in and they advised me that the Screen Actors Guild (SAG) had jurisdiction over the issue. If we were going to fight Disney, we would have to take our complaint to SAG. When we went to them, I was surprised to learn that the guild had received numerous complaints about Walt Disney over the years, and that he had always done what he wanted to do no matter what. After reviewing my iron-clad contract, SAG was delighted and felt that my winning was a foregone conclusion. SAG not only promised to stand behind me, but wanted to join me as a plaintiff in suing Walt Disney.

The legal sword rattling began as I readied myself to battle one of the most powerful men in Hollywood. It was clear to everyone that I was likely to prevail, and yet Disney refused to meet my demand that the studio honor our agreement. Days before I was going to file the papers in court, I was summoned to the Screen Actors Guild for a last-minute meeting with their key executives. Mr. Disney had sent me a message through the grapevine, and it was startlingly clear: "Sue me and I'll destroy you." SAG advised me to drop the matter. They said, "Maureen, you'll beat him in court, but you'll never work in the picture business again. Let it go." I knew Disney could make good on his threat, and that I would win the battle but lose the war. I've never been one to run from a fight if I believed the cause was right and the principle significant, but I didn't feel that the issue of how my name was displayed was worth gambling a career on. I let it go and tried to forget the whole ugly matter. I never have forgotten it though, and it still doesn't sit well with me.

The damage to my relationship with Walt Disney was done. I never worked for him or his studio again. A few years later, Charlie Fitz and I did attend a meeting with Disney to pitch an idea we had for a family movie that I wanted to star in. It was based on a popular character in Bronwyn's favorite book. Disney sat and listened, but barely spoke a word during the meeting. His people called a few days later and told us that Mr. Disney thought our idea was a heap of rubbish. But very shortly after that, they announced in the trades that Disney had bought the movie rights to the book we suggested. He made *Mary Poppins* exactly as we had pitched it.

Years later, Walt Disney was quite ill, in a Los Angeles hospital. His doctor just happened to be the brother of my new publicity agent, Helen Morgan. Helen had stopped by the hospital to see her brother and he'd taken her into Mr. Disney's room to wish him well. Helen introduced herself and told him that I was her client.

Disney was very weak but somehow mustered enough strength to sit up in his bed and force out his reply: "That bitch."

The Parent Trap cost $2 million to make in 1961 and earned nearly $10 million upon its initial release. It was a blockbuster, and I received some of the best reviews of my career. My favorite said that I had a flair for comedy not seen since Irene Dunne. At forty, I had a major hit on my hands, and suddenly found myself with many new opportunities.

I chose a western for my next project, one that was being produced by Charlie Fitz. Based on his novel, A. S. Fleischman wrote the screenplay for *The Deadly Companions,* about a drifter running from his past. When he accidentally kills a woman's young son, he tries to make up for it by escorting her through dangerous Indian territory so that she can bury the boy next to his father. No one believes there is a father. They all think the woman is a whore. I was cast as the dead boy's mother and Brian Keith agreed to play the drifter. He had only one condition: Sam Peckinpah had to direct the picture. Charlie Fitz wanted Brian in the movie very badly, so he agreed to hire the young, untested director. Peckinpah had established himself as a director of promise in a series of television westerns, including *Gunsmoke*, *The Rifleman*, and *The Westerner.* He had never directed a motion picture before, and *The Deadly Companions* was his feature-film debut.

It was a total fiasco. Peckinpah might have been a great television director, but he didn't have a clue as to how to direct a movie. He was oblivious to the fact that he was missing shots that were necessary to cut together a cohesive story in the editing room. Each day the editor came to Charlie and told him which reaction or cutaway shots he needed. Since the story involved a trek across the West, I had only one costume in the whole picture, and so I would perform the needed pickup shots at the end of the scenes Peckinpah wanted to shoot. I kept right on acting long after he called "cut." Everyone, except Peckinpah, knew what we were doing. Then one day, he finally noticed that I was still acting and asked me, "What the hell are you doing that for?" I finished what I had been asked to do by Charlie and answered, "I'm sorry, Mr. Peckinpah, I just got so caught up in the scene."

The biggest mistake that he made, though, the one that doomed the picture as "too artsy," as critics maintained, was that he never filmed the great fight sequence with the Indians. The script called for a dramatic action sequence where we fight for our lives on our way to the cemetery. The threat of an Indian attack was the great danger that drove the story, and it never happens in the picture. Peckinpah made a western about wild Indians without any Indians at all!

Peckinpah later reached icon status as a great director of westerns, but I thought he was just awful. I found him to be one of the strangest and most objectionable people I had ever worked with. He was mean and got a bizarre satisfaction on the set whenever something cruel happened to an animal. I remember watching him shoot the sequence where a horse tramples a snake to death. Peckinpah nearly worked himself into a frenzy with delight. But my most vivid memory of Sam Peckinpah, the one that has stayed with me over the years, is how terribly uncomfortable I felt watching him waste the day away relentlessly scratching his crotch.

Of course, by this stage in my career, I was an expert at surviving strange directors. I had made five films with John Ford, and there wasn't a more complicated director on the planet. I still visited Pappy and would stop by his office to visit with Meta and say hello to the gang. It was around the time I finished *The Deadly Companions* when I began noticing that John Ford seemed to be growing increasingly unhappy. He was complaining about his home life more than ever before. Then one day he told me, "I have over a million dollars stashed away in France. Why don't the three of us just run away and escape all of this?" I was so concerned for Mary and the kids that I called Jack Bolton at MCA and told him about the whole conversation. I was afraid that if anything happened to Pappy, and all that money really had been hidden, Mary would never know how to find it.

I also started seeing episodes of his periodic alcoholism firsthand. Pappy would show up at the house unannounced, brought there by his driver. He'd stagger to the door and bang on it until I let him in. There was no way I could turn him away. I'd send Bronwyn over to one of the neighbors while Pappy sat in the den on the sofa by the window, rambling on about Ireland and what he had done with his life and what he still wanted to do. Then he'd eventually demand, "Bring me coffee!" John Ford was miserable when he was drunk. The bad drunks usually are. I would no sooner bring the coffee to him than he'd stare at me while deliberately pouring it all over my carpet. He was daring me to challenge him, to stop him, but I never said a word.

On the one hand, Pappy was turning to my family and me for friendship and comfort. He'd stop by Daddy and Mammy's quite often to visit, cutting his cigar in half and sharing it with Daddy. He was always sober when he went there and would never dare be drunk in front of Daddy—he respected him too much. Daddy was the only man I ever saw put John Ford in his place, and I think Ford loved it. We were in Ireland at the time and Ford was staying with us at the house on Churchtown Road. Daddy was in his chair reading the newspaper while Pappy was sitting with him going on about the Irish freedom fighters. I was standing in the hallway, listening to this typical John Ford rambling. It went on and on until Daddy had finally had enough. He snapped the top half of his paper down, revealing his face, and said, "Why the hell don't you shut up talking about things you know nothing about!" Then he snapped the paper back up in front of his face again. I thought Ford would explode. I was ready to run, but he clammed up immediately and was quiet as a church mouse the rest of the night.

On the other hand, Ford was still doing things to hurt me. In late 1961, I was riding a wave of success as *The Parent Trap* continued breaking box-office records all across the country. Hoping to cash in on that, Darryl Zanuck cast me in the 20th Century-Fox comedy *Mr. Hobbs Takes a Vacation.* The picture marked the return of Jimmy Stewart to the kind of lighthearted comedy that had made him a national institution. Based on a novel by Edward Streeter, the picture is a simple story about a man and his wife who take a family vacation with their children and grandchildren in an old dilapidated house on the beach.

I was thrilled finally to have the chance to work opposite Jimmy Stewart. He was one of the biggest stars in the world and I was a huge fan. We started filming on October 1, and it was a fairly uneventful day. I didn't have a dialogue scene with Jimmy, and we only shot a walk-by sequence together. I was getting ready for bed later that night when Jack Bolton from MCA knocked on my door. He was quite upset.

"Jack, what are you doing here at this late hour?" I asked. His answer scared me. "I have to talk to you. It's very serious, Maureen." I didn't have a clue as to what it was about, so I asked him to come in. "Well, what is it? I have to get to bed. I've got an early call on the set tomorrow."

"That's what I want to talk to you about," he began. "Jimmy Stewart wants you off the picture right away." I was stunned. "What are you talking about? Why?"

"Well, Jimmy said that it was his understanding that you would eventually try to take over the picture and direct it." I couldn't believe it. I had never tried to direct a picture I was in, ever. I said, "How the hell could he possibly think that? I barely spoke to him the entire day. I said 'Good morning, Mr. Stewart,' and that was it. I did only one walk-by!"

That's when it hit me. There was only one person who would have said such a thing about me to Jimmy Stewart, and only one person whom Stewart would have believed—John Ford. Stewart and Ford had finished making *The Man Who Shot Liberty Valance* together only weeks before we began filming *Mr. Hobbs*. I knew they were still talking. Ford had done this kind of thing to me before, on many occasions.

Jack Bolton was one of John Ford's closest friends and so knew it was something Ford would do. Luckily, Jimmy had called Jack Bolton directly and hadn't mentioned it to the producer, Jerry Wald, or to Zanuck.

I said, "Look, Jack, you know the truth. You've got to speak to Mr. Stewart and straighten out this whole mess."

So I got up the next day and went to work as scheduled. I went in with my lines prepared but didn't go near Jimmy Stewart. I only said, "Good morning, Mr. Stewart. How are you today?" to which he answered, "I'm doing fine. Thank you."

I was never asked to leave the cast. What happened and who changed whose mind I still don't know. Within a matter of weeks, Jimmy was falling all over himself in an effort to be friendly. He was charming and nice and would ask me how I was and how I was feeling. He followed me around the set, showing me pictures of his trip to Africa, of him in the wild with his daughter. I responded, remaining friendly and charming. I'm sure that I left him with a positive impression when the film was finished, and over the years, Jimmy and I would become good friends. And he would later ask me to be in another picture with him.

But I learned a few things about working with Jimmy Stewart on *Mr. Hobbs Takes a Vacation.* I discovered that in a Jimmy Stewart picture, every scene revolves around Jimmy Stewart. I was never allowed to really play out a single scene in the picture. He was a remarkable actor, but not a generous one. *Mr. Hobbs Takes a Vacation* was a huge box-office smash and I won the Exhibitors Award for best performance by an actress in a comedy. How I won for this movie, I will never know.

Thanks to *The Parent Trap* and *Mr. Hobbs Takes a Vacation,* 1961 was a banner year for me. After twenty years of making movies, I had survived a two-year slump and was suddenly box-office gold again.

CHAPTER 20

DEPARTURES AND *McLINTOCK!*

I had every reason to be on top of the world as 1961 came to an end. My career was on the rise again; Bronwyn had grown into a terrific young woman; and I was finally in a happy and healthy relationship. Everything was going so well; then we got the news that Mammy had cancer.

She hadn't been feeling well for months, so doctors had begun a series of checkups and tests. Her symptoms strongly indicated that she had a malignancy, but the X rays were inconclusive. We were all clinging to that small bit of hope the day she went into surgery, but the doctors told us, "We know what we're looking for." I was on the set when the call came from Charlie Fitz: "It's everywhere, Maureen. There's nothing they can do."

Sorrow washed over me and I fell apart, collapsing in hysterics. Losing Mammy was too much to imagine. She and Daddy were part of my inner strength, something I relied on. They believed in me so much that I knew I could lick the world so long as they were in my corner. Mammy and I were more than just close; we lived in each other's pockets. I left the set and didn't return for a few days so I could be with my family and pray for a miracle.

I do believe in miracles. With conventional medicine leading us nowhere, we were more than willing to turn to divine sources for guidance and help. In January 1962, Charlie Fitz recalled a priest he had seen in Los Angeles who had performed a miracle by giving the gift of sight to a little boy who had been blind since birth. It was Father Aloysius, of Spain, who was gaining notoriety as having a special gift from God that allowed him to heal the sick.

The experience we had with Father Aloysius was remarkable. What he did for Mammy is a medical fact that can be explained only by faith. After she saw Father Aloysius, Mammy's tumors shrank to the size of a pea. She made a miraculous recovery and soon was up and about and feeling back to normal. We were suddenly full of hope. I wanted to do something special for her and decided to take her back to Ireland to see our homeland, relatives, and friends.

Before we could go, I had a live televised performance of *Spellbound* to do with Hugh O'Brian for NBC in New York. From there, I went to West Berlin to do *The Ed Sullivan Show*. By the time I returned to Los Angeles, in March, I had to start wardrobe and testing for my next picture at Warner Bros.—a family drama titled *Spencer's Mountain*, with Henry Fonda. While I was finishing up the testing, I took Mammy for a wonderful shopping spree for new clothes so that she could step off that plane dressed to the nines. We were only days from leaving when Mammy took a sudden turn for the worse. It was very unexpected, and she was no longer able to make the trip.

Sadly, Mammy didn't go quickly. She was riddled with cancer

at the end and we all waited for her to die. She went slowly, bit by bit, until she finally drifted away on June 27, 1962. Bronwyn had taken care of Mammy at the end and was absolutely wonderful. She bathed her, cooled her forehead, and held her hand. I was very proud of my daughter. Daddy and Mammy had been married for forty-five years, and I saw the sparkle in my father's eyes fade and go with her the day he lost his "little girl." For each of us, there is a small place in our hearts that died, leaving a void that remains empty to this day. Forty years later, I still find myself mourning and missing her.

Much to my surprise, no one showed more support and care for Daddy and our family than John Ford. Pappy attended every event, including the rosary and requiem Mass, and even joined us at Holy Cross Cemetery when Mammy was finally laid to rest. Throughout, he showed his deep affection for Mammy and his great respect for Daddy. It spoke volumes about his love for the entire FitzSimons clan, and revealed to me another one of his many unexplainable contradictions.

The one person who didn't call or write to offer sympathy was Will Price. It had been quite a long time since we had heard from him. He hadn't called Bronwyn to say hello, and hadn't sent her a birthday card, or even wished her a Merry Christmas for years. The last I had heard was that he had bounced from London to the Virgin Islands, then to New York, before eventually landing back in McComb, Mississippi. I heard rumors that his decline had only worsened and that he had been in and out of numerous hospitals.

Two days after the funeral, in early July, I was on location in Jackson Hole, Wyoming, shooting *Spencer's Mountain.* One week to the day Mammy died, on the Fourth of July, director Delmer Daves came into my trailer and found me going over lines with my longtime stand-in Lucille House. He gave me this jolting news: "Will Price is dead."

The call had come from Hollywood. I was told that Will had died of an apparent heart attack. It was only years later that I learned what his family had hoped to conceal: Will had taken his own life. I was shocked by the news of his death, though I must confess that I felt no sorrow at all. After a moment of silence, I looked up at Delmer and Lucille and could only say what I felt in my heart, "This is the happiest day of my life. Bronwyn is finally safe now."

My battles with Will had long ago become well known to the public. Delmer knew I was still grieving over Mammy, and he offered a comforting assessment: "Well, Maureen, it didn't take your mother long to get to work on it and get him out of your life once and for all."

It was fitting that I'd be on location making *Spencer's Mountain* at a time when so many changes were happening in my family life. In many ways, those changes were mirrored in the story we were about to tell on film. In *Spencer's Mountain,* Hank Fonda's father dies and our oldest son becomes a young adult and learns to stand on his own. The picture is loosely based on the novel by Earl Hamner Jr. about his life growing up in poverty on Spencer's Mountain, under the roof of God-fearing parents. They cling to the dream of one day sending their nine children to college. The film later inspired the critically acclaimed television series *The Waltons.*

I loved the script that had been adapted by director Delmer Daves. I liked the fact that it was a story with a strong married couple who were still playful and frisky with each other, but in a tasteful way. Just knowing they had nine children together provided all the sex appeal the picture needed. I knew it would make a lot of money for the studio. Hank, on the other hand, didn't like the script at all. He thought it was too old-fashioned and corny. The truth was, there was a play he was far more interested in doing, but his agent had already committed him to

Spencer's Mountain, and it was too late for him to get out of it. Playwright Edward Albee had written the role of George in *Who's Afraid of Virginia Woolf?* with Hank in mind. Had it not been for his commitment to *Spencer's Mountain,* he would have played the role. Fonda never got over it. He said years later, "I think I would have given up any role I've ever played—Tom Joad or Mister Roberts, any of them—to have had a crack at that part."

Henry Fonda and I hadn't worked together for nearly twenty years, not since we'd made *The Immortal Sergeant* together. He told me that he didn't know what he wanted to do with his life until Marlon Brando's mother persuaded him to try his hand at acting. She urged him to his first audition, and it didn't take long after that. I had been a huge fan of his ever since I'd seen him in *The Grapes of Wrath,* and I saw everything he ever did after that. While I was at West Point making *The Long Gray Line*, Meta Sterne and I once drove all the way to New York City just to see him perform *Mister Roberts* onstage.

I was thrilled to be working with him again. We used to call him "Ol' Weepy Eyes" on the set because he could make his eyes well up at the drop of a paper clip. He could cry on cue faster than any actor I've ever seen. What I appreciated most about him was that he cooperated with you in every way, and was never selfish in a scene. Henry Fonda was the gifted, tough, and classy kind of leading man that I most enjoyed working with.

Toward the end of production, Hank and I both found ourselves without powerful agents anymore. There had been complaints for a long time about MCA and how it had been exempted from the SAG rules that prohibited a talent agency from also engaging in film production. The rumor was that the exemption was part of a secret deal made between Lew Wasserman and Ronald Reagan while Reagan was still president of the Screen

Actors Guild. MCA had for years been in the unique position of being able to offer jobs to the actors it represented.

The Kennedy administration filed suit against MCA, but settled out of court. MCA was forced to choose between being a talent agency or a production company. Since its production company was more profitable, MCA closed its talent agency. Rumors were rampant around Hollywood as to why MCA was really taken down a notch. In private circles, many pointed to Marilyn Monroe's affair with President Kennedy. The gossip was that Marilyn was angry with MCA over their handling of her career and that she had asked the president to do it. Whatever the reason, Hank and I were no longer represented by the biggest agency in Hollywood. We both stayed with Jack Bolton when he went on his own.

After finishing *Spencer's Mountain*, I was well on my way to another smashing box-office success. I went right into the recording studio to cut my second record album—*Maureen O'Hara Sings Her Favorite Irish Songs*. I was much more comfortable with the music this time around and enjoyed the whole process much more than I had the first time. This time I picked every song myself except for one. The president of Columbia Records picked the last song on the record: "Come Back to Eirin," his favorite Irish song.

The album did very well, much better than my first, and I was very proud of it. I attended signings all over the country and actually got to shake hands with fans. It was wonderful. When I got back to Los Angeles, I was thrilled when an entire case of the albums finally arrived at my home. They were the only ones I got from Columbia for my private use and I had promised autographed copies to my family, friends, and a few special fans. Then, one night when I got home, I discovered that the entire box was gone. I searched the house and finally asked my housekeeper if she had seen them. "Oh yes," she replied. "Mr. Ford came by the house while you were gone and took the box home with him." I was heartbroken. John Ford had taken every single one, and I never knew what he did with them. I never saw them again.

Ford's good behavior after Mammy passed didn't last long. He was back to his bizarre antics by early September. This time he targeted my brother Jimmy instead of going after me directly. I was in Mexico City with Enrique and had invited Jimmy and his new girlfriend to come and visit. After a nice stay, Jimmy received a call from Meta Sterne saying that he was being summoned back to Los Angeles for an important casting meeting with Ford. Unfortunately, the flights out of Mexico City were all booked and we were only able to get one seat on the plane, for Jimmy. His girlfriend would have to wait a day and take another flight.

She blew her lid and threw a huge temper tantrum. Poor Jimmy was overcome. He caved in and refused to leave without her. That was a catastrophic mistake. I warned him, "Jimmy, you *have* to be on that plane. This is important business and you don't stand John Ford up." Her tantrum must have shattered his eardrums, for my pleas fell on deaf ears. Not only did Jimmy not take the flight, and miss the meeting, he didn't call Meta Sterne to inform Ford that he was trapped in Mexico. Jimmy and his girlfriend were able to get a flight out the following day, but the damage had been done and Ford had already set the wheels of retribution in motion.

Late that afternoon, I received an emergency call from Jimmy. He was sobbing.

"I'm in jail. They arrested me as soon as I got off the plane."

"Jail! What for?"

"It's crazy. I've been turned in as a draft dodger. I'm to be deported."

"That son of a bitch! I know who did it."

"You've got to help me, Maureen. You've got to get me out of here."

"Don't worry, Jimmy. I will."

I knew the culprit the minute I heard Jimmy's voice. There was only one person alive who would punish Jimmy so cruelly, and who had the power to do it so quickly and decisively—Rear Admiral John Ford. Ford wanted Jimmy to pay for what he saw as his insolence. I called Enrique, and we called his brother Fernando to ask for help. Fernando was close friends with the Kennedy family and it would now take those kinds of connections to foil Ford's plan. Fernando reassured me, "Don't worry. I'll call Bobby."

Luckily, the rear admiral was no match for the attorney general of the United States. Bobby Kennedy obliged his friend, and Jimmy was released from jail very shortly after that. We were given instructions for Jimmy to report to the federal building in Los Angeles. They gave us the name of a man to meet on a specific date, as well as a time for Jimmy to apply for his American citizenship. Fools that we were, we got the date mixed up and went to the federal building the day before we were supposed to. Thank God that we did. Ford wasn't finished yet. He had arranged for a large group of American veterans to parade outside the federal building with banners and signs in protest against Jimmy on the day we were supposed to arrive. Our mistake foiled his plan and Jimmy turned in his application for processing. Ford was too late. Whatever Bobby Kennedy had done, John Ford couldn't undo. Jimmy was given his American citizenship and was in the clear.

This wasn't the first time John Ford had used the authorities to lash out at those who had angered him. Long before the Jimmy incident, he had tried to do the same thing to me. I was in Mexico and got a call from Charlie Wendling. He sounded quite odd—all he said was, "I've got to come down and see you."

Naturally I was curious and asked, "What . . . what . . . what?"

"I can't discuss it on the phone."

Wendling arrived the next day and floored me with the reason for his visit. The Treasury Department had contacted him because they were angry. I had been reported to them by "a very credible source" as running a major jewelry-smuggling operation between Mexico and the United States. John Ford had apparently arranged for me to be arrested when I returned to the United States and went through customs. Officials at the Treasury Department told Charlie, "We are so disgusted. She thinks he is one of her closest and best friends, but he isn't."

The Treasury Department told me to go back to the United States through Fort Worth and put two pieces of my jewelry in a box and declare it as I went through customs. I booked a flight and did exactly as I was instructed. I put a bracelet and a pin in the box. When I arrived, I declared it and customs took it. I was let back into the United States. My bracelet and pin were returned later and I never again heard anything about it.

Sadly, Ford was still able to punish Jimmy for his disobedience. Before the incident, Jimmy had a bright and promising acting career ahead of him, having already made countless Westerns and having costarred with Sinatra. Suddenly, John Ford killed it. Aside from the small jobs Charlie Fitz or I were able to get him, Ford saw to it that Jimmy never really worked in the picture business again. I've never understood why he punished Jimmy with such a devastating blow. The mistake Jimmy made was foolish and disrespectful, but not worth ending a career over. No matter, Ford knew just how to hurt me. Instead of attacking my career, he ended my brother's and made me watch Jimmy's disappointment year after year.

Yet my career went on. In late 1962, I was approached by

Batjac Productions (Duke's production company) to star opposite John Wayne in the western comedy *McLintock!* It would be another blockbuster. The story, written by James Edward Grant, was tailor-made for Wayne and O'Hara. George Washington McLintock (Duke) is a rip-snorting cattle owner who has everything he could want except his proud and feisty wife (me). She left him years ago, suspecting infidelity, but has returned to meet her daughter (played by a young and talented Stefanie Powers) back from school in the East. He wants his wife back, and she wants a divorce—even though she still loves him. He finally snaps and chases her through town, gives her a public spanking that, for the moment, tames her, and they are happily reunited.

We began filming *McLintock!* in early November 1962, in Arizona, on location near Tucson, Nogales, and Tombstone. The sets were wonderful, and Duke wanted the picture to be 100 percent authentic.

There are so many great scenes in the picture. Audiences always rave about the fight sequence that takes place at the mine dump and ends in the mud. A total of forty-two cast members took part in the brawl, and nearly all of us ended up sliding down the bank into the mud pit below. I went down when my character takes a pin from her hat and jabs it into Duke's rear. He reacts from the pain and accidentally knocks me down the bank.

I had to slide down the bank on my back, headfirst. The stunt was much more dangerous for me than it looks. I had undergone surgery to remove more ovarian cysts only weeks before we started shooting *McLintock!* While I was readying to do the stunt, extra precautions had to be taken. Faye, Jimmy, and Duke's wardrobe man said, "Good God, we're not going to let you go backward down that slope without protecting you."

The resourcefulness of my gang was mind-boggling. Somehow they found a pair of waterproof fishing waders in my size.

They cut off the front and back aprons, then forced me into them so that if the operation incision opened up, everything would be held in place. My waist was wrapped tightly and I was put back into my costume. This took forever and I was running late. When I got to the set, Duke hollered, "What the hell kept you? Why were you so long?" I had never told Duke about my surgery, and did so only after my stunt. He was furious with me when he found out, and hollered, "Good God. Why didn't you tell me? We could have killed you!"

The far more dangerous stunts, though, took place at the end of the picture, during the sequence in which Duke chases me through the town before spanking me. These stunts were planned and coordinated with the help of a first-rate group of stuntmen: Cliff Lyons, Good Chuck Hayward, Bad Chuck Roberson, Boyd "Red" Morgan, Polly Burson, Lucille House, and Dean Smith. The first stunt starts the scene off as Duke kicks in my bedroom door and backs me off the balcony so that I fall down into a hay wagon. This stunt required precision falling and landing so I didn't snap my neck or spinal cord. The key to this stunt was hitting my departure mark and holding the backward rotation long enough. After I landed safely, I was far more concerned about breaking bones if Duke landed on me when he jumped down after me. Thankfully, he hit his mark too and missed me.

The most dangerous stunt I did perform in the picture was the fall from the ladder into the water trough. It looks so simple, but believe me, it was a highly risky proposition. How it got insured I'll never know. The scene calls for me, as I'm trying to escape Duke, to climb up a ladder that's leaning against a building. But as I reach the very top, which is two stories high, the ladder and I fall away from the building and I splash down into a water trough that breaks my fall. The stunt is so dangerous because I have only inches to spare. Had I fallen too long, I'd have snapped my neck.

Too short and I'd have snapped my spine and legs. If my elbows had not been tucked in tightly enough to my body, I'd have broken my arms and my shoulders as well. There was no margin for error. At forty-two years of age, you'd think I'd have known better.

I worked with the stuntmen before performing it and they instructed me in how to grip the ladder, with my palms turned up, not down. That's how I controlled the tuck. For days before I did the stunt, they drilled me all day long. "How are you gonna climb the ladder?" I'd answer, "Hands under the rungs, elbows in!" They fired off, "How you gonna fall?" They did it so often that it became second nature for me. "Let go with both hands at once, and keep my elbows in," I assured them. My stand-in, Lucille, was used to measuring the distance for the fall. She climbed the ladder and performed the test so I could first gauge the fall by sight. Lucille was as crazy as I was—God bless her!

Then it was my turn. I was confident as I climbed the ladder. Remember, fear is a killer. But as I hung from the ladder, Red Morgan whispered up to me, "For Godsakes, get down from there. You're gonna kill yourself."

"Well, it's bloody late to be telling me now as they're hauling me up," I answered.

The cameras rolled and before I started the fall I looked back and saw that the whole stunt team had gathered around the trough for support. You get these stunts on one take for obvious reasons, and I was thrilled when it was done. Everyone on the set applauded after the sequence was over, and Duke, in typical fashion, with a wisecrack and grin, let me know he was pleased: "You didn't get your hair wet." He was right. I didn't.

Of course, the scene finally ends with Duke getting a good lick in by throwing me over his knee and spanking me with a hand shovel. I'm always asked, "Did it hurt?" It sure as hell did. My behind was black and blue for days.

Unfortunately, *McLintock!* ended on a very sad note for me. On December 15, 1962, Bronwyn called to tell me that Charles Laughton had died of cancer. Charles had been sick for quite some time, and I had asked Bronwyn to call Elsa Lanchester every week to check on his condition while I was away on location. I had not been to see Charles toward the end because Elsa and I had had a bit of a tiff. She had accused me of sneaking into his hospital room and pinning St. Christopher medals under his bed. I hadn't done any such thing and the accusation was ludicrous. I told her, "Listen, Elsa, if you don't believe in God or want Charles surrounded by religion at this time, that's your business. I'll respect it, but I'm still going to pray for him. That's my business and between God and me." To her credit, when Elsa did call Bronwyn with the news, she told her, "Tell your mother that Charles did see a priest before he died." I know it took a lot for her to admit that to me and, in my eyes, it made her ten feet tall.

Losing Laughton was almost like losing a parent. He was more than my mentor and had always treated me like his daughter instead of his protégée. He taught me a great deal about acting and about life. Yet it's his immense talent that I will always remember most, and his unmistakably unique presence on-screen. His eloquent voice and that magical gleam in his eye will never be matched. It would be nearly thirty years until I would finally catch a glimpse of Laughton's essence again, and I would see it in the most unexpected of all places—in the eyes of a large and lovable comic from Canada.

CHAPTER 21

FROM THE GRASSY KNOLL

I love you too, but what if I wasn't here?" "If you ever leave me, I'll kill you."

"Enrique, you've got to have a male friend."

"I've got you. That's all I need."

"No. A man has to have a male friend to be his pal."

We'd had this conversation before, but it was never more true and necessary than now. Enrique was going through a very difficult time. Negrita's condition had worsened over the years and she had died of diabetes. He was absolutely devastated and heartbroken. In the end, when there was no hope, Negrita had accused Enrique of not finding her the best doctors and thus letting her die. He was in so much pain, and he never fully recovered.

It all happened at a time in Enrique's life when he was getting out of politics and that high-profile lifestyle. Many of his friendships—like that with President Aleman—were becoming less significant and part of his past. He didn't have any close friends other than me and I felt that he should. Enrique was a strong and prideful man and I believed that a male friend might be someone who could help him through the grieving process in a way that I wouldn't be able to.

I was the one who pushed Enrique to rebuild his old friendship with Manuel. I liked Manuel at the beginning. I was happy that Enrique finally had a friend I hoped he could trust. I thought Manuel was my friend too. I had been fooled, however; he wasn't my friend. I was about to discover that I had walked Enrique and myself straight into a lion's den.

I was planning to slow my career down a bit in 1963, but then Jack Warner approached me with a brilliant idea. The studio was about to begin production in August on the motion-picture version of the Broadway musical *My Fair Lady*. Rex Harrison had been cast as Professor Henry Higgins and Audrey Hepburn had been cast as Eliza Doolittle. Warner had a special role in the movie for me.

What Warner didn't know was that I had wanted to do the movie version of *My Fair Lady* for years. Harry Cohn at Columbia had once tried to buy the picture for me but was outbid by Hecht-Hill-Lancaster. When they were unable to raise the money to make the film, Jack Warner had ended up with the rights. The offer he made me was this: "Everyone knows that Audrey can't sing a note. We have to dub her; there's no way around it. How would you like to be the singing voice of Eliza Doolittle?" I almost fell out of my chair with excitement. I would have loved to play the whole role, but singing all those marvelous songs had always been why I wanted to do it most.

Jack Warner loved my singing voice. He had seen me perform the role of Mama from the stage play *High Button Shoes* on *The Garry Moore Show* and raved about it almost every time he saw me. But Warner knew that most people still didn't think of me as a singer, and that led to the second part of his idea. "Maureen, we want to have a contest all over the world asking people to guess who dubbed Audrey Hepburn. We're going to give this thing so much publicity, everyone will be talking about it. No one will ever guess that it was Maureen O'Hara!"

I thought it was a wonderful and brilliant idea. Unfortunately, Audrey Hepburn didn't agree and rejected it. I couldn't blame her really. She was the leading lady and certainly didn't want to share the spotlight with me. Had I been in her shoes, I'd have done the same thing. So Marni Nixon dubbed her and, once again, got to sing some of the most beautiful songs in movies.

It wasn't until nearly a year later that Warner found me another project to do and I was back to work. In late April 1964, I was on my way to Italy to make *The Battle of the Villa Fiorita* with Rossano Brazzi. Delmer Daves was set to direct me once again.

We started filming *The Battle of the Villa Fiorita* in early May. I was excited about making the picture because it was such a beautiful love story. Delmer Daves had once again adapted the screenplay, from the novel by Rumer Godden. The story is about an English wife and mother (played by me) who falls in love with a handsome Italian pianist (played by Rossano Brazzi) and leaves her family to live with him at the Villa Fiorita in Italy. Her children follow her there and battle to get their mother back.

I fell so in love with the script; it was one of the most beautiful love stories I had ever read. I began the picture with high hopes, but the picture quickly turned into a disaster. Rossano Brazzi wasn't right for the part. He was a native Italian, born and raised there, but had won fans all over the world with his performance as Emile de Becque opposite Mitzi Gaynor in *South Pacific*. He had fancied himself as a great screen lover ever since. Brazzi was not the first choice for *The Battle of the Villa Fiorita*. Delmer Daves wanted Richard Harris to play the part, but he was unavailable, which was a shame because I would have loved to work with Harris. Brazzi spent most of his time on the picture telling me about all of his lovemaking conquests, pampering his numerous toy poodles, and pretending to drop his trousers accidentally, in a vain attempt to make the script girl swoon.

I was photographed horribly in most of the picture and think it was done on purpose, payback for the most absurd thing you can possibly imagine—a soccer match. Early in the shoot, most of the cast and crew attended a local charity event. It was a soccer match between the Italian members of the cast and crew and the British members of the cast and crew, to benefit a small local children's hospital. Brazzi was playing goalie for the British team and so I thought it would be good public relations, and gracious, if I went and sat on the Italian side and showed support for our host's team. I had no idea that in doing so I had angered one very important person on the picture.

Later that evening at dinner, the picture's cameraman approached me at the table just before we were served. He was a charming man, a brilliant cameraman, and spoke with a thick English accent. "So, you sat with the I-talians, did ya?" His eyes narrowed in on me. "I'll getcha for that." I thought he was joking and laughed, but get me he did. From that day on, while we were filming, I would see him messing around with my key light just before the cameras rolled. Sometimes he'd give a signal to his assistant, and then he'd kick it so the light would drop down and shine on my stomach instead of my face. I was acting my heart out and giving a terrific dramatic performance, but when I saw the picture, I looked awful in it.

To make matters worse, the picture had been destroyed in the editing room. The cutter hated love scenes and cut out all the passion in the picture and ruined the love story. I was so upset at what the two of them had done that I cried when I finally saw the movie.

I was back in Mexico City by October and happy to be home, but I didn't receive the warm reception I was expecting. Something was troubling Enrique. He was cool and distant, and that was unlike him. He had never been that way with me before.

"Enrique, why are you upset with me? What did I do to make you so mad?"

"You know what you did!" he exploded. "How could you say those things about Quico? How could you say that about my son?"

I didn't know what the hell he was talking about. I had never said anything unkind about Quico. I loved his son and had ever since we'd first met. It was terrible. From that day on, Enrique and I were never as close as we had been. The first few bricks in the wall that would come between us had been laid. It didn't take long for me to figure out that someone was deliberately making Enrique upset with me. Enrique was constantly hearing mean and nasty things that I was supposed to have said but hadn't. I found myself in the daily position of defending myself against unfair and untrue accusations.

We both needed a break from it all. I went home to Los Angeles and left Enrique in Mexico. I was soul-searching and looking for answers to our problems. As I had for most of my life, I turned to Charlie Fitz for advice, and he told me to give it more time. I was relying more and more on my brother. We were going over some of my financial matters when he asked how my business relationship with Bill Duce was going.

I don't know why, but I had kept William B. Duce on as my business manager even after he had helped Will drain my bank account. He'd placed all the blame on Will and claimed he had only been following his instructions. Over the years, I kept a closer eye on Duce and he slowly regained my trust. Some years earlier, I had even formed a partnership with Bill Duce, Cal Cuba Enterprises, created to acquire oil leases and explore for oil and gas in Cuba. It had started off doing well but then had slowed quite a bit after Castro nationalized most of the businesses there.

Cal Cuba had been inactive for years but there was still quite a bit of my money in the partnership account. Charlie suggested I call the bank and verify the balance amounts that Duce had reported. It was a matter of prudence. Charlie's hunch was right on the money, so to speak. The account was short $500,000, and other valuable assets were missing as well. The paper trail led right to Bill Duce. In November 1964, I filed suit against him to dissolve our partnership and get my money back. I eventually settled out of court, because you can't get blood from a turnip and there was nothing left. I only recovered a small fraction of the money and some land and oil leases that were owned by the partnership. Every now and then, a $10 check rolls in from my big oil-well leases.

Enrique and I were talking on the phone a couple of times a week. Putting distance between us was doing some good, but our conversations still felt forced. We were walking on eggshells. He wanted to know when I'd be back in Mexico. I told him I'd be there when I finished the picture I was about to start.

In March 1965, I was back at work for Universal on another picture with Jimmy Stewart. This time he had asked for me, and I was very pleased. Jimmy had obviously liked working with me after all. *The Rare Breed* was a western and the last picture I made for almost four years. It is forgettable in every way except for a wonderful character performance by Brian Keith and the screen debut of Juliet Mills.

Jimmy—bless his heart—pulled another . . . well, Jimmy. You already know that as great an actor as he was, Jimmy was never one to happily share a scene. But this script gave me more screen time and the chance to play out a few scenes with him. I decided to make it count this time around. One day on the shoot, I poured everything I had into the scene we were doing and knew I had stolen it from Jimmy. I was thrilled with myself; stealing a scene from Jimmy Stewart is no easy task. We broke, and between takes, Jimmy went to his dressing room while my new makeup man, Whitey Snyder, came over to touch up my makeup. I was eagerly expecting compliments and feeling very full of myself. Instead, Whitey leaned over and whispered in my ear, "You'll be going home soon."

"Huh? What do you mean?" I asked.

"You'll see," he replied.

Sure enough, within a few minutes, the assistant director came to the set and announced that we were wrapping for the day. Mr. Stewart had suddenly come down with a mysterious illness and was unable to return to the set. When I showed up for work the next day to finish shooting the scene, new pages of script were handed out. The scene had been completely rewritten overnight and was now impossible for me to steal.

The picture wasn't a total flop, but it didn't quite live up to anyone's expectations. I didn't really care how well it did. My problems with Enrique were weighing on my mind as my pending return to Mexico City neared. I loved Enrique and was desperate to turn things around and get life back to the way it had been.

When I arrived, it was obvious that the time away had only widened the distance between us. Enrique was moving further and further away from me emotionally, and I couldn't seem to stop it. I didn't know what to do. I rationalized that it was best if I continued to act as I always had with him, to be myself. I didn't want to force the issue because that often sows the seeds of your own demise in a relationship.

As the end of 1965 neared, Enrique wasn't coming by the house for days at a time. I wouldn't see or hear from him at all. Our relationship was unraveling and my heart was breaking. I sank into sadness and depression. During the course of the following year, the distance between us widened. He was staying away now for longer periods of time. I knew all about this behavior from my time with Will, and also knew I couldn't and wouldn't put up with that again. I still loved Enrique, but was growing angry that he allowed others to ruin our life together. This was the man who had rescued me from the cold abyss of life with Will. I admired, respected, and deeply loved him. I didn't want that to change; I didn't want to ever feel resentment or bitterness toward him.

In February 1967, I left my things in Mexico City and flew to Los Angeles. Bronwyn stayed in Mexico, but I knew I was not coming back. My relationship with Enrique Parra was over.

It was the people closest to Enrique, those I had considered family and friends, who had finally succeeded in splitting us apart. They had conspired behind the scenes and fired at us from the grassy knoll. They wanted me out of the picture, and it was over the money, of course. It's always about money when there is a lot of it at stake. For some of them, the risk was too great. I'm certain there was great concern over what Enrique might have left to me if we had stayed together and I survived him.

As we reached the middle of 1967, I was in Los Angeles still feeling very down and depressed. I was avoiding everything, including life. Then one day I got a call from Charlie Fitz. An old family friend was in town on a layover with Pan Am during one of his around-the-world flights. Charlie Blair had called Charlie Fitz and asked him to meet him for dinner, but my brother was all tied up at the studio and couldn't go. Instead, he told Charlie Blair, "I can't, but Maureen's in town. Why don't you have her go with you?" But when Charlie Fitz called to ask me to have dinner with Charlie Blair, I really wasn't feeling up to it.

"Oh God no, I can't. I'm too depressed."

"Well, I can't either, and we can't leave the man here alone. I already told him you'd go."

"I'd be awful company."

"You need to get out of that house. So dust yourself off and be ready at eight because he's coming."

He was right. I needed to stop moping about and get on with it. I had dinner that night with Charlie Blair at my favorite Italian restaurant in Westwood, Matteo's. It was also one of Sinatra's favorite hangouts, but you had to go to the back room to see him. And no matter when I showed up, I always seemed to bump into George Burns there too. George was a Hollywood legend. He began in the early days of television as part of the famed husband and wife comedy team of George Burns and Gracie Allen. Sadly, Gracie died early in life but their marriage remains one of Hollywood's greatest love stories. He'd gossip the night away about Gracie, even long after she was gone. Over dinner, I found out that Charlie Blair was in the dumps too. He was going through a terrible breakup with a girlfriend at the same time I was breaking up with Enrique. We spent the whole night commiserating with each other and talking about how much we had loved the other person.

So this definitely wasn't a date. It's funny, but I don't think Charlie Blair and I ever had a date together our entire lives. We had been friends from the time we'd met, when he flew me back to Ireland after the war. We had stayed in touch ever since. But there was never any romantic interest between us—he was always taken and so was I. I knew and was friendly with both of his wives. When I heard he was divorced from the wife I liked most, I left a message for him: "Tell him he's a damn fool!"

When I was in London making *Britannia Mews,* he'd fly there as part of his scheduled route and we'd see each other. He'd bring either steaks or chops with him—some kind of meat—because there wasn't much available in Europe right after the war. From the time we met, every time he came to Los Angeles we'd see him or we'd leave messages for him when we went through New York. The whole FitzSimons clan knew and loved him. By 1967, we had been friends for over twenty years.

Charlie Blair was an extraordinary man. He was eleven years older than I, born in 1909 to Irish-Scottish parents in Buffalo, New York. He had dreamed of soaring across the sky from the time he was a little boy, and had flown his first solo flight by the age of nineteen. He entered naval flying school in 1931 after earning a degree in mechanical engineering, and graduated a year later as a naval aviator designation number 4748, with the rank of ensign in the United States Naval Reserve. At twenty-three, his first assignment was to be stationed at the Naval Air Station in San Diego, California. It would be the first of many assignments that would span a military career that lasted over forty-five years and earned him the rank of brigadier general in the air force. Over the course of his career, Charlie flew over 35,000 hours, and made more than 1,600 crossings of the Atlantic.

Charlie was released from active duty in 1933 and quickly joined the commercial aviation industry. For seven years, he received the most rugged education a young pilot possibly could, flying airmail routes for United Airlines. In the 1930s, airmail pilots were the most daring and were considered the elite of them all. In 1940, he joined the newly formed American Export Airlines (later American Overseas Airlines, or AOA) as its first chief pilot. He was responsible for all scheduled flights between the United States and Ireland, the British Isles, Europe, Africa, and South America.

After World War II broke out, Captain Charlie Blair flew for both the Naval Air Transport and the Air Transport Command. In 1942, he flew the first groundbreaking test flights in an S-44 Sikorsky seaplane, the *Excalibur I*. In June of that year, he made aviation history when he piloted *Excalibur I* from Foynes, Ireland, through Newfoundland, to New York in the first non-stop commercial flight to cross the Atlantic with passengers and mail. The following year, he flew the first North Atlantic winter flight nonstop between the United States and the British Isles. A year after that, he commanded the five fastest seaplane crossings of the Atlantic on five consecutive missions. The fastest was fourteen hours and seventeen minutes, at the time a mind-boggling feat.

After the war was over, Charlie not only flew as a pilot for AOA, but also owned and operated a small nonscheduled airline flying passengers between New York and Europe, the Middle East, and South America. The company had only a single plane in its fleet—a long-range C-46 that Charlie named *Excalibur II*. He eventually sold the airline, after logging sixteen million safe miles. He became a Pan Am pilot in 1950 when it acquired American Overseas Airlines and its pilots.

Charlie always said, "The sky is full of new frontiers," and he always wanted to break flying barriers. He used the money from the sale of his air-line to purchase a single-engine P-51 Mustang fighter he called *Excalibur III*. In January 1951, Charlie flew *Excalibur III* nonstop from New York to London with the goal of breaking the speed record. His plan was to use a then little-known phenomenon called "the jet stream" to increase his speed by catching the tailwind. The flight was the first time a specific jet stream had ever been targeted and found. He made it from New York to London's Heathrow Airport in an elapsed time of just seven hours and forty-eight minutes, shaving a full hour and seven seconds off the previous record. His remarkable time for a transatlantic crossing by a single-engine, single-seat plane is a record that still stands today.

Four months later, on May 29, Charlie blazed across the sky one more time in his P-51 and made the most important flight of his career. Beginning in Bardufoss, Norway, with a final destination of Fairbanks, Alaska, Charlie, in a single-engine aircraft, flew the first long-distance solo flight over any polar region. His 3,260-mile nonstop flight validated a navigational system that he had developed specifically for flying over polar regions.

Charlie's flight across the North Pole had staggering implications. It not only demonstrated that transpolar flights were possible, but proved that the Arctic Ocean was no longer a safe defense against possible air attacks on the United States of America. This achievement earned him the Thurlow Award for Navigation, the Distinguished Flying Cross, and the coveted Harmon International Trophy, which was presented to him during a special ceremony at the White House. As President Harry S. Truman handed him the award, he proclaimed Charlie "the world's outstanding aviator."

In 1952, Charlie was ordered to Strategic Air Command to help develop techniques for delivering thermonuclear weapons from long-range fighter aircraft. He resigned from the naval reserve to accept an air force commission with the rank of colonel. He was promoted to the rank of brigadier general in 1959. I believe his top-secret work in the nuclear weapons programs later placed his life in grave danger.

Later, Charlie was the only part-time fighter pilot in the regular air force. And on the weekends, he still flew passenger airliners to Europe as a Pan Am senior pilot. As they used to say, he wore two hats.

After our dinner at Matteo's that night, Charlie called me every time he came to town. Sometimes I'd see him once a week and other times once or twice a month. Over the next year and countless dinners, the warmth of our friendship grew. I had always known and loved him as a friend of the family and I still saw him that way. I didn't consider the time we were spending together as dates, and so I wasn't expecting it when he looked at me from across the table at Matteo's and said, "I'm going to retire from Pan Am soon. I'm hoping that when I do, you might consider marrying me. I'd like to marry you very much."

It's odd, but I wasn't at all shocked or surprised by his proposal. It gave me a warm, comfortable, and happy feeling. I was intrigued and fascinated by the prospects of it. I thought, By God, yes, I'll think about this. He's a remarkable man worth loving and this could really work out and be wonderful. I knew the kind of man Charlie Blair was—good, strong, kind, and intelligent. He was also brave, adventurous, and a hero. We shared the same sense of family. My clan adored him and he adored them. So I eventually told him, "I will marry you after you retire."

We didn't wait for him to retire after all. In the first week of March, in 1968, Bronwyn injured her foot and needed medical attention. She was still in Mexico City and so I flew there to bring her back. I packed up my belongings and left a final message for Enrique Parra:

Enrique,
I have packed up my things and I am leaving. I'm not coming back. I would like to see you before I go.

Maureen

Enrique never responded to my note. The truth is, I don't know what I would have done had he answered it and asked me to stay. I think I was so hurt by then that I would have left anyway, but I can't say for certain. I loved him very, very much. Enrique had saved me from the darkness of an abusive marriage and brought me back into the warm light of life again. Leaving him was one of the most painful things I have ever had to do.

I left Mexico City and Enrique Parra behind without ever saying good-bye. We never spoke again. As I left, I couldn't help but remember Enrique's threat: "If you ever leave me, I'll kill you." Over the years with Charlie, I remembered it more than once.

I flew straight to Charlie, on St. Thomas, part of the U.S. Virgin Islands. We were married there in a small, private ceremony one week later, on March 12, 1968. I loved Charlie the day I married him, but I would fall madly in love with him as his wife.

CHAPTER 22

THE GENERAL'S WIFE

*L*ife in the Virgin Islands was like a fairy tale. I was living in a tropical paradise at the side of a man who was about to make me happier than anyone or anything ever had. I think I became complete as a person for the first time in my life, so it was later very easy to walk away from acting, movie stardom, and Hollywood. As Charlie and I began our lives together, I was certain I had proved the old Gypsy wrong. I had everything a person could ever want—a loving husband, family, health, happiness, and success. I held all of life's riches tightly within my hands, and Charlie held me in his.

Shortly before we were married, Charlie started building a beautiful home for us on the island of St. Croix, in the U.S. Virgin Islands. It sat upon the very top of a hill overlooking the crystal-blue waters of the Caribbean and the quaint little town of Christiansted.

By the time I arrived on St. Croix, it was inhabited by the most culturally diverse and ethnically rich people in the Caribbean. Immigrants had come from Africa, England, Holland, Spain, France, India, the United States, and even Ireland. Irish political prisoners being sent to Australia often jumped ship in the Caribbean and made homes there. I found the people to be full of spice, quick to smile, and wonderful. I was given a warm welcome, and they didn't seem to mind or care that a movie star had moved into the neighborhood. In no time, I was one of them, and together, we worked and made our living off a bustling tourist trade.

From the day we were married, Charlie and I were inseparable. Just standing beside him, I felt his strength—physical, mental, spiritual—and that made me feel secure and content. We were a dynamite couple, and within months of being married, it was fireworks between us that never stopped. Charlie was a tall and handsome man, with silver-streaked hair, confident eyes, and a nice square jaw. I don't mind saying, we looked bloody good together.

I committed myself completely to our new life together on St. Croix. I joined the family business right away. Antilles Air Boats was a scheduled passenger and cargo airline founded by Charlie that linked the U.S. and British Virgin Islands with Puerto Rico and St. Martin. "The Goose," as it was called, thanks to its fleet of Grumman Gooses, was the largest seaplane airline in the world. Its convenient downtown-to-downtown service made it the major transportation link among the islands. Trips between the islands that had once taken a full day or more now took less than an hour, round trip.

It didn't take me long to figure out that operating an airline is a lot like making movies. The business of an airline, just like that of movies, is dealing with the public, selling them tickets and making them come back and buy more tickets. I knew how to do that, and so my job was working with the public and promotion. I just had to get better doing it up in the sky.

Besides, Charlie made no secret of the fact that he didn't want me to work in the picture business anymore. When an offer came in to make *How Do I Love Thee?* with Jackie Gleason, he wanted me to turn it down. As yet, I had not made my decision to leave acting altogether. It had been almost five years since I had made my last picture, and I thought I should make this one just to keep myself out there in front of the public. There was only one scheduling problem that had to be worked out and agreed to for me to do it. Charlie was retiring from Pan Am in the middle of the filming and the airline had planned a big farewell tour around the world for him. He would be flying his "Pan Am Number One Around the World," the most prized Pan Am flight, one final time. More than anything, he wanted me to be with him and I wanted to be there as well.

Thankfully, Jackie and the producers agreed to shoot around me during the week I needed off. We started filming the third week in June 1969, and as soon as I arrived on location, I was homesick for St. Croix and already missing Charlie. I couldn't wait to join him in the middle of July and leave on our journey. Pan Am gave us one hell of a send-off and planned to cap the tour with a big celebration upon our return to New York. It was going to be a big party, but in typical Charlie Blair fashion, we got off in San Francisco so he could avoid the fuss of it. Charlie hated being the center of attention where work was concerned. We flew the rest of the way back to New York as passengers on a different flight. It was just the way he wanted to retire—without a bang.

I soon wished I had never returned to Florida to finish the picture. It was a terrible film. The script was awful, and the director couldn't fix it. The first week I was back, my hand was seriously injured in a freak accident with Jackie. We were in the middle of a scene and I was sitting on a garden bench. The cushions had been removed, exposing the Cyclone fence type of wire that supported them. My right hand was resting on the wire, and as Jackie walked over to deliver his lines, he tripped and accidentally fell on top of my hand. The Cyclone fence wire gave way and the weight of his body crushed my hand. I was taken to the hospital and a removable cast was put on so that I could finish the picture. As they say in the picture business, "Don't die until the picture is in the can." My hand later required orthopedic surgery. As a result, I have no cartilage in the fingers of my right hand anymore and I'm missing a joint on the first index finger.

Despite the accident, which made Jackie feel awful, I liked him very much. He was a very kind and funny man, but he drank too much. The picture's problems proved insurmountable, and it was a dud at the box office.

It was good to be back home in St. Croix, but by the holidays, I was preoccupied with old memories and missing Ireland. I had dreamed for years of having a little cottage in Ireland that I could visit once a year, in the summertime. Charlie loved Ireland too because of the many flights he'd made to and from Shannon Airport over the years and because of his famous flight from Foynes. In early 1970, we flew to Ireland and went looking for our little cottage. We scoured the countryside and saw many beautiful homes, but none that really grabbed us. Toward the end of our trip, we were finally told of a beautiful place in West Cork, in a small village called Glengarriff.

Driving through the one-road village, I knew right away that it had all the cozy charm we were looking for. We turned down the long avenue and kept driving and driving for what seemed like miles, looking for the house. We still hadn't seen it when Charlie glimpsed the sea through the trees. His face lit up, and I knew. He said, "Oh, this is perfect. It's perfect! We're buying it." Ever sensible, I reminded him, "But, Charlie, we haven't even seen the house yet. How do you know?" He gave me a pilot's answer. "Oh, it's a perfect place to land a seaplane," and so we continued down the road and bought the house at the end of it. The house was called Lugdine, which means "Deep Pool."

Life just kept getting better. We were no sooner settling back into our routines at Antilles than we got a surprise call from Bronwyn. She was pregnant, so Charlie and I were expecting our first grandchild together. Charlie already had grandchildren from his previous marriages, but I didn't have any from my side of the family. Earlier, on October 15, 1968, just six months after I'd married Charlie, Bronwyn married too. Charlie and I attended the ceremony, in northern California. I really hadn't been happy about the marriage, but what do you say to a beloved daughter? The marriage didn't last, but it yielded precious fruit. My grandson, Conor Beau, was born on September 8, 1970. At fifty years of age, it was official: Maureen O'Hara was a granny.

Duke called to congratulate us on the new addition to the family, but he was also calling with an offer. He had just won an Academy Award for his performance in *True Grit* and was set to make another western in Mexico. He wanted me to play his wife. This time, Charlie was all for it, since he and Duke had become great friends. The funny thing about it is that Charlie Blair was a jealous husband. He hated it when other men even looked at me. He never made a fuss, but a wife knows when her husband is jealous. So what I realized was that Charlie Blair didn't like me to work unless the leading man was one of his good friends, and he had many in the picture business.

Charlie was no stranger to movie stars. In addition to marrying one, he had flown most of them somewhere in the world many times over the years. He liked Hank Fonda a lot, and was particularly fond of Humphrey Bogart. Charlie flew Bogie in and out of Africa many times during the war. They were friends until the day Bogie died. Charlie told me how he had once saved the life of Bogie's second wife, Mayo Methot, by pulling her off a hotel-room ledge after she'd learned of her husband's affection for Lauren Bacall. Charlie and Duke had an even closer relationship, and so I was free and clear to make the picture.

I wasn't crazy about playing the part of Martha McCandles in *Big Jake.* It was a small role and not central to the story, but it was Duke, so I agreed to do it. We shot the picture in October 1970, in Durango, Mexico. In addition to reuniting Duke and me in our last picture together, *Big Jake* also brought many of the old gang back together—members of the Ford stock company like Dobe Carey, Good Chuck and Bad Chuck, and a few of Duke's kids. It was fun to be out there doing stunts again, but with a little less spring in our step this time around. You can't beat Father Time, and the aches and pains of making a western took just a little longer to soothe on this picture. I didn't have much screen time in the movie because the film was too long, so some of my biggest scenes with Duke were left on the cutting-room floor. Fans of the Wayne-O'Hara team were a bit disappointed, and it was reflected at the box office. It was a good movie, but not a great one.

The interiors for *Big Jake* were filmed back in Hollywood, and on one of those days, Duke asked me, "Have you gone to see the old man yet?"

It had been more than a few years since I had seen or heard from John Ford. Our lives had gone in different directions. I was living a new life in St. Croix with Charlie, while he had remained in Hollywood. I also hadn't been in any great rush to see him. His mean and spiteful behavior toward me and then toward Jimmy had put a wedge between us. But I knew I couldn't stay angry with

Ford and that any self-imposed estrangement would eventually come to an end. Too much of our lives had been spent together, making great pictures and being friends and loyal Irish kinsmen. Pappy was in poor health now, either bedridden or in a wheelchair, having broken his hip falling over a laundry basket at home. It was time I went to see him.

Bronwyn and Conor Beau joined me in Los Angeles while I was doing some publicity for *Big Jake* in January 1971. I took them with me to see Pappy so he could meet my new grandson. I called Meta and was surprised when she told me that Mary Ford was not well either. She was struggling with Parkinson's disease and angina. Apparently, Barbara and Pat weren't doing all that well either and had problems of their own. I was sad that the whole Ford family was in poor health and battling their demons. We arrived at the Fords' new home on Copa de Oro, in Bel Air, in the early afternoon. I went in to see Mary first. She perked up as soon as she saw the four-month-old child in Bronwyn's arms. We stayed with her for a while and then went across the hall to see Pappy.

The old man was expecting us. We found him sitting upright in a makeshift hospital bed and being tended to by a nurse. He had the familiar cigar in his mouth and that crazy black patch over the left lens of his glasses. Ford had had cataracts removed twenty years before this and his eyesight was fine. He'd complained for years that his left eye was still sensitive to light, but it was rubbish, of course. I had seen him use that eye like a microscope whenever he wanted to. He'd flip the patch up, study something intently, then flip it down again. He liked the visual effect it provided and the yarn he could spin about it.

I walked in carrying the baby and Pappy didn't miss a beat: "I didn't even know you were pregnant." He knew I was bringing my grandson and must have given extra thought to how he would break the ice. Walking into the room felt very comfortable. There was no awkwardness at all. We started chatting as if it had been only days since we'd last seen each other. I set Conor Beau down on the bed beside Pappy and he went on and on about how fine a baby he was and how happy he was for Bronwyn and our family. It didn't take long before he had us on the subject of Ireland and the great time we all had while making *The Quiet Man.* Then I asked how Barbara was and he answered sadly, "Oh, she's *lán go leóir*," Gaelic for "good and full." It meant she was drunk. We could have stayed there gossiping for hours, but I could see that Ford wasn't well either. He had always looked old to me, but now he also looked sickly and frail. After an hour or so, we said good-bye and left him to rest.

On our way home in the car, Bronwyn and I were both feeling introspective. She had known John Ford her entire life and was as surprised by his frail appearance as I was. She broke the silence with an observation of something that I had always denied. "He's in love with you, Mom." I was quick to deny it again. "Oh, don't be silly. Of course he's not." But she was adamant and spoke with certainty. "I saw it, Mom. I saw the way he looked at you."

So here at last is the answer to a question that has been around for decades. Certainly, having read this far, you must be curious yourself. Was John Ford in love with Maureen O'Hara? I honestly believe the answer is no. He might have thought that he was, but he was only in love with an image. John Ford was in love with Mary Kate Danaher and I was his image of her. Later in life, he blamed me for not remaining her, and for not saving him from himself.

Six months after my visit with John Ford, he began complaining of abdominal pain. Everyone knew what it was before the doctors opened him up. The cancer was terminal, and Hollywood began to prepare for John Ford's final reel.

I was back soon enough in St. Croix with Charlie, working at Antilles. The airline was growing by leaps and bounds. Our new slogan was "Why lose an entire day on a boat going from one island to another, when a quick flight can get you there in the blink of an eye?" We called ourselves "The Streetcar Line of the Virgin Islands." Our small company had grown from just one pilot, one seaplane, and five employees to fourteen amphibious aircraft.

There's an old expression that wives of all the great pilots use. We refer to our husband's favorite plane as his girlfriend. Well, our Sikorsky VS-44 was Charlie's. He loved telling me with a grin, "She's the Queen of the Sky and I'm the King of the Sky," and they really were. With a twinkle in his eye, he would go on, "But the King of the Sky married the Queen of the Earth."

Over the years, I had taken comfortably to a very simple but rich and loving way of life with Charlie. For the first time, I had someone who wanted to take care of me and it was wonderful. As a military man, Charlie followed a strict regimen. He was up bright and early every morning, by six A.M., to do push-ups and sit-ups. Then it was off to the shower to get ready for the day. Every morning before he left for work, he made me a cup of tea and brought it to me in bed. He was out the door by six forty-five A.M., sharp and on his way to the Antilles base to make sure the guys were on the job and the Gooses were ready to fly. Some days he flew a Goose himself and other days he flew a desk as president of the airline. He worked a long day and came home only when the last Goose had come in. He ran a few miles every night before supper and took our dog, McGillicuddy, with him for company. We were always in bed early.

I was so content being the general's wife that I didn't miss being Maureen O'Hara at all. I didn't miss Hollywood or acting or anything else, for that matter. I hadn't made a picture since *Big*

Jake, and had turned down more than a few good ones over the years. There was nowhere I wanted to be more than with Charlie.

This bliss was interrupted briefly by the sudden passing of my father. Daddy died peacefully, in his sleep, on July 17, 1972, but I was comforted by the fact that he was now with Mammy and that he knew I was safe with Charlie.

Charlie knew I needed something to get my mind off losing Daddy, and he encouraged me to accept an offer to star opposite Henry Fonda in *The Red Pony*. I agreed to make the picture because you rarely find a story written better than John Steinbeck does it, and because I would get to work with Fonda one more time. It was a made-for-television picture for *Hallmark Hall of Fame* that aired on NBC in March 1973. Hank and I were never paid our full salary. We used to call each other from time to time and ask, "Did you get any money yet?" Still, I am particularly pleased with the picture and feel it is some of my best dramatic work. I received a lovely letter from actress Shirley Booth telling me that the scene with my son upstairs was one of the very best she had ever seen on film. I was quite flattered. The movie won the Peabody Award for Television Excellence. I ended on a high note with *The Red Pony* and wouldn't make another picture for twenty years.

Around the time *The Red Pony* aired, I was in Los Angeles finishing up some publicity and readying for another very important performance. The American Film Institute was about to honor John Ford with its first Lifetime Achievement Award. The award was established to honor filmmakers whose work had "stood the test of time." When the nominating committee met to make their selection, John Ford was the only name put up for a vote. No filmmaker deserved the honor more. It was also announced from the White House that on that very same evening,

President and Mrs. Nixon would be in attendance to award Pappy the Medal of Freedom.

On March 31, I attended *The American Film Institute Presents: A Salute to John Ford,* held at the Beverly Hilton Hotel in Los Angeles. It was a night that John Ford had waited for his entire life. All of Hollywood was there to honor him, and the president would thank him on behalf of a grateful nation.

The award ceremony began with the formal introduction, "Ladies and gentlemen, the president of the United States and Mrs. Nixon and tonight's guest of honor, Mr. John Ford." I was sitting on the dais with Duke, Jimmy Stewart, Jack Lemmon, Charlton Heston, Ronald Reagan, and Danny Kaye when they pushed Pappy's wheelchair into the ballroom. The president and Mrs. Nixon entered behind him as the orchestra played "Hail to the Chief." I was shocked by Pappy's appearance and knew instantly that death was not far behind him.

Pappy was wheeled over to the dais and seated next to me. The president, Mrs. Nixon, and Mary Ford were seated next to him so that Pappy would be at the president's right-hand side. As chairman of the board of trustees, Charlton Heston spoke first and introduced Danny Kaye, who was the night's emcee. Kaye gave a vintage performance by doing his trademark routine, which uses countless foreign accents. Then, one after the other, pillars of the filmmaking community rose to their feet and saluted John Ford and his remarkable career. Duke spoke, and then Jimmy Stewart and Jack Lemmon. Pretaped commentary from Clint Eastwood, Lee Marvin, and Roddy McDowall was played. When it was finally my turn, I saluted John Ford the only way I knew how:

Ladies and gentlemen, Mr. President, and if you'll forgive me, more importantly, Mr. Séan Aloysius Kilmartin O'Feeney, alias Mr. John Ford, sometimes Rear Admiral John Ford, but to all of us

who love him so very, very dearly, he'll always be Pappy. Pappy,
with your permission tonight, I'd like to salute you and the
Admiral's lady, Mary, by singing to you from the score of The Quiet
Man.

Ford always made me sing for him wherever we were, so what
could have been more fitting? My medley began with "The Humor
Is on Me Now," then "Young May Moon," and, finally, "The Isle of
Innisfree." When I returned to the dais, my songs seemed to have
breathed new life into the old man. It gave him the yearning to
pull one last John Fordism with me. Making sure President Nixon
could see and overhear him, Ford leaned over and began speaking into my ear in bogus Gaelic. I knew my cue and wasn't about
to let him down. As I always had, I nodded softly and replied,
"Seadh. Seadh." He went on and on until getting precisely the reaction from the president that he wanted. Nixon leaned over and
asked, "What are you two doing over there?" I could almost hear
the giddiness in Pappy's voice as he answered gruffly, "We're
speaking in our native language."

The AFI ceremony was the last time I saw John Ford. I returned home to St. Croix, and he died on August 31, 1973.

Ford's passing began a long period of confusion for me, and I
have wrestled with my thoughts about him ever since. I set out to
contribute to a deeper understanding of him in this book. I wanted
to come to terms with my feelings about this incredibly complex
man who had played such an important role in my life and in the
life of my family.

What made John Ford such a brilliant filmmaker? I don't
think the world will ever fully know, despite all the analysis of his
genius. I think his films were reflections of his own hopes and
dreams. He wished he had lived every one of those lives he
brought to the screen.

Of my acting abilities, he remained true to his contradictory form. He once wrote to me, "You are the best *fucking* actress in Hollywood." Then, when later asked by a young film student at UCLA about me, in front of Merian C. Cooper, he replied to his audience, "Her? That bitch couldn't act her way out of a brick shithouse." Yet he cast me in more films than any other of his leading ladies, so that will have to suffice as an answer for me.

Who was John Ford the man? To figure that out we must make sense of all his contradictions and reconcile the personal conflicts that he buried deep within himself and surrounded with walls built of secrecy, lies, and aggression. This labyrinth was built stone by stone, like the Pyramids, and I don't believe the old man ever wanted to be found out or exposed in any way. An enigma? Absolutely—and of his precise making.

For years, I wondered why John Ford grew to hate me so much. I couldn't understand what made him say and do so many terrible things to me. I realize now that he didn't hate me at all. He loved me very much and even thought that he was in love with me. Sadly, Mary Kate was only a character in a movie and could never be his salvation. So as I conclude my thoughts on John Ford, I reaffirm my respect, admiration, and friendship for him by saying, "I love you too, Pappy."

CHAPTER 23

RED BALL IN THE SKY

The world keeps turning, with or without us. Vietnam was over. Watergate had come and gone, and a gentle peanut farmer was poised to become president. After a long period of turmoil and unrest in the world, everything seemed to be settling down and finally getting back to normal.

My heart and mind were miles and miles away from Hollywood by now, and I was no longer interested in offers to act. My not running off to make pictures made Charlie deliriously happy. He had me all to himself, and that was just the way he wanted it. Me too. Still, he decided to hedge his bets and came home one night with a surprise. In February 1976, Antilles Air Boats purchased the *Virgin Islander*, a magazine that focused on Virgin Islands living—dining, fashion, entertainment, and culture. Everyone on the islands read it. "What are we going to do with it,

Charlie?" I asked. He grinned at me and replied, "You mean what are *you* going to do with it. You're running it."

Publishing a magazine was an exciting proposition, and I loved a good challenge, but I was wise to his motive. "Why me, Charlie?" I quizzed suspiciously. "Because I know you can do it," he replied, and then put all his cards on the table. "And this way you'll be far too busy to be tempted back to Hollywood." At least he was honest. I accepted my assignment from the general and happily became the new publisher of the *Virgin Islander.*

The truth is, I loved it. I loved the medium, its unique creative process, and the excitement of meeting a deadline each month, or "putting the issue to bed," as we say in the biz. I also added my own column in every issue and called it "Maureen O'Hara Says . . ." My monthly articles varied from commentary on lighthearted subjects like the heartache of cleaning my purse, to technical articles on aviation that discussed the inherent benefits of seaplanes. And of course, there was plenty about Hollywood and show business.

Of course, Charlie knew there were some things I just had to do when special requests came in from Hollywood. On November 6, Frank Sinatra hosted a star-studded extravaganza for the show-business charity Variety Boys Clubs International, honoring John Wayne. Very few people actually knew I was coming, and those who did were sworn to secrecy. Toward the end of the evening, after all the guests had entertained and spoken tributes to Duke, I descended the steps in a gorgeous dress—whirling black chiffon, embroidered with beaded orchids and pale green stems and leaves, with white organza ruffled collar and cuffs—and sang "I've Grown Accustomed to Your Face." Duke kissed both my hands and we stood together as I finished the song. It was a wonderful, magical moment between us. There wasn't a dry eye in the house.

A few weeks later, I was back in St. Croix when a postcard arrived in the mail. It was a picture of a Pan Am 747 flying into the sunset. On the other side, it read:

In the sunset of our lives, when the hell are you going to invite me to St. Croix?

—Duke

We called Duke right away and made plans. He had to go to Washington first and attend the inaugural gala for Jimmy Carter, but would come to St. Croix straight from there. He and his friend Pat Stacy arrived on St. Croix the last week in January 1977. We tried to sneak him off the plane so he could really rest and soak up the sunshine, but it was impossible. How do you hide John Wayne? Duke and Charlie loved spending time together playing chess and I rarely saw them the whole time Duke was visiting. They went fishing and flying in the big seaplane almost every day.

One day, they had apparently gone to Puerto Rico and almost landed themselves in big trouble. There was a pilot who worked for Antilles at the time who I never really liked or trusted. I think he knew that Charlie and Duke had flown to Puerto Rico and he called the FAA to lodge a complaint. He reported that they were flying in violation of FAA regulations. Well, the FAA boys came down to where the plane was docked and where Charlie and Duke were. They told them it had been reported that Charlie had made an illegal flight with only one certified pilot onboard. The regulations required two certified pilots for a seaplane of that size, and Duke wasn't a certified pilot. Charlie and Duke, those two bastards, bluffed their way out of it. Charlie's eyes widened in shock and disbelief, and he quipped with absolute astonishment, "Oh, come on. Haven't you guys ever seen *The High and the Mighty?*"

The two FAA men looked at each other, remembering the picture in which Duke had played an airline pilot on a troubled plane. They bought it hook, line, and sinker, and said, "Oh, oh yes. Of course. Of course. We're sorry, Mr. Wayne." Of course, Duke had never really flown a plane, and that spoke volumes about the actor he really was.

The last day of Duke's visit, he and Charlie were deep in another game of chess. They were whispering like schoolboys as I approached with their lunch. Duke looked at Charlie and then up at me with the most envious eyes. "You sure do love him, don't you?" I felt a little sad because I knew Duke hadn't found contentment and happiness. "I sure do," I replied. "All right then," Duke went on, "don't you think it's time you quit movies and stayed home?" I'm sure both of them were expecting me to raise holy hell, but I didn't. I knew Duke was right, and I was finally ready to walk away from acting. Life with Charlie on that island had brought me more happiness and joy than all my days in Hollywood ever had.

To their surprise, I answered with "Okay, fine. I quit . . . right now," and I meant it. Saying good-bye to Hollywood was the easiest decision I have ever made. I was set to live the remainder of my days with Charlie, but the old Gypsy wasn't through with me yet.

I always thought it was strange that all the pilots who worked for Antilles Air Boats were military men who had just retired. I wondered, With all the high-paying jobs that go to former officers, why would a bunch of ex-colonels and captains come to the Caribbean to fly little seaplanes?

In late 1977, I got my answer. We received from one of our vendors new billing instructions that I found quite odd. The monthly payments we made on our seaplanes, which had always been mailed to a company in the United States, were now to be routed to a Swiss bank account. All we had was an account number. The change in payments came right as the Central Intelligence Agency was receiving bad press over some covert operations that had gone terribly wrong. Maybe I have a suspicious nature, but I knew instantly that the two were linked. I started looking for some kind of proof that Antilles Air Boats was much more than a friendly little commuter airline in the Caribbean. After a bit of snooping, I found it several days later. Paperwork in Charlie's desk revealed that some of our seaplanes had actually been provided by the CIA.

General Blair had not retired at all. I'd be lying if I didn't admit that I believed all along that Charlie was still working for the United States government. I had seen too much, but chose to ignore it. I had gone with him to the home of Senator Barry Goldwater, in Arizona, on numerous occasions, and had sat in the parlor as they talked elsewhere about matters I wasn't privy to. Like Charlie, Barry Goldwater was an aviation pioneer who had flown 165 different types of aircraft by the time he retired from the air force as a general. Whenever these two old friends got together, they spoke behind closed doors about very important business. I had also often accompanied Charlie to the Pentagon. Again, I would sit on a bench and sew in the waiting area while Charlie was taken somewhere to meet with whoever had ordered him there. I never ever asked him his business—and if I had, he wouldn't have told me.

I had a theory, but kept it to myself. I believed that Antilles was not only a commercial airline, but was also a secret fleet used by the CIA. Under General Blair's command, I think Antilles pilots flew reconnaissance missions to monitor who and what was going in and out of Cuba. Antilles was founded in 1963, a very short time after the Cuban missile crisis. The United States was still very concerned about the small Communist island. I kept my eyes closed and my mouth shut from that moment on. A military wife learns to accept that there are some things about her husband she will never fully know.

In the spring of 1978, I started feeling absolutely awful. I had no aches, no pains, but I still felt terrible. If the phone rang, I wanted to smash it to smithereens. I knew something had to be wrong. I didn't tell anyone, not even Charlie, and flew out to California to see my family doctor, Blake Watson. He checked me over and said I was finishing my period. "What the hell are you still doing with this thing? That should have been finished with a long time ago. You're too old." I thanked him for the uncomplimentary compliment with a few very special words; he recommended that I have curettage, and that was just fine by me.

The operation is simple and it was done the very next day. I was downstairs a few hours later, sitting in the hallway of the hospital, waiting for more tests. Dr. Watson tapped me on the shoulder. "You'll be going back into surgery in a few days. You have cancer." His tone was so matter-of-fact that I couldn't believe I'd actually heard him right. Then he just walked away.

In fact, I had cancer of the womb, and it was quite serious. The surgical procedure was not a small matter, but I wanted it done fast. I also didn't want Charlie to know. We had just won a big charter contract at Antilles Air Boats (excellent money), and I knew Charlie would have canceled it and flown to be at my side if he knew. I decided to tell him after the operation was over and I was safe.

I had the surgery and the doctors were confident they had cut out all the cancer, although it was going to take me some time to recover. Charlie had finished the contract by this time and flew in to Los Angeles to be with me. My sister Florrie met him at the airport and told him about my cancer surgery. It nearly killed him and he fell to pieces. He came straight to the hospital and just held me tightly and cried and cried. "If anything ever happened to you," he wept, "I'd fill a Goose, fly out to sea, and keep flying until the fuel ran out."

"Don't worry. Everything's going to be fine, Charlie," I reassured him. "I won't leave you."

I was in the hospital for several days and stayed in Los Angeles for several weeks after that to finish all the checkups that were required. I still wasn't feeling that great, so I told Charlie, "I don't want to go back to St. Croix and face the heat just yet. I'm not up to it. Would you mind if I go to Lugdine for a while?"

He thought it was a good idea and suggested that Florrie go with me. "I'll fly out and join you as soon as I can."

By the time I made it to Ireland, it was the middle of June. Antilles was so busy that it took Charlie over a month to squeeze in time for a little rest and relaxation. He finally made it to Glengarriff in August, but then had to go back just a few days later. Florrie and I drove him up to Shannon Airport. As soon as we got to the gate, I had a very strange feeling. It overwhelmed me and I thought, Oh God, I wish he wouldn't go. I wish he would stay.

I didn't heed it. I didn't say the words. We said good-bye and I watched him walk down the ramp to board his plane. I still felt awful but let it pass. I wish I had shouted as loudly as I could for him to stop and come back. A few days later, Florrie and I were out running some errands in the car. There are three sets of gates at Lugdine along the way from the top of the driveway to the house. When we reached the first set, they were locked. I had to get out of the car to open them and that was strange. When we got to the second set of gates, they were locked too. When I saw that the gates in the second set were also closed, I knew then that something was wrong. I told Florrie, "I don't know what, but something terrible has happened." We never locked those gates, nor did the neighbors.

We got down to the gates at the house and they were locked too. I've never to this day found out who locked them. All the way to the house, and in the hallway as soon as we entered, I just kept saying, "Something's wrong. Something's wrong." Just then the phone rang. It was Charlie's oldest son, Chris.

"There's been an accident, Maureen," he began softly, "and Dad was flying the plane."

"Oh dear God! Is he badly hurt?"

"No. He's dead."

The words shattered me. I felt as if I were free-falling into darkness. I fell apart, sobbing uncontrollably over the phone. I don't remember how or when I hung up. We weren't on the phone long, if memory serves. I remember hearing the words come out of my mouth, "Charlie is dead."

Florrie took me in her arms and held me as we both cried. The great love of my life was gone, and a part of me died and went with him that very moment.

On September 2, 1978, Charlie was making a routine flight from St. Croix to St. Thomas in a two-engine Grumman Goose. He had made that flight hundreds of times over the years. Just one mile west of St. Thomas, on the approach to the Charlotte Amalie Harbor, the port engine exploded, killing Charlie instantly. Eyewitnesses watched a red ball fall from the sky. They said the plane struck heavy seas, flipped over, and sank within minutes. Tragically, three other passengers died with Charlie. There were seven survivors.

Bad news spreads fast and I knew I had to pull myself together. The very next morning, I boarded a plane to New York so I could accompany Charlie's kids back to St. Croix. I asked my sister Peggy to call Duke because I wasn't up to it. I was told he took the news very hard. I also asked my brother-in-law, Colonel Harry Edwards, USMC, to accompany us back to St. Croix. I wanted him to be with me when I went to see Charlie's body.

I had to see him one last time and say good-bye. I took holy water with me and blessed him with it during a baptism ceremony I had learned as a young girl in school.

"I baptize you, Charles Francis Blair, in the name of the Father, the Son, and the Holy Spirit." I sprinkled him with the holy water and spoke to him, but not out loud, only in my head, and I want what I said to remain private.

When I reached the house, I telephoned Charlie's mother. At one hundred years of age, Grace McGonegal Blair was still a lion of a woman. I started to cry, but she put an end to it quickly. "Stop that right now. He died doing what he loved to do."

A few hours later, the phone rang. When I answered it, a man whose voice I did not recognize said, "Mrs. Blair, I'm calling from Washington, D.C. We'd like to know the true story of the assassination of General Blair." I went into shock and started to cry. "I don't know what you're talking about," I blurted out through tears, then hung up the phone.

The idea that Charlie's death had been anything other than a horrible accident was inconceivable to me. I don't know who made that call. The man never identified himself, nor did he say who the "we" was. I called a friend in New York who was connected with the Secret Service and told him about the call. He warned me to keep my mouth shut. I was told, "Maureen, act dumb and ignorant if they call again. Have hysterics. Don't say anything about this to anyone. It's too dangerous. Keep your mouth shut!"

After that, I received two more calls about Charlie's "assassination." It was not the same person, but it was a man each time. Both times I did exactly as I'd been instructed and got off the phone as quickly as I could.

A few days after that, I was standing at the airport in St. Croix looking through a Cyclone fence at some planes coming in. Both of my hands were raised, my fingers gripping the Cyclone fence wire. I suddenly felt a presence behind me. Then a man—whose voice I did not recognize—said, "Mrs. Blair, I know who killed General Blair." His words turned my blood cold and my instincts warned me not to look back. I answered, "If you do, don't tell me. I'll have to kill whoever it was." The man walked away and I didn't turn to see him. I was too terrified.

I was never able to get any more information about Charlie's death. Nobody was willing to get involved, and I was told not to ask. And so I never did. I have never discussed it with anyone until now, not even my own daughter. For twenty-five years, I have kept my mouth shut, but I cannot remain silent forever. I owe it to Charlie and to myself at least to ask the questions. I honestly don't know if Charlie's death was an accident, as is the official explanation, or whether he was assassinated. I will say that I have serious questions and suspicions about how he died.

Why did Charlie end up on that flight? He wasn't scheduled to fly it. An important air force pilot was supposed to fly the plane that day, but at the last moment was unavailable. Since it was a full flight, Charlie didn't want to disappoint the passengers, so he said he'd take it. I can't help but wonder why that pilot backed out just minutes before they were scheduled for takeoff.

Why was the engine replaced in Puerto Rico before it exploded, and what happened to the plane after it crashed? When I arrived in St. Croix, I asked to see the plane that had killed Charlie. They told me, "Oh, it's gone. It doesn't exist anymore." I was never told why. I don't know where it is or who has it. Is it still at the bottom of the sea? I also found it strange that almost immediately after the accident, many of the pilots left the company. Within weeks, they were gone, scattered around the globe, some to Africa, some to the Middle East, and others to the Pacific Rim.

Why would someone want to kill Charlie? Perhaps Charlie simply knew too much. One thing I was told about Charlie by someone who knew his military background well was that he not only worked for years in a nuclear weapons think tank, but actually helped place the small nukes for the United States. I was told that Charlie knew where they were—their precise location—and that was very serious information during the Cold War.

I remembered a completely unrelated event, years earlier, which confirmed this for me. Pan Am was about to fly the first American commercial flight into the Soviet Union. Naturally, Charlie wanted to be the pilot to fly into Moscow because he loved being the first in everything to do with aviation. He requested that he be allowed to pilot the flight, but his request had to be made to Washington for approval. Washington refused and offered a warning as an explanation, "If Charlie Blair goes into Moscow, we'll never get him back."

There are just too many loose ends, too many unanswered questions. Something is fishy. I'm not looking to blame anyone, I'd just like to know what happened.

There were two services for Charlie. The first was held at the Catholic church in St. Croix. It was very sad. The second was also important to me, and not easy to achieve. I wanted Charlie buried with his peers at Arlington National Cemetery. I didn't want it for any reason other than that Brigadier General Charles F. Blair, the great American patriot and aviator, had earned it. Surprisingly, I was getting some resistance. I was told Washington was planning to open a new Arlington National Cemetery because the original was getting full. I didn't want Charlie laid to rest surrounded by people he never knew or served with. It wasn't right.

They gave me such a tough time that I enlisted a group of distinguished citizens to help me. The group, including Duke, Barry Goldwater, and columnist Frank Farrel, USMC, petitioned on my behalf for Charlie to be laid to rest with the honors he deserved.

It was all very strange. When they called the Pentagon for help, Curtis LeMay, a very big and important general, said, "Blair? Charlie Blair? Don't know him. Never heard of him." I know damn well he knew Charlie because I had answered the phone many times when he called. Charlie had worked with General LeMay at Strategic Air Command, and LeMay had called our home in St. Croix often when Charlie was alive.

I finally received a call from the assistant to the president. The president was at Camp David at the time, with Anwar Sadat and Menachem Begin, reaching the Camp David Peace Accord. The president's assistant asked me, "What are you going to do if President Carter denies your request?" My answer got his attention: "If the president denies it, I will bring Charlie Blair's body to Washington. I will pickle it, and then I will fight until permission is given."

"The president is at Camp David on matters of world peace," he replied in disbelief.

"Then please send him my message."

Shortly after that conversation, President Carter personally approved a well-located grave for Charlie in Arlington and a burial with full military honors. They must have warned President Carter that I'm not one to back down from a fight. I'm sure he said, "We had better do it or we'll have nothing but trouble from her." Would I really have done it? Yes, indeed, and I would have kicked up a holy stink and kept it on the front page of the papers until I won.

Charlie was buried at the original Arlington National

Cemetery with full military honors. A band played, guns saluted, and I was handed a tightly folded American flag. There is room for my name on his headstone, and I will be laid to rest with him when my time comes. All the top military and political brass were present. Senator Barry Goldwater delivered the eulogy. Halfway through it, he was moved to tears and couldn't finish.

I put on a brave face for the public and held myself together with as much grace as I could muster. Inside, though, I was an absolute basket case. Everything was happening so quickly that I hadn't had time to come to terms with my feelings and my grief. That would have to come later.

Antilles Air Boats was still a going concern, and its future was now in jeopardy. But the company was Charlie's dream and I couldn't let it die too. A meeting of the stockholders was called. I did not campaign for the presidency of Antilles Air Boats, but as Charlie's widow, I was the largest shareholder and the person closest to the business as its vice president. The shareholders placed my name in nomination and asked me to become president. There was nothing else for me to say or do but accept, and so I was made president of Antilles Air Boats by a vote of its shareholders. In doing so, they made me the first woman president of a scheduled airline in the United States of America. It's a feat of which I'm proud.

As the head of the company, I quickly found myself knee-deep in it. The Virgin Islands' Senator Sydney Lee, of St. Croix, introduced a bill asking for the appointment of a blue-ribbon committee to investigate the airline after the accident. The FAA stepped in also and conducted its own review of the incident. The FAA acted very strangely during this process and tried to do things I still don't understand. I couldn't believe it when they intimated that they wanted the man who had changed the engine on Charlie's plane in Puerto Rico—the engine that blew—to be made president of the airline. I refused. I didn't see how a newly hired mechanic was suddenly qualified to run the airline.

After its review, the FAA called a meeting with all the interested parties to discuss its proposal regarding the fate of Antilles Air Boats. Basically, they wanted to shut it down and put it out of business. They blamed it on the accident, but that was ludicrous. If that were a reason to close airlines, the skies would be empty.

The FAA administrator told me, "The airline has to be closed, and our decision is final. I have the papers to hand you, right here in my coat pocket, that will shut the airline down."

There was no way I was going to sit still and let that happen. I was not about to see Charlie's airline destroyed as long as I had anything to do with it. I pointed a finger at that man. "Don't you do it," I said. "Don't you dare put your hand in that pocket. If you do, God will cut your arm off!" I locked eyes with him. He never did put his hand in that pocket and pull those papers out. Over time, we worked it all out and the airline stayed open.

There were also lawsuits resulting from the accident, which had to be settled, and they were handled expeditiously. The lawsuits needed to be resolved so that we could go through with the sale of Antilles to Resorts International. Charlie had initiated discussions with them shortly before his death.

James Crosby was the founder and president of Resorts International, and he loved airplanes. I went to meet with him to close the deal. Crosby was a straight shooter and asked me, "Do you recommend that I buy the airline?" I answered confidently, "Yes, indeed I do." His next question shocked me. "Well, if I go through with this, can I tell everyone that I'm now a member of the CIA?" Mr. Crosby obviously had friends in high places and had done his homework well. I didn't skip a beat and replied, "If you want to." The deal was done and we shook hands on it. Resorts International acquired Antilles Air Boats within a matter of months. I was pleased that the stockholders didn't lose money and that the airline was in the hands of someone who would protect it.

Years later, Crosby died on the operating table. Resorts International was put up for sale, and talk-show king Merv Griffin bought it. He wasn't as fond of airplanes as Crosby was, and ultimately either shut Antilles Air Boats down or sold it. It's gone now, which makes me feel sad.

In the months that followed Charlie's death, we all tried to pick up the pieces of our lives and go on. Bronwyn was devastated, and little Conor Beau even more so. Charlie was the only father and male role model he had ever known.

It wasn't much of a holiday that year as Christmas came and went. Soon New Year's Eve was upon me and it made me even sadder.

I don't like New Year's Eve. I never have. Only once in my life did I ever go to a New Year's Eve party. I was fifteen years old, and the party was held at the Royal Marine, an elegant old-world hotel in Dublin. I was with Daddy and Mammy and feeling conspicuous in my pink taffeta ball gown. It was a marvelous time at first, as we all danced the night away. But when the stroke of midnight came, I wished that I could be anywhere else but at that party.

The bells were tolling the death of the old year, a year I had loved, a year that had felt comfortable and safe. That year was gone now. It would bring no more happiness. We were all turning our backs on it, forgetting it and leaving it in the past for a New Year hardly born a second ago, the unknown, the untried, the unpromising New Year. I missed that old year, just as I would miss my husband. I would never turn my back on it or on him.

As 1979 began, I was grieving hard for Charlie. I'm still grieving to this day. But then there came a point when I had to say to myself, "Enough of this. Life goes on, so get to it. There is a future. There has to be." I struggled for a bit and asked myself, "If I come out of this fog, where will I be? What lies ahead for me now?" I didn't know the answer to that question. I just knew that I had to take my first step. I had to open my eyes again and see.

CHAPTER 24

JOHN WAYNE, AMERICAN

he evening of May 20, 1979, was especially dark as I looked outside my airplane window and watched the lights of San Juan fade to black. I was on my way to Washington, D.C., at the urgent request of Congressman Barry Goldwater Jr. of California. The day before, Goldwater had called me in a panic. "Where the hell are you? You testify tomorrow." Goldwater had introduced legislation to award Duke the Congressional Gold Medal, an honor rarely given. At that time, in the history of the United States, only eighty-four of these medals had been issued. The first went to George Washington. Duke would be joining other such distinguished Americans as Andrew Jackson, Thomas Edison, and the Wright brothers.

I was hell-bent on doing everything I possibly could to see that Duke received it. There were those who thought it was silly to give such a prestigious medal to an actor, but they were small-minded and lacked the vision to see John Wayne in his proper context. Duke was much more than an actor. He had come to represent the American experience—how the West was won, victories in war—so I felt deeply that it was right that Congress should honor him.

But I had more selfish reasons than that for being on this flight. The truth is, I thought the medal was the perfect "sock in the jaw" to all of Duke's critics who had ridiculed him for years for being so politically active and outspoken. There were many within the liberally slanted Hollywood community who didn't like Duke because of his conservative views, views that in many ways hurt his professional career. But Duke never gave a damn; he served his country as his country wanted him to.

Far more important to me, though, was something I knew that most of the world didn't know at the time: Duke was dying of cancer. I wanted Congress to honor him with the medal while he was still alive to see it. I knew it would mean more to him than any of the films he had made.

On January 10, Duke had been admitted to the UCLA Medical Center for an operation to remove his gallbladder. The nation's best surgeons performed it. What the surgeons found when they opened him up was terrifying—advanced stomach cancer. I knew Duke hadn't been feeling well, but I had no idea how serious it really was. We were both trying to age gracefully— to stand up straight and never mind the crow's-feet. Duke used to joke that we were two old Rolls-Royces, and mileage never hurt a Rolls.

In reality, the immortality we'd felt in our youth was beginning to fade, but neither of us was willing to admit that. I could try to be cute and say that when I learned Duke's life was coming to an end, my sun stopped shining and I heard the birds stop singing their songs. I suppose that all happened too. But I'm O'Hara, so

I'll give it to you straight. It knocked me on my rear and sent me spiraling into a deep depression that took me years to crawl out from. There are not enough numbers available to count the times I have wanted and needed to pick up the phone and hear his voice.

I fidgeted in my seat for hours and sipped lukewarm tea, realizing that this wasn't going to be like the first time he'd had cancer, when he'd lost a lung but had survived. He beat that villain, as he had so many on-screen. It was a knock-down, fist-swinging fight in the mud, but then it was over, with Duke riding off once again into the sunset. This battle was going to be very different, and I was struggling to come to terms with it. I couldn't believe Duke was going to die. As close as we were as friends, even I still saw him as invincible. He was too damn tough to let God take him before they both agreed it was time to go.

I was also still in a state of shock from losing Charlie. It was less than a year after that awful night. I couldn't accept Charlie's death, and now I was faced with Duke's. I wasn't strong enough to lose them both in the same year. It wasn't fair. But then, life rarely is.

Of course, Duke's was going to be a longer good-bye. I found some comfort in knowing I was going to have the chance to bring some kind of closure, that I could reaffirm my love for him. I never had that chance with Charlie, and I sure as hell wasn't going to miss it with Duke. I had to acknowledge the unique bond between us and let him know he had made a profound difference in my life.

This was the real journey on my way to Washington. Believe me, it was a journey much longer than the distance that separated that city from San Juan. It spanned nearly forty years of memories, as I struggled to find the right way to describe him to Congress. Duke and I were not just friends; we were best friends. I knew him as well as anyone alive, and I knew him better than any other actor did. I gazed out the window as if watching some magical silver screen that was showing images of Duke during all the stages of his life.

Duke was a nickname given to him as a boy. I saw that little boy standing before me just as he had described himself so many times. He was a lonesome child whose best pal was a dog named Duke, and everyone called them Duke and Little Duke. Little Duke became John Wayne. He grew to become a deeply caring person, but one who was often loyal to a fault. He was smart but not shrewd, and was cheated out of a fortune more than once. He lost millions. He loved ladies and liked women, but only tolerated dames. Duke was terribly unlucky in marriage and never understood why. It was his greatest disappointment.

He made up for it as a father, though. He was overly doting with his kids, and a very proud grandfather. He loved having all twenty-one of his grandchildren around him. He was self-indulgent to the extreme, and very opinionated, also to the extreme. Duke was one of the most decent men I have ever known. He had a short and explosive temper and could holler louder than anyone else I've ever heard. Rugged, gutsy, and determined—John Wayne was definitely a man's man.

He hated his legs and thought they were like tree trunks. He had hands like hams and a big nose that looked smaller on-screen. As he grew older, he was self-conscious about the way his eyes puffed up, and he wore a toupee in public when his hair got thin on top. He felt forever a slave to his image.

His legendary swagger was real and God given. It was not created for the camera, like some have said. That's rubbish. It was a strong step and stride that came from the way he clenched his buttocks, like the fold in the seed of a date. We called it his date-seed fanny walk. Not so with the way he lifted his eyes and wrinkled the top of his brow—that signal in his films that told us he'd had enough and that the action was about to start. He created that for the camera and never used it off-screen.

Professionally, Duke was the hardest-working actor I've ever been on a picture with. He was always on time and prepared, and expected you to be as well. He was intolerant of those who didn't follow a director's instructions. I saw him blow his top more than once and shout, "Goddammit! Why don't you listen to the man?" He was an awesome presence on the set and would easily mow down a weak and insecure actor. He was not generous with scenes, but he wasn't selfish either. If you wanted a scene from Duke, then you had to take it, and if you did, he was the first to praise you for it.

The nicest thing he ever said about me was, "There's only one woman who has been my friend over the years, and by that I mean a real friend, like a man would be. That woman is Maureen O'Hara. She's big, lusty, absolutely marvelous—definitely my kind of woman. She's a great guy. I've had many friends, and I prefer the company of men. Except for Maureen O'Hara."

As I've said, our chemistry on-screen was so magical because Duke never had to defer to me as a woman. I was strong enough to stand up to him and be his equal. He used to say that I was the greatest guy he ever knew.

We were so convincing together in our films that many fans believed Duke and I were married in real life. I remember arriving at the premiere of *McLintock!* and hearing a woman shout to me as I made my way down the red carpet, "Miss O'Hara, Mr. Wayne and your children have just gone in." It happened to both of us all the time.

Duke and I were never involved romantically. We were never lovers. I know this is going to disappoint some people, but I'm sorry, it's the truth. No, I never saw the Duke with his boots off. And yes, there were plenty of rumors over the years. I've heard that our illegitimate daughter is living at an undisclosed location somewhere in California's San Fernando Valley. I sure would like to meet her one day.

While we were shooting *The Quiet Man* in Ireland, a story was released in the United States that Duke and I were fooling around on the set. Normally, I would have let it roll off my shoulders, but this hurt because Duke's whole family was on location with us. The article said an anonymous source present on the set provided the details. I was furious and stormed into John Ford's office, demanding to know, "Who would do such a terrible thing?" The old man answered without a blink, "I did. It'll sell more tickets."

Like most great friendships, ours withstood the years even when it was seriously tested. Most of the time, we were so close that when we saw each other, we wanted to hug and never let go. But there were also times when we would have crossed the street to avoid bumping into each other. We were once so mad at each other that we didn't speak for almost a year.

It happened right after we finished filming *The Wings of Eagles*. I was in John Ford's office making arrangements to attend the premiere in New York City. I noticed that no arrangements were being made for Duke and asked when he would be arriving. Ford's answer shocked me. "He's not going. Duke can't stand you. He wouldn't be seen at the same premiere as you. He wouldn't walk on the same street as you. Hell, he wouldn't even be in New York City at the same time you were. He hates your guts."

I went home and cried for hours. I couldn't believe that Duke would say those things about me. Then my sadness turned to anger and I decided not to see or speak to Duke again. I didn't hear from him for months, so I assumed everything Ford had told me was true. I was heartbroken.

A little less than a year later, I was attending a movie premiere in Hollywood and spotted Duke sitting in front of me. The event was packed with other stars and executives from the picture business, but I decided to confront Duke anyway. When he got up and made his way up the aisle, I cut him off and confronted him. "Duke, I want to talk with you. I want to know why you said all those terrible things about me." He answered, "Well, I want to know why you said all those things about—"

The truth hit us at the same time. We pointed our index fingers at each other and said those all too familiar words in unison, "John Ford." Ford had made it all up. Neither of us had ever said anything bad about the other. Duke and I hadn't spoken to or seen each other for almost a year, and it was all because of that manipulative old bastard. We never knew why he did it. But then, that was John Ford.

As I continued to stare out the window, I remembered how Duke had come to my aid while I was facing my own cancer in Los Angeles. I was in my hospital bed waiting to be taken to the operating room and wishing I were with Charlie back in St. Croix. They had already given me some medication to make me groggy, and I sure was. I watched orthopedic oxfords shuffle by in slow motion while my IV dripped and imploded. I lay there alone for what seemed like hours and was scared half out of my wits. The phone rang and I fumbled for the receiver. It was Duke.

I don't know how he knew I was having surgery. Everyone had strict instructions to keep their mouths shut. But I was so relieved to hear Duke's voice. It put me at ease. We chatted for a while about simple things. It was all upbeat and positive. We laughed and got caught up on the kids, and then Duke grew silent. It caught me off guard and sobered me. Several moments passed, then he started to cry. It was soft and loving, like a little boy. Finally he whispered, "Why you? Why me?"

I felt a tidal wave of love roll over me. It was as if this powerful man had reached out through the phone and had wrapped his strong arms tightly around me. I started to cry, and we both remained there for a long while and wept. It was the only time I can remember Duke ever breaking down. I tried to lighten things up and sobbed, "Well, goddammit! What are you doing calling me up and doing this for? I'm about to go upstairs."

We laughed again and chatted for a few more minutes. Then we hung up and I was wheeled off to wherever it was they took me. I have always believed Duke must have known that his cancer had come back.

As my plane continued toward the coast, I couldn't help but think about the irony of Duke's situation. I remembered one of the last pictures that he'd made. It was called *The Shootist,* and in it Duke played an old gunslinger who was told by his doctor, played by Jimmy Stewart, that he was dying of cancer. Stewart's character described the fate that awaited him. Duke's character chose a different way out. He'd go out as he had lived—in a blaze of glory, guns blasting. In the film, Duke's character dies setting the world to rights, in a final saloon shoot-out with a gang of heavies. But that was a movie. Though I know he would have preferred it, Duke in real life wasn't going to be as lucky.

After I found out his cancer was back, I called often to talk to him and see how he was doing. He was in a great deal of pain. By then it had been several months since my surgery, and my doctors in Los Angeles were checking me every few months. This gave me the chance to go see Duke the last week in April at his home in Newport Beach. I called Duke as soon as I arrived in Los Angeles. He told me to come down, and gave me directions even though I had been there a hundred times before. I've never been good with directions and could easily get lost in my own house, just on the way to the kitchen. If you put me in a maze, I'm sure I'd die there.

Of course, I did get lost. The crush of southern California traffic made me feel rushed and unsure of myself. Did I miss the turnoff? No. Definitely not. I don't think I did. I'm not sure. Damn. I was frantic and pulled off to the side of the road. I just sat there in my car feeling terribly stupid and looking like some dame with more fingers and toes than IQ points. After a while, two highway patrolmen pulled up and wanted to know what the hell I was doing. I told them I was lost and trying to get to John Wayne's house to see him. I flashed my movie-star smile, hoping to be recognized and praying for help. Their eyes widened as I registered. "You are? Well, come on, follow us." They took me the rest of the way—a police escort. Thank God, or I'd probably still be there by the roadside.

As we pulled into the cobblestone driveway, I didn't know this would be the last time I would see Duke. He was a touchstone of mine, an ever present constant that I could always trust and rely on. I was neither ready nor willing to say good-bye.

Duke's home was a small but spacious French Regency that sat on the point of the harbor so he would have easy access to the sea in his *Wild Goose*. The *Wild Goose* was the only thing Duke ever felt was truly his and his alone. He loved to sit in the garden on nice days, watching the other boats go by and waving to those who had tooted their whistles at him, hoping to be acknowledged by an American icon.

I walked through the garden to the door at the side of the house and knocked. Pat Stacy greeted me. I adored Pat. She loved Duke very much, and I was thrilled he'd found someone to share his final years with, even though I knew he'd never marry again. We made our way to the large central room of the house where many of Duke's awards and trophies were displayed. Gorgeous bronze statues of cowboys were scattered about. Duke's three children by his third wife, Pilar, were there. I didn't stop to speak with them then, but went straight down the hallway to Duke's bedroom. The walk felt unnaturally long.

I paused at the door, took a deep breath, stood up straight, and entered his room. There was a strange quietness and my feet added no sound. Once inside, I was caught by the staleness of the air. It made my mouth dry and my lips rise up tightly against my gums. I fought hard to withstand it and that's when I knew this would be our last time together. I walked up beside his bed and looked down on him. He was half propped up. The position was familiar to me from the visits he had made to my home in St. Croix. Duke couldn't lie flat on his back or his remaining lung could fill with fluid, a common problem for those who have lost a lung.

I was shocked by his appearance. He was skin and bones. He looked up at me, stirred his shoulders in salutation, and said, "Maureen." I replied, "Duke." Then we smiled at each other. I showed no sign of concern. He needed support, not sympathy. Our friendship had grown over the years beyond the need for that. This was my oldest friend and the man I'd made movie history with.

I moved to the small chair next to his bed and sat down. He reached his hand out to me and I took it in mine. Then I put my head, facedown, on the bed beside him. My heart was crying out, Oh damn—oh hell—oh God, please help me. I can't handle this anymore. I became overcome with heartbreak and started to cry. Duke put his hand on top of my head and asked, "Is that for Charlie?" I half-lied and said, "Yes." I didn't have the courage to tell him that it was not only for Charlie, but for him, and even for me too. Then he asked me, "Maureen, why did you and I have such lousy luck?" I didn't answer. The words rang too true to me. Duke was never able to find true love, and I had just lost it.

We remained like this, in silence, for a while. We were content to just be with each other. We knew what the silence meant. It meant, I love you, you're not alone, life is splendid yet brief, so spread your wings and fly—but no good-byes.

After a while, we broke the silence. I don't remember who spoke first. We gabbed like two magpies. We talked about my love for Charlie and his and Charlie's love of chess and steak dinners, and flying off together for adventures in the sky. I thanked him for his help in getting President Carter's approval for Charlie to be buried at Arlington. He smiled and nodded the way he did whenever he had done something nice for a friend. There was a smile still on his face as he drifted off to sleep. And for me, at that moment, the world stood still and was suspended in time.

Later on, Duke got up and I said I'd better get back on the freeway. Duke wanted me to stay. "No. You're staying." A decree, not a request. No ands, ifs, or buts. Pat offered to let me stay with her. She had a small home across the street from Duke's, but Duke said, "No way. She's staying right here, in this house, in the bedroom next to mine." So I stayed.

That night, we feasted on a wonderful Mexican meal prepared by his cook, Rosa. Duke didn't eat much, but was in high spirits. He was content to be with his family and an old and dear friend. Afterward, I washed my shirt and underwear in the bedroom sink and hung it on a hanger to dry. I crawled into bed exhausted by the weight of the day and was out in an instant.

The next morning, Duke and I sat outside at the water's edge surrounded by the kids, Ethan, Aissa, and Marissa. They listened as Duke and I talked about the old days in Hollywood, working with that tough old bastard John Ford.

I told them the story of how we had once been invited to a dinner party at Pappy Ford's in the early 1940s. Pappy kept insisting that Duke have another drink and then another. Soon he was feeling little pain. At the end of the evening, Pappy told me that I had to take Duke home. "You're responsible for him." I tried to get out of it and told Pappy that I couldn't handle Duke like that. It was no use, of course. The order had been given, and you never dared disobey an order from Ford.

Duke was poured into my car and off we went. I decided to take him to the Lakeside Country Club, a favorite Hollywood hangout. I was sure I could find some help there. As we made our way down Ventura Boulevard, Duke suddenly hollered for me to pull over. "I need another drink." I thought, What the hell is he going to do now? Foolishly, I pulled over. What a mistake! The next thing I knew, Duke was out the door and charging up the walkway to somebody's house. I got out of the car and raced to the porch after him. Too late—he was already banging on the door. I stood there just praying to God that he knew the people inside.

After a few minutes, the porch light came on and a middle-aged couple in pajamas opened the door. The look on their faces said it all—they were strangers. Just imagine their expressions when they found John Wayne and Maureen O'Hara standing on their porch in the dark of night. Their jaws dropped open. "Good evening. We need a drink," Duke declared with a loud slur. They didn't know what to do, so they invited us in.

Duke swaggered inside and we all made very absurd small talk. It was as if we were old and dear friends. I was mortified, thinking, What the hell have I gotten myself into? No—what had *he* gotten me into? The nice man made Duke a drink and we continued with our chatty and jovial conversation.

I've often wondered what happened to that couple and what they must have really been thinking, as we sat in their living room, Duke finishing off his cocktail. When the last drop was swallowed, Duke stood up, thanked them very courteously, and we were back on our way to Lakeside.

In the early 1940s, the Lakeside Country Club was a favorite hangout for the rich and famous. It was loud and convivial, smoke-filled rooms reveling in Hollywood camaraderie. When we arrived, Duke and I mingled, saying hello to people. We had been there only a few minutes when Duke noticed three pretty girls who were leaning against the bar. I saw that glitter in his eye and thought, Thank God. I'm off the hook. As Duke made his way in their direction, I grabbed the manager and said, "I got him this far. He's your responsibility now. You get him home." Then I got the hell out of there so fast you'd have thought someone had yelled, "Fire!"

Duke's kids loved the story and we all laughed. They asked him if it was true. Did he really do that? Duke paused and then answered with an amused roll of the eyes, "Well, if your auntie Maureen says I did . . . I guess I did."

A little later, I got ready to leave. I had to be on a plane the next morning to return to St. Croix. I put on my bright red coat and walked over to Duke. He used both hands to grab the collars of my coat. "That's a gorgeous coat. It looks beautiful on you." Our love and tears were in our hearts, but there were no good-byes. Then we kissed, and I was gone. Those were the last words John Wayne ever said to me.

When I arrived in St. Croix, I learned that Duke had been taken to Hoag Hospital the day after my visit and had had surgery again. The hospital issued a statement confirming that Duke was suffering from "diffuse carcinomatosis" or cancer everywhere visible to the eye. Duke was in God's hands now.

So it was vital that I come up with the right definition of John Wayne on that flight. It would be my final tribute to him, as well as the country's. John Wayne: "Actor" wasn't enough; neither was "cowboy." He was and he wasn't. Duke's cowboys were often loners, and he was a man rich in children and grandchildren. They were the most important part of his life. "Activist"? Too controversial and narrow. Even "patriot" missed the mark and seemed understated. I drifted in and out of thoughts, allowing the memories to guide me to my decision. By the time we reached the coast of the United States, the answer had finally come to me. It was perfect and I couldn't wait to drop my request on that committee. Only then did I close my eyes and finally fall asleep.

Unfortunately, poor weather caused my flight to be diverted through New York. The whole thing had been so rushed that I'd had no time to prepare anything. My hair was full of bobby pins and I had no money with me. No credit cards, nothing. When I arrived in New York, I had to sleep on a bench in the airport. Some glamorous movie star. I was sure people were waiting for me to pull food from a garbage bin.

I took the first flight to Washington in the morning and was met by one of Goldwater's aides. We went straight to the Capitol. As soon as we arrived, I rushed to the bathroom to remove the pins and comb my hair. I was doing it as quickly as I could when Goldwater barged through the door. "Come on. You're on! We've got to go." I answered in a panic, "But my hair isn't combed and—" No time. "Sorry. Now!"

We raced up the long hall in the congressional building, into the room, and sat down. I could hardly breathe and had to start talking about Duke almost immediately.

The group present before the committee was impressive. Kathleen Nolan, president of the Screen Actors Guild, and General Albert Coady Wedemeyer were scheduled to speak. Elizabeth Taylor, then married to Senator John Warner of Virginia, was also there and scheduled to speak. At the time, her husband was running for reelection. Numerous letters and telegrams had already been read into the record from President Jimmy Carter, former president Gerald Ford, Ronald Reagan, Lady Bird Johnson, General Omar Bradley, Frank Sinatra, Katharine Hepburn, Gregory Peck, and many, many others. I was disappointed that they were not able to come in person.

I had no written statement and let my feelings and words just flow from my heart. I give you the guts here of what I said:

Mr. Chairman, I am happy, thrilled, delighted, and very proud to be here. In my lifetime, I have been very privileged to have known and to have met many great and famous men, starting with my beloved father and then my husband, Charlie Blair, and John Wayne. I think they are perhaps the three greatest men I have ever been privileged to know.

I have known John Wayne for thirty-nine years, and in those thirty-nine years, I have called him my dearest friend, my best friend. I cannot tell you the kind of man he is.

You have listened to many eloquent speeches about Duke. But it is the man you really don't know about. I can speak to you here as an immigrant to the United States, because I am. I can speak for the people around the world outside the United States. And, since I am now an American citizen, I can speak for the people of the United States. I hope they will grant me permission to do that. I think they will.

To the people of the world, John Wayne is not just an actor, and a very fine actor, John Wayne is the United States of America. He is what they believe it to be. He is what they hope it will always be. It is every person's dream that the United States will be like John Wayne and always be like him.

I believe Duke lives by a phrase that I learned as a schoolgirl in Ireland: "Breathes there the man with soul so dead who never to himself hath said, This is my own, my native land."

Tears began to roll down my cheeks as I prepared to reveal my request.

I beg you to strike the medal for Duke; to order the president to strike it. And I feel that the medal should say just one thing: "John Wayne, American."

My request was met with stunned silence as I wiped the tears from my eyes and collected myself. My suggestion had to be seconded within a few minutes or it would not be accepted by the committee. It felt like a million years as I waited. I wanted to yell, "Dammit! One of you second this. If you don't, you'll be destroying my final gift to Duke." Finally, Congressman Henry Hyde, of Illinois, to whom I will always be grateful, stood and raised his hand: "I second it." Then he offered an amendment to the bill, permitting the inscription that I had requested.

I cannot describe to you what that moment meant to me. That I, as an immigrant to the United States of America, would be permitted to name the Congressional Gold Medal for one of the country's greatest Americans. When the vote finally came, it was unanimous. John Wayne would become the eighty-fifth person in history to receive the Congressional Gold Medal.

Duke watched the proceedings on television, from his hospital room. The medal meant more to him than all of the hundreds of awards he had received. The full House of Representatives approved the medal on May 23, 1979. The president signed it three days later, on Duke's birthday.

I returned to the Virgin Islands and called Duke regularly over the next few weeks. He was too weak to speak to me, so the children kept me posted on his condition. They wanted to keep his last few days private. They had shared their father with the world their entire lives and deserved to have him to themselves in his final hours. On June 10, I phoned Duke's hospital room one last time and spoke to his son Patrick. I told him to give his father a kiss and tell him it was from me. "I don't think he'll hear me." Duke had slipped into a coma. "He will," I said. And I know he did.

I hung up the phone and went into my living room, where I had guests. We had been having days of unusual fog in the Virgin Islands, and as I sat there, a terrible gloom crept over me. Suddenly, I heard myself saying to my dinner guests, "The fog will go and take Duke with it." I broke down crying in front of them.

I went to bed early that night. I couldn't sleep, and stood at the window for hours, looking out through the fog at the lights of Christiansted. Then a moment came when I knew in my heart that Duke had died. I crawled back into bed and closed my eyes, waiting for the telephone call. Within the hour, the phone rang out. I answered it and an unfamiliar voice said softly, "Duke just died." "I know," I said. I got out of bed and moved back to the window. The fog was lifting, up toward the heavens, and taking my dear friend John Wayne with it.

What a hell of a game of chess must have been played by Charlie and Duke in heaven that night. And then I said, "Goodbye, you two bastards . . . please miss me."

CHAPTER 25

ONLY THE LONELY

*M*iss me? I'm quite positive that all those guys—Charlie, Duke, Laughton, Fonda, Ty Power, all my other leading men, Pappy Ford, and even Daddy—have all gotten together up in heaven and talked to God and said, "Please don't let her up here. Give us a little peace just for a while." I can't say I blame them.

It's hard when you outlive most of the people who were closest to you. You count on them being there. I went through quite a bout of loneliness after they had gone—and I still sometimes feel a bit blue. But I'm not a whiner and I don't mope. I have a daughter and a grandson, two sisters, stepchildren and stepgrandchildren, nieces and nephews whom I love very much. They are all I need to keep going every day.

I've spent much of my life since Charlie passed loving him and missing him, honoring his memory and preserving the historical record of his great aviation achievements. This legacy is important to the future of aviation and for all the young pilots who will follow.

After Charlie died, I received countless letters from aviators who had been inspired and touched by him. One of the many I received went like this:

Dear Ms. O'Hara,

Every guy who ever flew an airplane looked up to Charlie Blair as one of the great pioneers in aviation. I was a young man in the Eighth Air Force in the summer of 1944 just after D-Day when my squadron commander asked me to fly to London on a stand down day to pick up a friend of his by the name of Blair. I flew to London and coming back to Bungay, Charlie flew in the right seat and I flew in the left seat. He had never been in a B-24 before. I asked him if he wanted to land and he said yes. After I identified the field among the many in East Anglia at that time, he flew upwind over the landing runway then made a sweeping 360° turn to a perfect power-on landing that was a marvel of precision and technique.

The next day Charlie got up early with the combat crews and flew over occupied France with our group. We chatted that night in the officers club. Charlie never talked about his vast experiences—only asking us questions of formation and AA defensive tactics. He made us feel important.

He was a role model to the young men of our generation, and it was an exciting day when he flew with us.

I am sorry that he had that fatal accident—but I will always remember the tall, calm guy who told us we were great pilots and were lucky to be in the Eighth Air Force.

Sincerely,
K. S. Valis

One of the first things I found myself doing after Charlie and Duke were gone was questioning the accident findings of the representative of the National Transportation Safety Board. After months of review, the board representative had concluded that the accident was a result of pilot error.

His report alleged that Charlie should have made an emergency landing at sea instead of trying to reach the harbor base. The investigator claimed that after the engine blew up, Charlie attempted to fly the plane in "ground effect," an aerodynamic technique in which the pilot keeps the aircraft very close to the surface of the water. He concluded that Charlie was unable to maintain the ground effect and so the seaplane struck the water with full power on the right-engine side. The left-wing float then struck the water, causing the plane to cartwheel and break apart. The engine that blew was on the pilot's side, only a couple of feet from Charlie's head. He was killed instantly from the explosion. How could he have flown the plane in ground effect or maintained it when he was already dead?

I quickly learned that when you go through an airline-accident investigation, there is no precise science to rely on. Perhaps they've become much better over the last twenty-five years. I found that quite a few of the conclusions drawn were based on a set of assumptions and suppositions that might have been plausible, but were not necessarily true. The qualifications of some of the investigators are not always up to snuff. At its conclusion, there still remains quite a bit of uncertainty because there had been a great deal of guesswork involved. Lost lives understandably call for answers and conclusions and accountability. Sometimes, though, reputations can be tarnished unfairly, forever, in this process.

I'm not about to let that happen to Charlie.

Charlie made countless emergency landings at sea over the

course of his flying career. He knew the signs and conditions under which one was necessary and possible. I know in my heart that if Charlie could have landed that plane, he would have. He didn't get the chance to try.

But the charge that really made me boil was the claim that, as president of Antilles, Charlie had "violated or condoned violations of federal regulations in the interest of company objectives, and key company managers were aware of the falsification of records."

Huh? I was vice president of the airline and this was all news to me. The very idea that a man of Charlie's character and background would do such a thing is a disgrace. That kind of man isn't fit to fly or even to shine Charlie's shoes. I'm mad as hell right now and should have sued! General Blair was a career military man who lived every day of his life under the strict discipline of a military regimen. He lived by a military code of conduct that was beyond reproach. He exemplified it. If Charlie did all these things, then the man I lived with was an impostor.

And so here I am again, with more questions than answers. Given the mysterious nature of his death, and all that happened afterward, am I to believe that the man President Truman once called "the world's outstanding aviator" was not fit to wear his uniform? Or is this the final nail in a carefully constructed coffin, leaving Charlie as the documented cause of his own demise?

Bloody rubbish. It all seems a little too clean and tidy to me.

I also found myself honoring Duke's memory after he passed. I loved sharing my experiences with his fans, and they still wanted more of him. Duke had been the spokesman for Great Western Savings at the time of his death, and had done some really great commercials for them. Fans were writing in asking if the ads would continue. Some of Duke's friends in the business—John Huston, Ben Johnson, Glenn Ford, and me—were approached to make a commercial as a follow-up salute to Duke. I did it as a tribute to him, but even that brief appearance before the cameras raised the old questions again: With Charlie gone, was I resuming my acting career and returning to Hollywood? I absolutely was not. As for Maureen O'Hara, well, quite frankly, I was sick of her.

All I wanted was peace and quiet and my memories of Charlie. I had no desire to be in the public eye anymore. In 1980, I sold the *Virgin Islander* to *USA Today*. I wanted the freedom to spend all of my time with Bronwyn and Conor Beau and the rest of my family. But we were all so spread apart, and now I found myself a frequent flier on airplanes going between St. Croix, New York, Los Angeles, and Glengarriff. I always use New York as a resting point to break my flights into two shorter trips. I have a studio apartment there and get to see Charlie's kids when I pass through. I also make sure to have dinner at least once at Neary's Pub whenever I'm in New York City. Not to is a crime, and you won't find better crispy lamb chops anywhere on the planet.

One of the first things I did to honor Charlie was to establish the General Charles F. Blair and Maureen O'Hara Golf Classic in Glengarriff. Patrick Carey and Luke Flanagan of the golf club approached me with the idea and the National Dairy Board was the original sponsor, followed by Murphy's Stout. I thought it would be great and something Charlie would have enjoyed. In its twentieth year now, it's an open tournament in which anyone who pays the small entrance fee can play. Golfers and tourists from all over the world come to our little village in June. At the end of the tournament, I get up in a very official capacity and present the trophies and gifts to the winners. One of the benefits of doing it is that it always guarantees that I will make it home to Lugdine at least once a year. I still spend the whole summer there.

There's also a funny thing that happens when an actor retires and reaches his sixties. Awards and accolades start chasing you around. Sometimes they give them to you just so that you'll attend the dinner and they can sell tickets, but usually they are on the up-and-up. Some awards are for you and others are for friends. Over the years, I have been blessed with many.

In 1985, it was Roddy McDowall's turn. I was in Glengarriff when I received a call from Roddy, saying, "I'm being honored with the Career Achievement Award by the American Cinema Foundation. It's a very big affair and I wanted to ask you if you would come and present the award to me." Roddy and I had been friends for forty-five years, so I couldn't refuse. I told him I would make my flight arrangements right away. I would be there to give him the award.

I packed my bags and left Ireland early that year in order to be at the affair. I worked on the presentation speech for a few weeks and coordinated my presentation with the film clips from his career that would run while I spoke. I thought I would open my remarks with:

Ladies and gentlemen,
    It is my pleasure to have traveled from a small village in Ireland to be here with Roddy tonight—
    Roddy and I first met when we were cast by the great director John Ford as brother and sister in How Green Was My Valley—*and we have been brother and sister ever since . . .*

The remarks that followed were a tribute to his great talent as an actor and his generosity as a human being. Roddy had been very good to me, especially after Charlie and Duke passed. He was one of the Hollywood friends I had left but still saw often.

I was so thrilled to be there that night. I sat in my seat backstage and waited for them to announce me. I waited and waited and waited but never got to give him the award or address my remarks to the audience. Right as the introduction was about to begin, Elizabeth Taylor walked up and took the award off the table. I was so stunned I couldn't say a word. I just sat there with my mouth open and watched her. She needed no introduction and so the audience applauded, never being the wiser. She presented Roddy with that award and gave a glowing speech of her own. I was heartbroken and furious. I had flown all the way from Ireland just for this event and I had been cheated out of it. What could I do? I couldn't cause a scene with Miss Taylor and ruin Roddy's special night. For all I knew, she had also been asked to present the award and didn't know I had flown all the way from Ireland to present it.

It seems I split most of my time between events honoring my film career and those honoring Charlie. I enjoy attending his fetes much more than mine. These tributes have been so wonderful. They have given me a little bit more of Charlie over the years. Honoring him at these ceremonies is therapeutic and one of the most important things I do. It's getting harder to fly all over the world as the years mount up, but I always seem to find the grit.

Sadly, one of the most important symbols of my marriage to Charlie was lost in September 1989. I was in Ireland when Hurricane Hugo hit St. Croix. The devastation it left in its wake was all over the news and so I tried to call the island to find out if there had been any damage to our home. This was the house that Charlie had built for us—the one we had lived in together—and it meant everything to me. Nearly all of my memories and remembrances of those years were there. It was full of things of little value to anyone else, but they were priceless to me.

I caught the first plane to New York, then on to St. Croix. As soon as I arrived, Chris Blair met me at the airport and took me straight to the house. As we turned onto the road that led up to the house, I could see that it was not completely destroyed. It would have been a wiser business move to write it off as a loss, but I just couldn't do it. I stayed in St. Croix long enough to get architects and contractors working on the plans to rebuild it and put it back together as it was. I was heartbroken over the loss of Charlie and Duke's chess set, Duke's hats that he had given me, and Natalie Wood's wonderful ceramics. They are all up there, floating around in the sky.

When I boarded the plane to head back to New York, I wasn't feeling at all well. Chris came to New York with me on his way back to Boston and helped me get some information from the bank for reconstructing the house.

We walked to the bank, like all New Yorkers do, but halfway there I sensed that something was terribly wrong. All of a sudden, my body froze. I couldn't move anything. I couldn't breathe or think or cry out for help. There was no pain. I was suddenly paralyzed while still on my feet. After a few minutes, the paralysis went away as suddenly as it had struck me. I was able to walk again. I thought it was strange, but talked myself out of being concerned. We continued on to the bank and concluded our business there.

The next day was Sunday and so I was up early to go to Mass. My church was just up the street, and so I walked there, as I always did. It happened again. I stopped and couldn't move. No pain, but total paralysis. I waited it out, and it passed again and I went to Mass. Later that evening, I was going out to dinner with my old friend Jane Rady Lynes (her father produced one of my record albums). I took a taxi uptown to the apartment where we were going to have dinner. In the cab, I started feeling ill again and had a panic attack. I somehow got the insane idea that the taxi driver was going to kill me. I don't know why I thought that, but I did. I must have been delirious.

When we reached the apartment, I got out of the cab as fast as I could and started across the street. In the street, I saw two young men coming toward me with two large knives in their hands. I was hallucinating. I started running and dashed into the building I was headed to. I sat in the hallway and went into hysterics. Jane and her friend came downstairs and wanted to take me to the hospital right away. I was stubborn and said, "No. There's nothing wrong with me. I don't know what this is all about, but I'm fine." So I stayed and ate dinner and then went straight home. I felt fine. I went right to bed and slept soundly that night. I woke in the morning and thought, Well, whatever the hell it was, it's gone. I feel great.

I sat up to get out of bed, and that's when I felt pain for the first time. It was a sharp, awful pain in my chest. I knew instantly that it was my heart. I fell on the bed and reached for the phone on the nightstand. I dialed Jane and said, "I'm having a heart attack, Jane. You had better get an ambulance over here." I was starting to panic, but calmed myself down. I was settling down, so I changed my mind. "No. Just come over and we'll get to the hospital in a taxi." Jane rushed over, and we did take a taxi to the hospital. We got there, and rather than take me right in, I was put in a waiting room. I didn't want to be difficult, so I sat there until I had another attack—by this time, my fifth.

Jane lost it and went up to the desk, calling out, "Look, you guys. You have to see this woman immediately. We've got an emergency here!" They took one look at me and got the picture. I stopped acting brave for the medical staff; otherwise they might have left me there for hours.

I was rushed to the cardiac-care unit and was full of tubes and connected to wires in the blink of an eye. They ran a series of tests and decided to go with an angioplasty. If it was successful, we had a good chance of avoiding open-heart surgery. I was on the table

having it done within a few hours. I was awake during the procedure, listening to the attending nurse go on and on about her
famous chocolate cookies. It was over in no time and I got some of
those cookies as my reward. She was right; they were delicious.

My doctors were pleased with the results and said there was
no need to perform open-heart surgery. They took me back to my
room, and while they were busy congratulating themselves on the
great job they had done, I had my sixth attack. I was rushed back
to the operating room and they performed a second angioplasty. It
was done twice in the same day.

I don't know if the stress of losing Charlie and Duke, and then
the house, caused my heart problems or if I had a natural block-
age and it was only a matter of time before it would happen. I
really don't. I only know that it felt as if the pressure had reached
a breaking point and something had to give. I suffered six back-
to-back attacks during this incident, but I'm not surprised that
I'm still here. As I said in the beginning, I have always been a
tough and strong woman. These are my most dominant characteristics, and so I survived—thank God. I haven't had a problem
since. Charlie must have had a long chat with the angels and God
himself.

The following year, I received another telephone call from
Charlie Fitz that changed my life all over again. "I've just read a
script for you," he said, "and this you do." I was a little intrigued
by the fact that Charlie Fitz loved the script so much that he
wanted me to do it. He was well aware of the fact that I wasn't interested in the picture business anymore.

"No way. I don't want to go back to work," I insisted. "I'm finished with movies, Charlie. I'm through." He sent the script to me
anyway.

It had come to him in an unusual way. Acclaimed film director Chris Columbus had apparently been a fan of mine for years

because of *The Quiet Man*, and he had written the role in this film specifically for me. *Only the Lonely* is the story of a lovable Chicago cop who at age thirty-eight still lives at home with his tough Irish mother. When Chris sat down to write the role of Rose Muldoon, he asked himself, What would Mary Kate Danaher be like if she were an older widow living in Chicago with her son? Chris apparently had been looking all over the country for me, but with no luck. He finally stumbled on an old family friend, journalist Joe Murphy, who directed him to Charlie Fitz.

The script sat on my table in Glengarriff for a few days, taunting me while I tried to ignore it. It was like a giant elephant sitting in my living room and refusing to go away. Curiosity finally got the better of me, and so I picked up the damn thing and read it.

I called Charlie back as soon as I finished it. "You're right. This I do." Rose Muldoon was wonderfully tough, mean, strong, nasty, sad, and funny. An actress knows when a great role is staring her in the face, and this one was too good to turn down.

I called Chris Columbus and told him how much I loved his script and that I would play the part if I liked the people involved in the project. It made no sense for me to go back to work and be miserable with people I couldn't stand. Chris had already cast Canadian comedy actor John Candy in the role of the son, Danny Muldoon. I said, "That sounds wonderful, but I'd like to meet you and John Candy before I give you my final answer." Candy was in northern Canada and I was in Ireland, so we all agreed that the easiest place for all of us to meet the following week was in Chicago.

I was picked up at the airport and taken straight over to the studio. I liked Chris Columbus and John Candy instantly. In less than ten minutes, I turned to Candy and said, "All right, I'll be your mother."

In October 1990, I arrived in Chicago to begin filming my

first picture in twenty years. Technology might have advanced, but the process of making a movie was still very much the same. One observation I did make, though, was that budgets were more tightly controlled in the studio-system days. Directors have more latitude now to spend money on creative choices. Trying different things usually translates into more takes for the actors, and so making a movie still meant hard work and long hours. I also thought people worked a little slower than we did in the old days. There was much more of a whip over you when men like Darryl Zanuck had their hands on the reins.

The cast and crew welcomed me very warmly. Chris Columbus couldn't have been more gracious, and made sure I really got the star treatment. *Only the Lonely* had a terrific cast for comedy. In addition to Candy and myself, Ally Sheedy costarred as Candy's love interest, and Tony Quinn costarred as mine. Jim Belushi and Milo O'Shea provided character-actor repartee, and Macaulay Culkin and his brother Kieran played my young grandsons. Roddy McDowall came to visit me one day on the set and got talked into a brief cameo, but I think that scene was cut from the picture. Everyone was terrific to work with and it was particularly interesting to watch Macaulay milk Chris Columbus out of pocket money with every take.

Before he would act, Macaulay stood in front of Chris with his hand out, and the director would have to dig into his pockets and come up with something. A couple of coins was all it took, and Macaulay would be thrilled with himself. Chris Columbus has a special gift when working with child actors. They adore him and in their performances will do anything to please him. Chris, of course, had skyrocketed to fame directing Macaulay in the first two *Home Alone* movies for producer John Hughes. Hughes agreed to produce *Only the Lonely* for Chris in return for the blockbuster success of those two pictures. Most recently,

Chris hit it big again directing and producing the *Harry Potter* movies.

You might be surprised by the fact that John Candy was one of my all-time favorite leading men. People always want to know if he was funny on the set, and I hate bursting their bubble when I tell them the truth. You don't monkey around on a movie set. It's bloody hard work, and if you're a professional, you keep busy and do your job. Candy was a pro and didn't clown around. He was busy learning lines and preparing for his performance between takes and scenes. He was pleasant and courteous. Do I sound like a crotchety old lady?

The depth of John Candy's talent did surprise me. I didn't expect it to be so great. It didn't take long for me to see that his reservoir of emotion was deep, and that he was not only a comedic genius but an actor with an extraordinary dramatic talent. I'm sure that even he didn't fully understand how good he really was. He reminded me a great deal of Charles Laughton. I have often thought that John Candy could have become one of the great dramatic actors if he had remade some of Laughton's old pictures. Each morning on the set, I greeted Candy with a simple question, "Who came to work today, John, John Candy the funnyman or John Candy the actor?" He always looked down sheepishly, then raised his head proudly, saying, "The actor."

The one thing that had been bothering me about the picture was that as the script was written, it contained quite a bit of profanity. Before we started shooting, I approached Candy and said, "Listen, I don't think you need those four-letter words. If we play these scenes without them, we'll have a much better movie." I know pictures today have "eff" this and "eff" that in them, but I just don't think it's necessary. I think they offend part of the audience. Candy earned my respect on the very first day when he agreed to cut out all of the heavy swearwords. From that day on, I knew he was one class act.

I grew very fond of John Candy. Maybe it was because he was half Irish! He was just a genuinely kind and decent man, and we got along. We liked working together so much that we agreed to make another picture together after *Only the Lonely*. There was actually a script we both liked, in which John would be playing a father who rents a grandmother for his kids. I have no doubt that we would have worked together again had he not died so suddenly. But then, he saw the end coming before any of us did.

Shortly after the picture wrapped, I attended a party for John to celebrate his fortieth birthday. Most of the cast and crew from the picture were there. That night, John Candy the funnyman was released from his cage. He entertained the party with comic characters and zany improvisation. He was absolutely outlandish and brilliant. It was so unlike what I was used to from him on the set that I finally grabbed him by the arm and asked, "What are you doing all this crazy stuff for?" His answer surprised me. He said sadly, "Maureen, all the men in my family died at a very young age. I'm on borrowed time."

Candy called me the day before he left for Durango, Mexico, to make *Wagons East*. He didn't want to go. He didn't even want to make the picture. He knew something bad was going to happen on location there and told me, "I'm scared." He died there just a few weeks later. Sometimes the brightest stars burn fast and furious, then are extinguished suddenly, leaving us wishing for more. That was certainly true of John Candy.

Only the Lonely was a delightful experience. The film was well received—it grossed $25 million—and I got some of my very best reviews. Right away, those around me brought up the possibility of an Oscar nomination. I was told that times had changed and that actors now had to campaign for Academy Awards. It would cost $30,000 and there was no guarantee I would get one. I called Roddy McDowall and asked for his advice. He was on the Academy board and would know what I should do. He talked me out of it. He said, "If you have that kind of money to throw around, then put it in a nice interest-earning CD. Maureen, I've been your friend for fifty years, so believe me when I tell you this. You will never—*ever*—receive any recognition for anything you do from Hollywood."

I was so surprised by this. I didn't and still don't know what I could possibly have done over the years to make him say that. Whom have I offended so egregiously?

"But, Roddy, why?"

"I promise I'll tell you before I die."

He never did. I was on my way from Ireland to see him, and Roddy passed away from cancer just as my plane was landing at LAX.

I was so pleased with *Only the Lonely* that it renewed my interest in acting all over again. I have since ended my self-imposed exile from Hollywood and got the word out that my status has changed from retired to semi-retired. What that really means is that Maureen O'Hara will act in a movie if the script is good, if my character is important to the story, and if I like the people involved.

It's hard for older actresses to find exciting projects, and so I hold out for something special. Over the last ten years, I have made three more pictures. They were all made-for-television movies that aired on CBS and were produced by the Polson Company. The first was the holiday tearjerker *The Christmas Box*, based on the *New York Times* best-selling novella by Richard Paul Evans. It was one of the highest-rated movies of the year and proved to the network brass that the old girl still had a fan base she could deliver. We were number one and beat *Monday Night*

Football in the ratings, which is a real television coup. I followed that project with *Cab to Canada* and *The Last Dance*, and each film won its time slot, proving that the first one wasn't a sentimental fluke.

It astounds and flatters me that I'm still in demand after all these years. I owe a great many thanks to cable networks like American Movie Classics and Turner Classic Movies for frequently airing my old pictures and keeping me eternally young and in the public eye. Though I must admit, they often don't give me the proper billing when announcing the movie. Sometimes it sounds as if I'm not in the movie at all, and it's a little frustrating. Still, these channels and videocassettes and DVDs have helped me reach a new and younger audience.

Sometimes I'll go to dinner and a young girl will approach me and say, "You're Maureen O'Hara." She will then go down the list of my movies, and it feels good to know that the films and my work have survived the test of time. I particularly enjoy it when a young actress stops to speak with me. These girls have such hope in their eyes. I always give them the same advice: "Never give up. Stick to it, and hustle. Have a second profession so you aren't desperate when you walk in to an audition."

All this attention for O'Hara makes me feel wonderful, but I prefer avoiding the fuss people still make over her. I now love the quietness of being Maureen FitzSimons Blair. Then I'll get a call or hear about a delicious and rare part that's out there for a veteran actress with my mileage, and the old fire in my belly starts burning again. I tell it to go away and let me be, but the fire is inextinguishable. God has a most wicked sense of humor.

CHAPTER 26

THE EMPTY PAGES

Oh love, could thou and I with fate conspire
To grasp this sorry scheme of things entire,
Would we not shatter it to bits—and then
Remold it nearer to the heart's desire?

Oh yes, I would like to "remold it nearer to the heart's desire." And what is that? You'd have to be a fool not to know. It's to have my Charlie beside me. Every heartbeat would be precious. Daddy taught me this poem many years ago. Maybe he knew why, but I didn't until now.

I wish I had many more empty pages to fill. There are so many more stories I could tell you of my wonderful Irish family, from my childhood and youth to my contract with Charles Laughton. I could pen volumes more on my experiences in the theater and making movies, and of the birth of my daughter and my grandson, of my marriage to Charlie, and from then until now.

I used to put a pad and pen beside my bed every night in case I woke up with brilliant ideas. I was going to record them on my pad and be sure that everything found its way into this book. I would wake up, but I'd turn over and go back to sleep.

As our journey together nears the end, it feels strangely incomplete. I have not shared everything with you. But then, there is no way I can in only one book. I've left out details of the lives of my daughter and grandson and Charlie's kids, out of respect for their privacy. I am a public person and, thankfully, they are not.

I've thought often of the old Gypsy and wondered if her final prediction has come true. I think it is best that I leave that answer to you.

I've done a lot of living over the years. I've stood up for the principles that meant the most to me, and fought hard when I had to, usually going it alone. I'm stubborn that way. Through it all, I've tried to face the fire with bravery, honor, and honesty. Most of all, I'm proud that I have never wilted or cowered when it mattered the most.

I have never lost my faith in God. In times of sadness, *He* has given me the courage to face the world and carry on. In happy times, especially the wonderful days with my Charlie, I thanked Him every night before I closed my eyes to sleep. I know that *He* will take care of me.

And what, dear reader, are your intentions? How will you fill your empty pages? I pray that all you young people, middle-aged people, and old people like me live each day and enjoy each day, and when God calls you, that you answer *Him* and go willingly. But leave your mark on the world, on your children and on all the people you leave behind so that they will be brave and leave brave memories.

Some time ago, I told Larry King that I planned to live to be 102. I still do. I dreamed as a little girl in Dublin of growing into a wonderfully eccentric, tough, cantankerous, and sometimes mean old lady who thumps her cane loudly to get what she wants and to express her thoughts. I've already been known to use a cane to get around from time to time—the thumping is still to come.

Index

Photo Credits

All photographs are courtesy of the Maureen O'Hara Collection, unless otherwise noted.

page ii (frontispiece): Courtesy of Batjac Productions.

8: *The Hunchback of Notre Dame* © 1940, RKO Pictures, Inc. All rights reserved.

11, 12: *Dance Girl, Dance* © 1940 RKO Pictures, Inc. All rights reserved.

13, 14, 16: *How Green Was My Valley* © 1941, Twentieth Century Fox. All rights reserved.

15: Courtesy of the Estate of John Ford.

18, 22: *The Black Swan* © 1942, Twentieth Century Fox. All rights reserved.

23: *The Spanish Main* © 1945, RKO Pictures, Inc. All rights reserved.

26, 27: *Miracle on 34th Street* © 1947, Twentieth Century Fox. All rights reserved.

28, 31: *The Quiet Man* © Paramount Pictures. All rights reserved.

34: *At Sword's Point* © 1952, RKO Pictures, Inc. All rights reserved.

40: Courtesy of Tennessee Ernie Ford Enterprises, LP.

44, 45: *The Parent Trap* © Disney Enterprises, Inc. All rights reserved.

46: *Mr. Hobbs Takes a Vacation* © 1962, Twentieth Century Fox. All rights reserved.

48: *Spencer's Mountain* © 1963, Warner Bros. Pictures, Inc. All rights reserved.

49, 50, 51: Courtesy of Batjac Productions.